W9-BZK-781

JUL 2000

JUN 2004

WITHDRAWN

JUN 09

JUL X X 2015

10.00
sch.

WITHDRAWN

Women in Literature:
Criticism of the Seventies

by

CAROL FAIRBANKS MYERS

REFERENCE

Not to be taken from this room

The Scarecrow Press, Inc.

Metuchen, N.J.   1976

CUMBERLAND COUNTY COLLEGE
LEARNING RESOURCE CENTER
P. O. BOX 517
VINELAND, N. J. 08360

Ref
Z
6514
C5
W64

76- 630

Library of Congress Cataloging in Publication Data

Myers, Carol Fairbanks.
  Women in literature.

  Includes index.
  1. Women in literature--Bibliography. 2. Women
authors--Bibliography. I. Title.
Z6514.C5W64   [PN56.W6]   809'.933'52   75-35757
ISBN 0-8108-0885-4

Copyright © 1976 by Carol Fairbanks Myers

Printed in the United States of America

For Edna S. Hood and Helen X. Sampson

CONTENTS

NOTE TO THE READER

This bibliography includes material published in the 1970s relating to women in literature:

1) Literary criticism examining women characters in relation to other women, to men, to family, to work, to community, to the times and cultures in which they live.

2) Literary criticism examining women characters as myth and symbol.

3) Essays appraising feminist criticism as an approach to literature.

4) Biographical and critical studies of women writers.

5) Interviews with women writers.

6) Selected reviews of the works of women writers.

The coverage of the bibliography for selected books and periodicals dates from January 1970 through Spring 1975.

The "General Bibliography" includes works which are comprehensive in nature, providing insights into the literature of a particular period or genre, or providing historical, sociological, psychological and philosophical backgrounds for the study of women in literature.

ACHEBE, CHINUA

Ackley, Donald G. "The Male-Female Motif in Things Fall Apart." Studies in Black Literature 4 (Winter 1974): 1-6.

AIDOO, AMA ATA

Bamikunle, Adermi. "The Two Plays of Aidoo--A Commentary." In Work in Progress: I, pp. 170-183. Department of English. Zaria, Nigeria: Ahmadu Bello University, 1972.

Brown, Lloyd W. "Ama Ata Aidoo: The Art of the Short Story and Sexual Roles in Africa." World Literature Written in English 13 (November 1974): 172-183.

Burness, Donald Bayer. "Womanhood in the Short Stories of Ama Ata Aidoo." Studies in Black Literature 4 (Summer 1973): 21-23.

Conde, Maryse. "Three Female Writers in Modern Africa." Présence Africaine no. 82 (April-June 1972): 132-143.

AKHMATOVA, ANNA

Driver, Sam. "Anna Akhmatova: Early Love Poems." Russian Literature Triquarterly 1 (1971): 297-325.

_____. Anna Akhmatova. New York: Twayne, 1972.

"An Interview with Victor Andreevich Gorenko, Brother of Anna Akhmatova, with Unpublished Letters of Akhmatova." Russian Literature Triquarterly no. 9 (Spring 1974): 497-520.

Mihailovich, Vasa D. , ed. Modern Slavic Literature:
A Library of Literary Criticism. New York: Frederick Ungar, 1972.

Nedobrovo, N. V. "Anna Akhmatova. " Translated by
Alan Myers. Russian Literature Triquarterly no. 9
(Spring 1974): 221-236.

Taubman, Jane Andelman. "Tsvetaeva and Akhmatova:
Two Female Voices in a Poetic Quartet. " Russian
Literature Triquarterly no. 9 (Spring 1974): 355-
369.

Verheul, Kees. "Public Themes in the Poetry of Anna
Axmatova. " In Tale Without a Hero and Twenty-
Two Poems by Anna Axmatova. The Hague: Mouton,
1973.

_____ . The Theme of Time in the Poetry of Anna
Axmatova. The Hague: Mouton, 1971.

ALAS, LEOPOLDO

Tyrmand, Mary Ellen. "Women and Society in the Nineteenth-Century Spanish Novel. " Ph. D. Dissertation,
Yale University, 1974.

ALBEE, EDWARD

Dollard, John. "The Hidden Meaning of 'Who's Afraid
... ?'" Connecticut Review 7 (October 1973): 24-28.

Hayman, Ronald. Edward Albee. London: Heinemann
Educational, 1971.

Martin, Richard. "One v. One, or Two Against All. "
Die Neueren Sprachen 72 (N. S. 22): 535-537, October 1973.

Paolucci, Anne. From Tension to Tonic: The Plays of
Edward Albee. Carbondale and Edwardsville: Southern Illinois University Press, 1972; London and Amsterdam: Feffer & Simons, 1972.

Quinn, James P. "Myth and Romance in Albee's Who's
Afraid of Virginia Woolf. " Arizona Quarterly 30
(Autumn 1974): 197-204.

Taylor, Charlene M. "Coming of Age in New Carthage: Albee's Grown-up Children." Educational Theatre Journal 25 (March 1973): 66-70.

ALCOTT, LOUISA MAE

Diamont, Sarah Elbert. "Louisa May Alcott and the Woman Problem." Ph. D. Dissertation, Cornell University, 1974.

Forrey, Carolyn. "The New Woman Revisited." Women's Studies 2 (1974): 37-56.

Manley, Seon and Susan Belcher. "The Pens that Rocked the Cradle and the World: Louisa May Alcott and Harriet Beecher Stowe." O, Those Extraordinary Women! Philadelphia: Chilton, 1972, pp. 157-171.

Moers, Ellen. "Money, the Job, and Little Women." Commentary 55 (January 1973): 57-65. Reply with rejoinder: E. Kaledin 55 (May 1973): 26.

Spacks, Patricia M. The Female Imagination. New York: Knopf, 1975.

_____. "Take Care: Some Women Novelists." Novel 6 (Fall 1972): 36-51.

ALERAMO, SIBILLA

Pacifici, Sergio. "Women Writers: Neera and Aleramo." The Modern Italian Novel from Capuana to Tozzi. Carbondale and Edwardsville: Southern Illinois University Press, 1973.

ALUKO, T. M.

Stegeman, Beatrice. "The Divorce Dilemma: The New Woman in Contemporary African Novels." Critique 15, no. 3: 81-93.

ANGELOU, MAYA

Butterfield, Stephen. Black Autobiography in America. Amherst: University of Massachusetts Press, 1974.

Essence, September 1974, p. 38. (Review of Gather

Together in My Name.)

Gottlieb, Annie. New York Times Book Review, 16 June 1974, p. 16. (Review of Gather Together in My Name.)

Julianelli, J. "Angelou: Interview." Harper's Bazaar, November 1972, p. 124.

Smith, Sidonie Ann. "The Song of a Caged Bird: Maya Angelou's Quest for Self-Acceptance." Southern Humanities Review 7 (Fall 1973): 365-374.

_____. Where I'm Bound: Patterns of Slavery and Freedom--Black American Autobiography. Westport, Conn.: Greenwood Press, 1974.

Washington, Mary Helen. "Black Women Image Makers." Black World 23 (August 1974): 10-18.

Weller, Sheila. "Work in Progress: Maya Angelou." Intellectual Digest 3 (June 1973): 11.

AQUILERA-MALTA, DEMETRIO

Siemens, William L. "The Devouring Female in Four Latin American Novels." Essays in Literature (Macomb, Ill.) 1 (Spring 1974): 118-129.

ARNOLD, JUNE

Morgan, Ellen. "Humanbecoming: Form and Focus in the Neo-Feminist Novel." In Images of Women in Fiction, pp. 192-197. Edited by Susan Koppelman Cornillon. Bowling Green, Ohio: Bowling Green University Press, 1972.

ARNOW, HARRIETTE

Oates, Joyce Carol. New Heaven, New Earth: The Visionary Experience in Literature. New York: Vanguard Press, 1974.

ATHERTON, GERTRUDE

McClure, Charlotte Swain. "The American Eve: A Tragedy in Innocence." Ph.D. Dissertation, University of New Mexico, 1973.

ATWOOD, MARGARET

Allen, Dick. "Shifts." Poetry 120 (July 1972): 239-240.

Bell, Millicent. "The Girl on the Wedding Cake." New York Times Book Review, 18 October 1970, p. 51.

Bowering, George. "Get Used to It." Canadian Literature no. 52 (Spring 1972): 91-92.

Delany, Paul. New York Times Book Review, 4 March 1973, p. 5. (Review of Surfacing.)

DeMott, Benjamin. "Recycling Art." Saturday Review of the Arts, April 1973, pp. 85-86.

Gibson, Graeme. Eleven Canadian Novelists. Toronto: Anansi, 1973.

Gleicher, David. "Female Chauvinism." New Leader, 3 September 1973, pp. 20-21.

Jonas, George. "Cool Sounds in a Minor Key." Saturday Night, May 1971, pp. 30-31. (Review of Power Politics.)

Kroetsch, Robert. "Unhiding the Hidden: Recent Canadian Fiction." Journal of Canadian Fiction 3, no. 3 (1974): 43-44. (Review of Surfacing.)

Laporte, Linda. "From Reality to Selfhood: Margaret Atwood's Fiction." M.A. Thesis, McGill University, 1973.

Larkin, Joan. Ms. 1 (May 1973): 33-35. (Review of Surfacing.)

McKenna, Isobel. "Women in Canadian Literature." Canadian Literature no. 62 (Autumn 1974): 69-78.

Mitchell, Sr. Beverley. Journal of Canadian Fiction 2, no. 4 (1973): 112. (Review of The Edible Woman.)

Morley, Patricia. Journal of Canadian Fiction 1, no. 4 (1972): 99. (Review of Surfacing.)

Onley, Gloria. "Margaret Atwood: Surfacing in the Interests of Survival." West Coast Review 7, no. 3

(1973): 51-54. (Review Essay.)

_____. "Power Politics in Bluebeard's Castle." Canadian Literature no. 60 (Spring 1974): 21-42.

Piercy, Marge. "Margaret Atwood: Beyond Victimhood." American Poetry Review, November/December 1973, pp. 41-44.

Pritchard, William H. Hudson Review 26 (Autumn 1973): 586-587. (Review of Power Politics.)

Rogers, Linda. "Margaret the Magician." Canadian Literature no. 60 (Spring 1974): 83-85.

Rosenthal, D. H. Nation, 19 March 1973, p. 374. (Review of Surfacing.)

Schaeffer, Susan Fromberg. "'It is Time that Separates Us': Margaret Atwood's Surfacing." Centennial Review 18 (Fall 1974): 319-337.

Sellers, Jill. The Spokeswoman, 15 June 1974, p. 6. (Review Essay.)

Stein, Karen F. "Reflections in a Jagged Mirror: Some Metaphors of Madness." Aphra 6 (Spring 1975): 2-11.

Stone, E. Crawdaddy, December 1973, p. 88. (Review of Surfacing.)

Van Duyn, Mona. "Seven Women." Poetry 115 (March 1970): 430-439.

Wimsatt, Margaret. Commonweal, 7 September 1973, p. 483. (Review of Surfacing.)

_____. "The Lady as Humphrey Bogart." Commonweal, 9 July 1973, pp. 483-484.

Woodcock, George. "Surfacing to Survive: Notes of the Recent Atwood." Ariel: A Review of International English Literature 4 no. 3 (1973): 16-28.

Zinnes, Harriet. "Seven Women Poets." Carleton Miscellany 14 (Spring-Summer 1974): 122-126.

AUSTEN, JANE

Acabal, Perla G. "Jane Austen's Moral Vision: Form and Function. " Ph. D. Dissertation, Indiana University, 1973.

Ames, Carol. "Fanny and Mrs. Norris: Poor Relations in Mansfield Park. " Dalhousie Review 54 (Autumn 1974): 491-498.

_____. "Love Triangles in Fiction: The Underlying Fantasies. " Ph. D. Dissertation, State University of New York at Buffalo, 1973.

Amis, Kingsley. What Became of Jane Austen? And Other Questions. New York: Harcourt Brace Jovanovich, 1970, pp. 13-17.

Anderson, Walter E. "The Plot of Mansfield Park. " Modern Philology 71 (August 1973): 16-27.

Beer, Patricia. Reader, I Married Him: A Study of the Women Characters of Jane Austen, Charlotte Bronte, Elizabeth Gaskell, and George Eliot. New York: Harper, 1975.

Birky, Wilbur Joseph. "Marriage as Pattern and Metaphor in the Victorian Novel. " Ph. D. Dissertation, The University of Iowa, 1970.

Brown, Lloyd W. Bits of Ivory: Narrative Techniques in Jane Austen's Fiction. Baton Rouge: Louisiana State University Press, 1973.

_____. "Jane Austen and the Feminist Tradition. " Nineteenth-Century Fiction 28 (December 1973): 321-338.

Burgan, Mary Alice. "Feeling and Control: A Study of the Proposal Scenes in Jane Austen's Major Novels. " In The English Novel in the Nineteenth Century, pp. 25-31. Edited by George Goodin. Urbana: University of Illinois Press, 1972.

Bush, Douglas. Jane Austen. New York: Collier Books, 1975.

Colby, Vineta. Yesterday's Woman: Domestic Realism in the English Novel. Princeton, N. J.: Princeton University Press, 1974.

Constantine, Annette Vincze. "Wit in Jane Austen's Novels: An Expression of Conflict Between Duty and Desire." Ph. D. Dissertation, University of Illinois at Urbana-Champaign, 1972.

Corwin, Laura. "The Concept of Self in the Novels of Jane Austen." Ph. D. Dissertation, University of Pennsylvania, 1970.

DeRose, Peter Louis. "Jane Austen and Samuel Johnson." Ph. D. Dissertation, Indiana University, 1974.

Devlin, D. D. "Mansfield Park." Ariel: A Review of International English Literature 2 (October 1971): 30-43.

Donovan, Josephine. "Feminist Style Criticism." In Female Studies VI: Closer to the Ground, pp. 139-149. Edited by Nancy Hoffman, Cynthia Secor, Adrian Tinsley. Old Westbury, N. Y.: Feminist Press, 1972.

Duckworth, Alistair M. The Improvement of the Estate: A Study of Jane Austen's Novels. Baltimore: Johns Hopkins University Press, 1971.

Edge, Charles. "Emma: A Technique of Characterization." In The Classic British Novel, pp. 51-64. Edited by Howard M. Harper, Jr. and Charles Edge. Athens: University of Georgia Press, 1972.

Eisner, Seth Alan. "Jane Austen's Characters: Manners of Being." Ph. D. Dissertation, University of Pennsylvania, 1973.

Fowler, Mirian E. "The Courtesy-Book Heroine of Mansfield Park." University of Toronto Quarterly 43 (Fall 1974): 31-46.

_____. "Patterns of Prudence: Courtship Conventions in Jane Austen's Novels." Ph. D. Dissertation, University of Toronto, 1970.

Glucksman, Stuart. "The Happy Ending in Jane Austen." Ph. D. Dissertation, State University of New York at Stony Brook, work in progress.

Gubar, Susan. "Sane Jane and the Critics: 'Professions and Falsehoods.'" Novel 8 (Spring 1975): 246-259. (Review Essay.)

Halperin, John, ed. Jane Austen: Bicentenary Essays. New York: Cambridge University Press, 1975.

_____. The Language of Meditation: Four Studies in Nineteenth-Century Fiction. Devon: Arthur H. Stockwell, 1973.

_____. "The Victorian Novel and Jane Austen." Egoism and Self-Discovery in the Victorian Novel. New York: Burt Franklin, 1974. pp. 1-30.

Hamilton, Jack. "A Conversation with Jane Austen." Intellectual Digest 3 (May 1973): 16-18.

Hardwick, Michael. A Guide to Jane Austen. New York: Scribner, 1973.

_____. The Osprey Guide to Jane Austen. Reading: Osprey, 1973.

Hartzler, Sara K. K. "Marriage as Theme and Structure in Jane Austen's Novels." Ph. D. Dissertation, The Pennsylvania State University 1970.

Heilbrun, Carolyn G. Toward a Recognition of Androgyny. New York: Knopf, 1973, pp. 50, 73, 74-8.

Hennedy, Hugh L. "Acts of Perception in Jane Austen's Novels." Studies in the Novel 5 (Spring 1973): 22-38.

Higbie, Robert Griggs. "Characterization in the English Novel: Richardson, Jane Austen, and Dickens." Ph. D. Dissertation, Indiana University, 1973.

Hodge, Jane. Only a Novel: The Double Life of Jane Austen. New York: Coward, McCann & Geoghegan, 1972.

Horwitz, Barbara. "A Young Lady is a Delicate Plant: Structure and Characterization in the Novels of Jane Austen." Ph. D. Dissertation, State University of New York, work in progress.

Hummel, Madeline. "Emblematic Charades and the Observant Woman in Mansfield Park." Texas Studies in Literature and Language 15 (Summer 1973): 251-265.

Katz, Judith Nina. "Rooms of Their Own: Forms and Images of Liberation in Five Novels." Ph. D. Dissertation, The Pennsylvania State University, 1972.

Kauvar, Elaine M. "Jane Austen and The Female Quixote." Studies in the Novel 2 (Summer 1970): 211-221.

Kestner, Joseph A., III. "The 'I' Persona in the Novels of Jane Austen." Studies in the Novel 4 (1972): 6-16.

Kissane, James. "Comparison's Blessed Felicity: Character Arrangement in Emma." Studies in the Novel 2 (Summer 1970): 173-184.

Kormali, Sema Günisik. "The Treatment of Marriage in Representative Novels of Jane Austen and Henry James." Ph. D. Dissertation, Texas Tech University, 1974.

Krier, William John. "A Pattern of Limitations: The Heroine's Novel of Mind." Ph. D. Dissertation, Indiana University, 1973.

Kroeber, Karl. Styles in Fictional Structure: The Art of Jane Austen, Charlotte Brontë, George Eliot. Princeton, N. J.: Princeton University Press, 1971.

Lauber, John. "Heroes and Anti-Heroes in Jane Austen's Novels." Dalhousie Review 51 (Winter 1971-72): 489-503.

Leeming, Glenda. Who's Who in Jane Austen and the Brontës. New York: Taplinger, 1974.

Linder, C. A. "The Ideal Marriage as Depicted in the

Novels of Jane Austen and Charlotte Brontë." Stand-punte 96 (1971): 20-30.

Litz, A. Walton. "Recollecting Jane Austen." Critical Inquiry 1 (March 1975): 669-682. (Review Essay.)

McMaster, Juliet. "The Continuity of Jane Austen's Novels." Studies in English Literature 1500-1900 10 (Autumn 1970): 723-739.

_____. "Surface and Subsurface in Jane Austen's Novels." Ariel: A Review of International English Literature 5 (April 1974): 5-24.

Mansell, Darrel. The Novels of Jane Austen: An Inter-pretation. New York: Barnes & Noble, 1973.

Mise, Raymond Winfield. "The Gothic Heroine and the Nature of the Gothic Novel." Ph. D. Dissertation, The University of Washington, 1970.

Moers, Ellen. "Money, the Job, and Little Women." Commentary 55 (January 1973): 57-65. Reply with rejoinder: E. Kaledin 55 (May 1973): 26.

Munday, M. "Jane Austen, Women Writers, and Black-wood's Magazine." Notes and Queries 20 (August 1973): 290.

Myers, Sylvia H. "Womanhood in Jane Austen's Novels." Novel 3 (1970): 225-232.

Nardin, Jane. Those Elegant Decorums: The Concept of Propriety in Jane Austen's Novels. Albany: State University of New York Press, 1973.

Newman, Ronald Bruce. "Life Style in the Novels of Jane Austen." Ph. D. Dissertation, The University of Michigan, 1972.

O'Neill, Judith. Critics on Jane Austen. Coral Gables, Fla.: University of Miami Press, 1970.

Page, Norman. The Language of Jane Austen. New York: Barnes & Noble, 1972.

Pikoulis, John. "Jane Austen: The Figure in the

Carpet. " Nineteenth-Century Fiction 27 (June 1972): 38-60.

Pinion, F. B. A Jane Austen Companion: A Critical Survey and Reference Book. London: Macmillan, 1973; New York: St. Martin's Press, 1973.

Podis, JoAnne Med. "'The Way They Should Go': Family Relationships in the Novels of Jane Austen. " Ph. D. Dissertation, Case Western Reserve, 1974.

Rackin, Donald. "Jane Austen's Anatomy of Persuasion." In The English Novel in the Nineteenth Century, pp. 52-80. Edited by George Goodin. Urbana: University of Illinois Press, 1972.

Robinson, Lillian S. "Who's Afraid of a Room of One's Own?" In The Politics of Literature, p. 374. Edited by Louis Kampf and Paul Lauter. New York: Pantheon Books, 1972.

Ross, Mary Beth. "The 'Bisexual' World of Jane Austen." Aphra 6 (Winter 1974-75): 2-15.

Roth, Barry and Joel Weinsheimer. An Annotated Bibliography of Jane Austen Studies 1952-1972. Charlottesville: The University Press of Virginia, 1973.

Rothstein, Eric. "The Lessons of Northanger Abbey." University of Toronto Quarterly 43 (Fall 1974): 14-30.

Rudolph, Jo-Ellen Schwartz. "The Novels that Taught the Ladies: A Study of Popular Fiction Written by Women, 1702-1834. " Ph. D. Dissertation, University of California, San Diego, 1972.

Sabiston, Elizabeth. "Prison of Womanhood. " Comparative Literature 25 (Fall 1973): 336-351.

Spacks, Patricia M. The Female Imagination. New York: Knopf, 1975.

Speakman, James Stewart. "Wit, Humor and Sensibility in Evelina, Belinda and Northanger Abbey. " Ph. D. Dissertation, University of California, Davis, 1972.

Steig, Michael. "Psychological Realism and Fantasy in Jane Austen: Emma and Mansfield Park." Hartford Studies in Literature 5 (1973): 126-134.

Stoller, Annette Linda. "Jane Austen's Rhetorical Art: A Revaluation." Ph.D. Dissertation, Brown University, 1974.

Stone, Donald D. "Victorian Feminism and the Nineteenth-Century Novel." Women's Studies 1 (1972): 65-92.

Tave, Stuart M. Some Words of Jane Austen. Chicago and London: University of Chicago Press, 1973.

Wagner, Geoffrey. Five for Freedom. Rutherford, Madison, Teaneck, N.J.: Fairleigh Dickinson University Press, 1972, pp. 18, 33, 40, 41, 44, 55, 82, 95.

Waidner, Maralee Layman. "From Reason to Romance: A Progression from an Emphasis on Neoclassic Rationality to Romantic Intuition in Three English Woman Novelists." Ph.D. Dissertation, The University of Tulsa, 1973.

Weinsheimer, Joel. "Chance and the Hierarchy of Marriage in Pride and Prejudice." ELH 39 (September 1972): 404-419.

_____. "In Praise of Mr. Woodhouse: Duty and Desire in Emma." Ariel 6 (January 1975): 81-95.

_____. "Three Assays of Jane Austen's Novels." Ph.D. Dissertation, Ohio University, 1973.

Wiltshire, John. "A Romantic Persuasion?" Critical Review no. 14 (1971): 3-16.

Wolfe, Thomas P. "The Achievement of Persuasion." Studies in English Literature 1500-1900 11 (Autumn 1971): 687-700.

AUSTIN, MARY

Berry, J. Wilkes. "Characterization in Mary Austin's Southwest Works." Southwestern American Literature 2 (Winter 1972): 119-124.

_____. "Mary Austin: Sibylic Gourmet of the South-
west." Western Review 9 (Winter 1972): 3-8.

Edwards, Lee R. and Arlyn Diamond. "Introduction."
American Voices, American Women. New York:
Avon, 1973.

Johnson, Lee Ann. "Western Literary Realism: The
California Tales of Norris and Austin." American
Literary Realism 1870-1910 7 (Summer 1974): 278-
280.

-B-

BALDWIN, JAMES

George, Felice. "Black Woman, Black Man." Harvard
Journal of Afro-American Affairs 2 (1971): 1-17.

Rosenblatt, Roger. Black Fiction. Cambridge: Harvard
University Press, 1974.

BALZAC, HONORE de

Bolster, Richard. Stendhal, Balzac, et le Féminisme
Romantiques. Paris: Lettres Modernes, 1970.

Frappier-Mazur, Lucienne. "Balzac and the Sex of
Genius." Renascence 27 (Autumn 1974): 23-30.

Prendergast, C. A. "Antithesis and Moral Ambiguity
in 'La Cousine Bette.'" Modern Language Review
68 (April 1973): 315-332.

Prendergast, Christopher. "Melodrama and Totality in
Splendeurs et Misères des courtisanes." Novel 6
(1973): 152-162.

Puge, Anthony R. Balzac's Recurring Characters.
Toronto: University of Toronto Press, 1974.

Smith, Elyzabeth Marie-Pierre Richer. "Nana, Santa,
et Nacha Regules: Trois Courtisanes Modernes."
Ph. D. Dissertation, University of Georgia, 1974.

Wagner, Geoffrey. Five for Freedom: A Study of Feminism in Fiction. Rutherford, Madison, Teaneck, N.J.: Fairleigh Dickinson University Press, 1972, pp. 15, 26, 40, 54, 77, 79, 91-102 passim, 109, 178.

BAMBARA, TONI CADE

Book World, 18 November 1973, p. 5. (Review of Gorilla, My Love.)

English Journal 63 (January 1974): 66. (Review of Gorilla, My Love.)

Washington, Mary Helen. "Black Women Image Makers." Black World 23 (August 1974): 10-18.

BARNES, DJUNA

Baxter, Charles. "A Self-Consuming Light: Nightwood and the Crisis of Modernism." Journal of Modern Literature 3 (July 1974): 1175-1187.

Gunn, Edward. "Myth and Style in Djuna Barnes's Nightwood." Modern Fiction Studies 19 (Winter 1973-74): 545-555.

Johnson, William A. "Modern Women Novelists: Nightwood and the Novel of Sensibility." Bucknell Review 21 (Spring 1973): 29-42.

BAROJA, PIO

Lamonte, Rosalie Salerno. "The Characterization of Woman in the Novels of Pio Baroja." Ph.D. Dissertation, Columbia University, 1974.

Patt, Beatrice P. Pio Baroja. New York: Twayne, 1971.

BARRENO, MARIA ISABEL

Ascherson, Neal. New York Review of Books, 20 March 1975, p. 11. (Review of The Three Marias: New Portuguese Letters.)

Barreno, Marie Isabel, Maria Teresa Horta, and Maria

Velho da Costa. "The Three Marias: New Portuguese Letters." Ms. 3 (January 1975): 86-87.

de Figueiredo, A. "Portugals' Three Marias: Literary Repression by the Government." Nation, 2 (March 1974, pp. 268-269.

Fonesca, Mary Lydon. "The Case of the Three Marias." Ms. 3 (January 1975): 84-85, 108.

Kramer, Jane. New York Times Book Review, 2 February 1975, p. 1. (Review of The Three Marias: New Portuguese Letters.)

Prescott, P. S. Newsweek, 27 January 1975, p. 61. (Review of The Three Marias: New Portuguese Letters.)

BARRIERE, THEODORE

Lee, Barbara G. "The Courtesan in the Drama of Théodore Barrière." Southern Quarterly 11 (April 1973): 191-206.

BAUDELAIRE, CHARLES

Barnett, Richard Lance. "Baudelaire and the Ambiguity of Women." Renascence 25 (Winter 1973): 59-66.

Beamish-Thiriet, Françoise Marie-Odile. "The Myth of Woman in Baudelaire and Blok." Ph. D. Dissertation, University of Washington, 1973.

BEAUMARCHAIS, PIERRE-AUGUSTIN CARON de

Berneck, Betty. "Feminism in the Works of Beaumarchais." Ph. D. Dissertation, Yale University, 1973.

BEAUVOIR, SIMONE de

Beauvoir, Simone de and Betty Friedan. "Sex, Society, and the Female Dilemma: A Dialogue Between Simone de Beauvoir and Betty Friedan." Saturday Review, 14 June 1975, pp. 14, 16-18, 20, 56.

Brée, Germaine. Women Writers in France: Variations on a Theme. New Brunswick, N. J.: Rutgers University Press, 1973, pp. 54-58.

Cottrell, Robert D. Simone de Beauvoir. New York: Frederick Ungar, forthcoming.

Fong, Anne Curtiss. "Exis and Pracis: Woman's Dilemma in the Works of Simone de Beauvoir." Ph. D. Dissertation, Duke University, 1973.

Gallant, Mavis. New York Times Book Review, 21 July 1974, p. 4. (Review of All Said and Done.)

Gontier, Fernande. "Les images de la femme dans le roman français de l'entre-deux-guerres." Ph. D. Dissertation, University of Virginia, 1973.

Hoerchner, Susan Jane. ""I Have to Keep the Two Things Separate'; Polarity in Women in the Contemporary Novel." Ph. D. Dissertation, Emory University, 1973.

McDowell, Margaret B. "Reflections on the New Feminism." Midwest Quarterly 12 (April 1971): 309-333.

Marks, Elaine. Simone de Beauvoir: Encounters with Death. New Brunswick, N. J.: Rutgers University Press, 1973.

O'Sullivan, Deborah Ann. "Janus and Narcissus: Woman's Situation as Depicted in The Second Sex, the Works of Fiction, and the Autobiography of Simone de Beauvoir." Ph. D. Dissertation, The University of Arizona, 1972.

Pagès, Irène M. "Beauvoir's Les Belles Images: 'Désubstantification' of Reality through a Narrative." Forum for Modern Language Studies 11 (April 1975): 133-141.

Pratt, Annis. "Women and Nature in Modern Fiction." Contemporary Literature 13 (Autumn 1972): 477.

Pritchett, V. S. New York Review of Books, 8 August 1974. p. 24. (Review of All Said and Done.)

Robinson, Lillian S. "Who's Afraid of a Room of One's Own?" In The Politics of Literature, pp. 376, 382-384. Edited by Louis Kampf and Paul Lauter. New York: Pantheon Books, 1972.

Rossi, Alice S. The Feminist Papers: From Adams to de Beauvoir. New York: Columbia University Press, 1973, pp. 672, 674.

Rubino, Elizabeth Ann. "Restrictions on Freedom Themes in the Fictional Works of Simone de Beauvoir." Ph. D. Dissertation, Case Western Reserve University, 1973.

Schwartzer, Alice. "The Radicalization of Simone de Beauvoir." Ms. 1 (July 1972): 60-63, 134. Also in The First Ms. Reader. New York: Warner Paperback Library, 1973, pp. 250-261.

Spacks, Patricia M. The Female Imagination. New York: Knopf, 1975.

Warnock, Mary. New Statesman, 24 May 1974, p. 731. (Review of All Said and Done.)

BEHN, APHRA

Kramer, Rita. "Aphra Behn: Novelist, Spy, Libertine." Ms. 1 (February 1973): 16-18.

Lindquist, Carol Ann. "The Prose Fiction of Aphra Behn." Ph. D. Dissertation, University of Maryland, 1970.

Miner, Earl, ed. Stuart and Georgian Moments. Berkeley: University of California Press, 1972, pp. 272, 273.

Novak, Maximillian E. "Some Notes Toward a History of Fictional Forms: From Aphra Behn to Daniel Defoe. " Novel 6 (Winter 1973): 120-133.

Scott, Clayton S., Jr. "Aphra Behn: A Study in Dramatic Continuity. " Ph. D. Dissertation, Texas Southern University, 1972.

Suwannabha, Sumitra. "The Feminine Eye: Augustan Society as Seen by Selected Women Dramatists of the Restoration and Early Eighteenth Century. " Ph. D. Dissertation, Indiana University, 1973.

BEHRMAN, S. N.

Baxter, Marilynn Ruth. "Modern Woman as Heroine in

Representative Plays by S. N. Behrman." Ph. D.
Dissertation, University of Wisconsin, 1973.

Shafer, Y. B. "Liberated Women in American Plays of
the Past." Players Magazine 49 (Spring 1974): 95-
100.

BENNETT, ARNOLD

Birky, Wilbur Joseph. "Marriage as Pattern and Metaphor in the Victorian Novel." Ph. D. Dissertation,
The University of Iowa, 1970.

Drabble, Margaret. Arnold Bennett. New York: Knopf,
1974.

Siegel, Paul W. "Revolution and Evolution in Bennett's
The Old Wives' Tale." CLIO 4 (February 1975):
159-172.

Wright, Walter F. Arnold Bennett: Romantic Realist.
Lincoln: University of Nebraska Press, 1971.

BERGSTEIN, ELEANOR

Avant, J. A. New Republic, 23 February 1974, p. 26.
(Review of Advancing Paul Newman.)

Martin, Wendy. "Eleanor Bergstein, Novelist--An Interview." Women's Studies 2 (1974): 91-98.

Rosenthal, Lucy. Ms. 2 (May 1974): 40-42. (Review
of Advancing Paul Newman.)

Sellers, Jill. The Spokeswoman, 15 March 1974, pp.
405. (Review of Advancing Paul Newman.)

BERNSTEIN-ROSMER, ELSA

Scholtz, Sigrid Gerda. "Images of Womanhood in the
Works of German Female Dramatists 1892-1918."
Ph. D. Dissertation, Johns Hopkins University, 1971.

BERTIN, CELIA

Brèe, Germaine. "Interviews with Two French Novelists: Nathalie Sarraute and Célia Bertin."

Contemporary Literature 14 (Spring 1973): 137-146.

Lipton, Virginia Anne. "Women in Today's World: A Study of Five French Women Novelists." Ph. D. Dissertation, The University of Wisconsin, 1972.

BHATTACHARYA, BHABANI

Fisher, Marlene. "The Women in Bhattacharya's Novels." World Literature Written in English 11 (1972): 95-108.

BLAKE, WILLIAM

Derderian, Nancy Cebula. "Against the Patriarchal Pomp! A Study of the Feminine Principle in the Poetry of William Blake." Ph. D. Dissertation, State University of New York at Buffalo, 1974.

Taylor, Irene. "The Woman Scaly." Bulletin of the Midwest Modern Language Association 6 (Spring 1973): 74-87.

White, Mary Elizabeth. "Woman's Triumph: A Study of the Changing Symbolic Values of the Female in the Works of William Blake." Ph. D. Dissertation, University of Washington, 1972.

BOURGET, PAUL

Easterly, Joan Elizabeth Triplett. "Women in the Novels of Paul Bourget." Ph. D. Dissertation, Vanderbilt University, 1973.

BOWEN, ELIZABETH

Austin, Allan E. Elizabeth Bowen. New York: Twayne, 1971.

Coles, Robert. Irony in the Mind's Life: Essays on Novels by James Agee, Elizabeth Bowen, and George Eliot. Charlottesville: University Press of Virginia, 1974.

Parrish, Paul A. "The Loss of Eden: Four Novels of Elizabeth Bowen." Critique 15, no. 1 (1973-1974): 86-100.

Stern, Joan Oberwager. "A Study of Problems in Values and the Means by Which They Are Presented in the Novels of Elizabeth Bowen. " Ph. D. Dissertation, New York University, 1974.

BOWLES, JANE

Kazin, Alfred. "Cassandras: Porter to Oates. " Bright Book of Life: American Novelists and Storytellers from Hemingway to Mailer. Boston, Toronto: Little, Brown, 1973, pp. 175-178.

BRADDON, MARY

Gorsky, Susan. "The Gentle Doubters: Images of Women in Englishwomen's Novels, 1840-1920. " In Images of Women in Fiction, pp. 32, 36, 48. Edited by Susan Koppelman Cornillon. Bowling Green, Ohio: Bowling Green University Press, 1972.

_____. "Old Maids and New Women: Alternatives to Marriage in Englishwomen's Novels, 1847-1915. " Journal of Popular Culture 7 (Summer 1973): 68-85.

BRADSTREET, ANNE

Eberwein, Jane Donahue. "The 'Unrefined Ore' of Anne Bradstreet's Quarternions. " Early American Literature 9 (Spring 1974): 19-26.

Keeble, Neil H. "Anne Bradstreet: The First Colonial Poet. " Literary Half-Yearly 13 (1972): 13-28.

Laughlin, Rosemary M. "Anne Bradstreet: Poet in Search of Form. " American Literature 42 (March 1970): 1-17.

Requa, Kenneth A. "Anne Bradstreet's Poetic Voices. " Early American Literature 9 (Spring 1974): 3-18.

_____. "Public and Private Voices in the Poetry of Anne Bradstreet, Michael Wigglesworth, and Edward Taylor. " Ph. D. Dissertation, Indiana University, 1971.

Schulman, Grace. "Women the Inventors. " Nation, 11 December 1972, pp. 594-596.

Walker, Cheryl Lawson. "The Women's Tradition in
American Poetry." Ph.D. Dissertation, Brandeis
University, 1973.

Waller, Jennifer R. "'My Hand a Needle Better Fits':
Anne Bradstreet and Women Poets in the Renaissance."
Dalhousie Review 54 (Autumn 1974): 436-450.

White, Elizabeth Wade. Anne Bradstreet, The Tenth
Muse. New York: Oxford University Press, 1971.

BRAEME, CHARLOTTE

Gorsky, Susan. "The Gentle Doubters: Images of Women
in Englishwomen's Novels, 1840-1920." In Images
of Women in Fiction, pp. 39, 46. Edited by Susan
Koppelman Cornillon. Bowling Green, Ohio: Bowling
Green University Press, 1972.

_____. "Old Maids and New Women: Alternatives
to Marriage in Englishwomen's Novels, 1847-1915."
Journal of Popular Culture 7 (Summer 1973): 68-85.

BRANNER, H. C.

Mishler, William. "The Theme of Reflection in H. C.
Branner's Ariel." Scandinavian Studies 47 (Winter
1975): 42-51.

BRECHT, BERTOLT

Cronin, Mary J. "The Politics of Brecht's Women
Characters." Ph.D. Dissertation, Brown University,
1974.

BRONTË, CHARLOTTE

Allott, Miriam, comp. The Brontës, the Critical Heritage. London, Boston: Routledge & Kegan Paul,
1974.

_____, ed. Charlotte Brontë: Jane Eyre and Villette.
London: Macmillan, 1973.

Arndt, Frances Cole. "Villette: Another Turn of the
Wheel." Ph.D. Dissertation, Duke University,
1972.

Auerbach, Nina. "Charlotte Brontë: The Two Countries." University of Toronto Quarterly 42 (Summer 1973): 328-342.

Basch, Françoise. Relative Creatures: Victorian Women in Society and the Novel. New York: Schocken, 1974.

Beer, Patricia. Reader, I Married Him: A Study of the Women Characters of Jane Austen, Charlotte Brontë, Elizabeth Gaskell, and George Eliot. New York: Harper, 1975.

Benvenuto, Richard. "The Child of Nature, the Child of Grace, and the Unresolved Conflict of Jane Eyre." ELH 39 (December 1972): 620-638.

Berndt, David Edward. "'This Hard, Real Life': Self and Society in Five Mid-Victorian Bildungsromane." Ph. D. Dissertation, Cornell University, 1972.

Birky, Wilbur Joseph. "Marriage as Pattern and Metaphor in the Victorian Novel." Ph. D. Dissertation, The University of Iowa, 1970.

Blom, M. A. "Charlotte Brontë, Feminist Manquée." Bucknell Review 21 (Spring 1973): 87-102.

_____. "Jane Eyre: Mind as Law Unto Itself." Criticism 15 (Fall 1973): 350-364.

Brayfield, Peggy Lee. "A New Feminist Approach to the Novels of Charlotte Brontë." Ph. D. Dissertation, Southern Illinois University, 1973.

Bromley, Laura Ann. "...The Victorian 'Good Woman' and the Fiction of Charlotte Brontë." Ph. D. Dissertation. Rutgers University, The State University of New Jersey, 1973.

Burkhart, Charles. Charlotte Brontë: A Psychosexual Study of Her Novels. London: Gollancz, 1973.

_____. "The Nuns of Villette." Victorian Newsletter no. 44 (Fall 1973): 8-13.

Cazamian, Louis. The Social Novel in England 1830-1850.

London and Boston: Routledge & Kegan Paul, 1973.

Colby, Vineta. Yesterday's Woman: Domestic Realism in the English Novel. Princeton, N. J.: Princeton University Press, 1974.

Eagleton, Terry. "Class, Power, and Charlotte Brontë." Critical Quarterly 14 (Autumn 1972): 225-235.

Figes, Eva. Patriarchal Attitudes. New York: Stein & Day, 1970.

Gérin, Winifred. The Brontës: The Creative Work. New York: British Book Center, 1974.

_____. The Brontës: The Formative Years. New York: British Book Center, 1974.

Gorsky, Susan. "The Gentle Doubters: Images of Women in Englishwomen's Novels, 1840-1920." In Images of Women in Fiction, pp. 29-30, 40, 43, 49. Edited by Susan Koppelman Cornillon. Bowling Green, Ohio: Bowling Green University Press, 1972.

_____. "Old Maids and New Women: Alternatives to Marriage in Englishwomen's Novels, 1847-1915." Journal of Popular Culture 7 (Summer 1973): 68-85.

Hagan, John. "Enemies of Freedom in Jane Eyre." Criticism 13 (Fall 1971): 351-376.

Halperin, John. Egoism and Self-Discovery in the Victorian Novel. New York: Burt Franklin, 1974, pp. 45-61.

Hannah, Barbara. Striving Towards Wholeness. New York: Putnam's for the C. G. Jung Foundation for Analytical Psychology, 1971.

Hardwick, Elizabeth. Seduction and Betrayal. New York: Random House, 1974, pp. 1-29.

_____. "Working Girls: The Brontës." New York Review of Books, 4 May 1972, pp. 11-18.

Heilbrun, Carolyn G. Toward a Recognition of Androgyny. New York: Knopf, 1973, pp. 50, 58-59, 73, 78-79.

Hoffman, Leonore Noll. "A Delicate Balance: The
Resolutions to Conflicts of Women in the Fiction of
Four Women Writers of the Victorian Period."
Ph. D. Dissertation, Indiana University, 1974.

Katz, Judith Nina. "Rooms of Their Own: Forms and
Images of Liberation in Five Novels." Ph. D. Dissertation, The Pennsylvania State University, 1972.

Kroeber, Karl. Styles in Fictional Structure: The Art
of Jane Austen, Charlotte Brontë, George Eliot.
Princeton, N. J.: Princeton University Press, 1971.

Leeming, Glenda. Who's Who in Jane Austen and the
Brontës. New York: Taplinger, 1974.

Linder, C. A. "The Ideal Marriage as Depicted in the
Novels of Jane Austen and Charlotte Brontë."
Standpunte 96 (1971): 20-30.

Manley, Seon and Susan Belcher. "The Moor Was
Mightier than the Men." In O, Those Extraordinary
Women! Philadelphia: Chilton, 1972, pp. 108-130.

Millett, Kate. Sexual Politics. New York: Avon, 1970,
pp. 130, 140-147.

Moers, Ellen. "Money, the Job, and Little Women."
Commentary 55 (January 1973): 57-65. Reply with
rejoinder: E. Kaledin 55 (May 1973): 26.

Ohmann, Carol. "Charlotte Brontë: The Limits of Her
Feminism." In Female Studies VI: Closer to the
Ground, pp. 152-163. Edited by Nancy Hoffman,
Cynthia Secor, Adrian Tinsley. Old Westbury, N. Y.:
Feminist Press, 1972.

Osborne, Marianne Muse. "The Hero and Heroine in the
British Bildungsroman: David Copperfield and A
Portrait of the Artist as a Young Man, Jane Eyre
and The Rainbow." Ph. D. Dissertation, Tulane
University, 1971.

Peters, Margot. Charlotte Brontë: Style in the Novel.
Madison: University of Wisconsin Press, 1973.

Peterson, M. Jeanne. "The Victorian Governess:

Status, Incongruence in Family and Society." Victorian Studies 14 (September 1970): 7-23.

Platt, Carolyn Virginia. "The Female Quest in the Works of Anne, Charlotte, and Emily Brontë." Ph. D. Dissertation, University of Illinois at Urbana-Champaign, 1974.

Rich, Adrienne. "Jane Eyre: The Temptations of a Motherless Woman." Ms. 2 (October 1973): 68.

Showalter, Elaine Cottler. "The Double Standard: Criticism of Women Writers in England, 1845-1880." Ph. D. Dissertation, University of California, Davis, 1970.

Spacks, Patricia M. The Female Imagination. New York: Knopf, 1975.

Stone, Donald D. "Victorian Feminism and the Nineteenth-Century Novel." Women's Studies 1 (1972): 65-92.

Sudrann, Jean. "Hearth and Horizon: Changing Concepts of the 'Domestic' Life of the Heroine." Massachusetts Review 14 (Spring 1973): 235-255.

Wagner, Geoffrey. Five for Freedom: A Study of Feminism in Fiction. Rutherford, Madison, Teaneck, N. J.: Fairleigh Dickinson University, 1972, pp. 34, 41, 55, 103-137 passim, 138, 159, 167, 168, 186, 218.

Waidner, Maralee Layman. "From Reason to Romance: A Progression from an Emphasis on Neoclassic Rationality to Romantic Intuition in Three English Women Novelists." Ph. D. Dissertation, The University of Tulsa, 1973.

Winnifrith, Tom. The Brontës and Their Background: Romance and Reality. New York: Macmillan, 1973.

Yeazell, R. B. "More True than Real: Jane Eyre's Mysterious Summons." Nineteenth-Century Fiction 29 (September 1974): 127-143.

BRONTË, EMILY

Allott, Miriam Farris, comp. The Brontës, the Critical

Heritage. London, Boston: Routledge & Kegan Paul, 1974.

Ames, Carol. "Love Triangles in Fiction: The Underlying Fantasies." Ph. D. Dissertation, State University of New York at Buffalo, 1973.

Basch, Françoise. Relative Creatures: Victorian Women in Society and the Novel. New York: Schocken, 1974.

Burns, Wayne. "In Death They Were Not Divided: The Moral Magnificence of Unmoral Passion in Wuthering Heights." Hartford Studies in Literature 5 (1973): 135-159.

Gérin, Winifred. The Brontës: The Creative Work. New York: British Book Center, 1974.

_____. The Brontës: The Formative Years. New York: British Book Center, 1974.

_____. Emily Brontë: A Biography. Oxford: Clarendon Press, 1971; New York: Oxford University Press, 1971.

Hannah, Barbara. Striving Towards Wholeness. New York: Putnam's for the C. G. Jung Foundation for Analytical Psychology, 1971.

Hardwick, Elizabeth. Seduction and Betrayal: Women and Literature. New York: Random House, 1974, pp. 1-29.

Heilbrun, Carolyn G. Toward a Recognition of Androgyny. New York: Knopf, 1973, pp. 58, 59, 62, 63, 79-82, 126.

Krier, William John. "A Pattern of Limitations: The Heroine's Novel of Mind." Ph. D. Dissertation, Indiana University, 1973.

Manley, Seon and Susan Belcher. "The Moor Was Mightier Than the Men: The Brooding Brontës." O, Those Extraordinary Women! Philadelphia: Chilton, 1972.

Mitchell, Giles. "Incest, Demonism and Death in

Wuthering Heights." Literature and Psychology 23 (1973): 27-36.

Moglen, Helene. "The Double Vision of Wuthering Heights: A Clarifying View of Female Development." Centennial Review 15 (Fall 1971): 391-405.

Ohmann, Carol. "Emily Brontë in the Hands of Male Critics." College English 32 (May 1971): 906-913.

Petit, Jean Pierre, ed. Emily Brontë: A Critical Anthology. Harmondsworth: Penguin, 1973.

Platt, Carolyn Virginia. "The Female Quest in the Works of Anne, Charlotte and Emily Brontë." Ph.D. Dissertation, University of Illinois at Urbana-Champaign, 1974.

Spacks, Patricia M. The Female Imagination. New York: Knopf, 1975.

Sucksmith, H. P. "The Theme of Wuthering Heights Reconsidered." Dalhousie Review 54 (Autumn 1974): 418-428.

Winnifrith, Tom. The Brontës and Their Background: Romance and Reality. New York: Macmillan, 1973.

BROOKE, FRANCES

New, William H. "The Old Maid: Frances Brooke's Apprentice Feminism." Journal of Canadian Fiction 2 (Summer 1973): 9-12.

Shohet, Linda. "Love and Marriage--Canada 1760." Journal of Canadian Fiction 2 (Summer 1973): 101-103. (Review Essay.)

BROOKS, GWENDOLYN

Brooks, Gwendolyn. Report from Part One. Detroit: Broadside, 1972.

Dobbs, Jeanine. "Not Another Poetess: A Study of Female Experience in Modern American Poetry." Ph.D. Dissertation, University of New Hampshire, 1973.

Furman, Marva Riley. "Gwendolyn Brooks: The 'Un-
conditioned Poet.'" CLA Journal 17 (September 1973):
1-10.

Kent, George E. Blackness and the Adventure of Western
Culture. Chicago: Third World Press, 1972, pp.
104-138.

_____. "The Poetry of Gwendolyn Brooks, Part I."
Black World 2 (September 1971): 30-43. "Part II."
2 (September 1971): 36-48.

Stravos, George. "An Interview with Gwendolyn Brooks."
Contemporary Literature 11 (Winter 1970): 1-20.

Walker, Cheryl Lawson. "The Women's Tradition in
American Poetry." Ph.D. Dissertation, Brandeis
University, 1973.

BROUGHTON, RHODA

Gorsky, Susan. "The Gentle Doubters: Images of Women
in Englishwomen's Novels, 1840-1920." In Images
of Women in Fiction, p. 45. Edited by Susan Koppelman Cornillon, Bowling Green, Ohio: Bowling Green
University Press, 1972.

BROWN, ALICE

Toth, Susan A. "A Forgotten View from Beacon Hill:
Alice Brown's New England Short Stories." Colby
Library Quarterly 10 (March 1973): 1-17.

_____. "Sarah Orne Jewett and Friends." Studies in
Short Fiction 9 (Summer 1972): 233-242.

Walker, Dorothea. Alice Brown. New York: Twayne,
1974.

Wood, Ann Douglas. "The Literature of Impoverishment:
The Women Local Colorists in America 1865-1914."
Women's Studies 1 (1972): 3-46.

BROWN, CHARLES BROCKDEN

Carlson, Constance Hedin. "Heroines in Certain American Novels." Ph.D. Dissertation, Brown University,
1971.

Cicardo, Barbara Joan. "The Mystery of the American Eve: Alienation of the Feminine as a Tragic Theme in American Letters." Ph. D. Dissertation, St. Louis University, 1971.

Cunningham, Judith Ann. "Charles Brockden Brown's Pursuit of a Realistic Feminism: A Study of His Writings as a Contribution to the Growth of Women's Rights in America." Ph. D. Dissertation, Ball State University, 1971.

Earnest, Ernest. The American Eve in Fact and Fiction, 1775-1914. Urbana, Chicago, London: University of Illinois Press, 1974, pp. 31-33.

Franklin, Wayne. "Tragedy and Comedy in Brown's Wieland." Novel 8 (Winter 1975): 147-163.

Krause, Sydney J. "Ormand: Seduction in a New Key." American Literature 44 (1973): [570]-584.

McCay, Mary Ann Dobbin. "Women in the Novels of Charles Brockden Brown: A Study." Ph. D. Dissertation, Tufts University, 1973.

Montgomery, Judith Howard. "Pygmalion's Image: The Metamorphosis of the American Heroine." Ph. D. Dissertation, Syracuse University, 1971.

Nelson, Carl. "A Just Reading of Charles Brockden Brown's Ormond." Early American Literature 8 (Fall 1973): 163-178.

Rodgers, Paul C., Jr. "Brown's Ormond: The Fruits of Improvisation." American Quarterly 26 (March 1974): 3-22.

Tomlinson, David Otis. "Women in the Writing of Charles Brockden Brown: A Study in the Development of an Author's Thought." Ph. D. Dissertation, The University of North Carolina at Chapel Hill, 1974.

Witherington, Paul. "Brockden Brown's Other Novels: Clara Howard and Jane Talbot." Nineteenth-Century Fiction 29 (December 1974): 257-272.

BROWNING, ELIZABETH BARRETT

Basch, Françoise. *Relative Creatures: Victorian Women in Society and the Novel.* New York: Schocken, 1974.

Lupton, Mary Jane. *Elizabeth Barrett Browning.* Old Westbury, N. Y.: Feminist Press, 197?.

————. "The Printing Woman Who Lost Her Place: Elizabeth Barrett Browning." *Women: A Journal of Liberation* 2 (Fall 1970): 2-5.

Radley, Virginia L. *Elizabeth Barrett Browning.* New York: Twayne, 1972.

Showalter, Elaine Cottler. "The Double Standard: Criticism of Women Writers in England, 1845-1880." Ph.D. Dissertation, University of California, Davis, 1970.

Thomson, Patricia. "Elizabeth Barrett and George Sand." *Durham University Journal* 33 (June 1972): 205-219.

Zimmerman, Susan. "*Sonnets from the Portuguese*: A Negative and Positive Context." *Mary Wollstonecraft Newsletter* 2 (December 1973): 7-20.

BUCHANAN, CYNTHIA

Gottlieb, Annie. *New York Times Book Review*, 9 January 1972, p. 6. (Review of *Maiden.*)

Stimpson, Catherine. *Nation*, 24 January 1972, p. 117. (Review of *Maiden.*)

BURNEY, FANNY

Halsband, Robert. "'The Female Pen': Women and Literature in Eighteenth-Century England." *History Today* 24 (October 1974): 702-709.

Hemlow, Joyce, Curtis D. Cecil and Althea Douglas, eds. *The Journals and Letters of Fanny Burney (Madame D'Arblay),* vol. 1. New York: Oxford University Press, 1972.

Hemlow, Joyce and Althea Douglas, eds. A Catalogue of the Burney Family Correspondence, 1749-1878. Montreal: McGill-Queen's University Press, 1971.

_____, eds. The Journals and Letters of Fanny Burney (Madame D'Arblay), vols. 2-4. New York: Oxford University Press, 1972, 1973.

Katz, Judith Nina. "Rooms of Their Own: Forms and Images of Liberation in Five Novels." Ph.D. Dissertation, The Pennsylvania State University, 1972.

Manley, Seon and Susan Belcher. "Bluestockings and Bon Wits." In O, Those Extraordinary Women! Philadelphia: Chilton, 1972, pp. 57-84.

Moler, Kenneth L. "Evelina in Vanity Fair: Becky Sharp and Her Patrician Heroes." Nineteenth-Century Fiction 27 (September 1972): 171-181.

Pratt, Annis. "Archetypal Approaches to the New Feminist Criticism." Bucknell Review 21 (Spring 1973): 3-14.

Rubenstein, Jill. "The Crisis of Identity in Fanny Burney's Evelina." New Rambler (Johnson Society, London) 112 (1972): 45-50.

Rudolf, Jo-Ellen Schwartz. "The Novels That Taught the Ladies: A Study of Popular Fiction Written by Women, 1702-1834." Ph.D. Dissertation, University of California, San Diego, 1972.

Spacks, Patricia Meyer. "'Ev'ry Woman is at Heart a Rake.'" Eighteenth Century Studies 8 (Fall 1974): 27-46.

_____. The Female Imagination. New York: Knopf, 1975.

_____. "Reflecting Women." Yale Review 63 (October 1973): 26-42.

Speakman, James Stewart. "Wit, Humor and Sensibility in Evelina, Belinda and Northanger Abbey." Ph.D. Dissertation, University of California, Davis, 1972.

Steeves, Edna L. "Pre-Feminism in Some Eighteenth Century Novels. " <u>Texas Quarterly</u> 16 (Autumn 1973): 48-57.

BYRON, GEORGE GORDON, LORD

Boken, Julia Barbara. "Byron's Ladies: A Study of <u>Don Juan</u>. " Ph. D. Dissertation, Columbia University, 1970.

Hull, Gloria Thompson. "Women in Byron's Poetry: A Biographical and Critical Study. " Ph. D. Dissertation, Purdue University, 1972.

Schlosstein, Sallie Elizabeth. "Byron: The Inverted Role of the Female in His Poetry. " Ph. D. Dissertation, University of Cincinnati, 1974.

-C-

CABALLERO, FERNAN

Klibbe, Lawrence H. <u>Fernán Caballero</u>. New York: Twayne, 1973.

Tyrmand, Mary Ellen. "Women and Society in the Nineteenth-Century Spanish Novel. " Ph. D. Dissertation, Yale University, 1974.

CABRERA INFANTE, GUILLERMO

Siemens, William L. "The Devouring Female in Four Latin American Novels. " <u>Essays in Literature</u> (Macomb, Ill.) 1 (Spring 1974): 118-129.

CALLAGHAN, MORLEY

Atwood, Margaret. "Ice Women vs Earth Mothers. " In <u>Survival: A Thematic Guide to Canadian Literature</u>. Toronto: Anansi, 1972, pp. 195-212.

Jones, D. G. <u>Butterfly on Rock: A Study of Themes and Images in Canadian Literature</u>. Toronto and Buffalo: University of Toronto Press, 1970.

Moss, John. Patterns of Isolation in English Canadian Fiction. Toronto: McClelland & Stewart, 1974.

Walsh, William. A Manifold Voice: Studies in Commonwealth Literature. New York: Barnes & Noble, 1970.

CAMBRIDGE, ADA

Roe, Jill. "'The Scope of Woman's Thought is Necessarily Less': The Case of Ada Cambridge." Australian Literary Studies 5 (October 1972): 388-403.

CAMUS, ALBERT

Grainger, Inslee Ebissa. "Women in the Imaginative Works of Albert Camus." Ph.D. Dissertation, University of North Carolina at Chapel Hill, 1973.

CAPECIA, MAYOTTE

Clark, Beatrice Stith. "The Works of Mayotte Capécia." CLA Journal 16 (June 1973): 415-425.

CAREY, R. N.

Gorsky, Susan. "The Gentle Doubters: Images of Women in Englishwomen's Novels, 1840-1920." In Images of Women in Fiction, p. 39. Edited by Susan Koppelman Cornillon. Bowling Green, Ohio: Bowling Green University Press, 1972.

_____. "Old Maids and New Women: Alternatives to Marriage in Englishwomen's Novels, 1847-1915." Journal of Popular Culture 7 (Summer 1973): 68-85.

CARY, JOYCE

Brown, Patricia Sant. "Creative Losers: Blacks, Children, and Women in the Novels of Joyce Cary." Ph.D. Dissertation, University of Massachusetts, 1973.

Reed, Peter J. "'The Better the Heart': Joyce Cary's Sara Monday." Texas Studies in Literature and Language 15 (Summer 1973): 356-370.

CATHER, WILLA

Adams, Theodore S. "Willa Cather's My Mortal Enemy: The Concise Presentation of Scene, Character, and Theme." Colby Library Quarterly 10 (September 1973): 138-139.

Barba, Sharon Rose. "Willa Cather: A Feminist Study." Ph. D. Dissertation, University of New Mexico, 1973.

Bash, James R. "Willa Cather and the Anathema of Materialism." Colby Library Quarterly 10 (September 1973): 157-168.

Carlson, Constance Hedin. "Heroines in Certain American Novels." Ph. D. Dissertation, Brown University, 1971.

Ditsky, John. "Nature and Character in the Novels of Willa Cather." Colby Library Quarterly 10 (September 1974): 391-412.

Eichorn, Harry B. "A Falling Out with Love: My Mortal Enemy." Colby Library Quarterly 10 (September 1973): 121-137.

Fleming, Patricia Jean. "The Integrated Self: Sexuality and the Double Role in Willa Cather's Fiction." Ph. D. Dissertation, Boston University Graduate School, 1974.

Fox, Maynard. "Symbolic Representation in Willa Cather's O Pioneers!" Western American Literature 9 (November 1974): 187-196.

Gelfant, Blanche H. "The Forgotten Reaping Hook: Sex in My Antonia." American Literature 43 (March 1971): 60-82.

McClure, Charlotte Swain. "The American Eve: A Tragedy of Innocence." Ph. D. Dissertation, University of New Mexico, 1973.

McFarland, Dorothy T. Willa Cather. New York: Frederick Ungar, 1972.

Mattern, Claire. "The Themes That Bind." Willa

Cather Pioneer Memorial and Educational Foundation 18 (Winter 1974): [1].

Moers, Ellen. "Willa Cather and Collette: Mothers of Us All." World, 27 March 1973, pp. 51-53.

Murphy, John J. "The Respectable Romantic and the Unwed Mother: Class Consciousness in My Antonia." Colby Library Quarterly 10 (September 1973): 149-156.

Parker, Jeraldine. "'Uneasy Survivors': Five Women Writers 1896-1923." Ph. D. Dissertation, University of Utah, 1973.

Pratt, Annis. "Women and Nature in Modern Fiction." Contemporary Literature 13 (Autumn 1972): 476-490.

Schneider, Lucy. "Artistry and Instinct: Willa Cather's 'Land-Philosophy.'" CLA Journal 16 (June 1973): 485-504.

Slote, Bernice and Virginia Faulkner, eds. The Art of Willa Cather. Lincoln: University of Nebraska Press, 1974.

Stouck, David. Willa Cather's Imagination. Lincoln: University of Nebraska Press, forthcoming.

Stuckey, W. J. "My Antonia: A Rose for Miss Cather." Studies in the Novel 4 (1972): 473-483.

Wells, Nancy. "Women in American Literature." English Journal 62 (November 1973): 1159-1161.

Whaley, Elizabeth Gates. "Cather's My Mortal Enemy." Prairie Schooner 48 (Summer 1974): 124-133.

Willa Cather: A Pictorial Memoir. Photos by Lucia Woods and Others. Text by Bernice Slote. Lincoln: University of Nebraska Press, 1973.

Woodress, James Leslie. Willa Cather: Her Life and Art. New York: Pegasus, 1970.

CENDRARS, BLAISE

Szautner, Kathleen Anne Marschang. "The Mystery of

Woman in the Works of Blaise Cendrars. " Ph. D.
Dissertation, Bryn Mawr College, 1970.

CENTLIVRE, SUSANNAH

Burke, Terrence William. "Susanna Centlivre's A Bold
Stroke for a Wife: A Re-Evaluation. " Ph. D. Dissertation, Case Western Reserve University, 1971.

Miner, Earl, ed. Stuart and Georgian Moments. Berkeley, University of California Press, 1972, pp. 272,
273.

Suwannabha, Sumitra. "The Feminine Eye: Augustan
Society as Seen by Selected Women Dramatists of the
Restoration and Early Eighteenth Century. " Ph. D.
Dissertation, Indiana University, 1973.

CHALLE, ROBERT

Forno, Lawrence J. "Challe's Portrayal of Women. "
French Review 47 (April 1974): 865-873.

CHARLOTTE ELIZABETH (Mrs. Tonna)

Cazamian, Louis. The Social Novel in England 1830-
1850. London and Boston: Routledge & Kegan
Paul, 1973.

Colby, Vineta. Yesterday's Woman: Domestic Realism
in the English Novel. Princeton, N. J. : Princeton
University Press, 1974.

CHARRIERE, MME. de

Braunrot, Christabel Pendrill. "Madame de Charrière
and the Eighteenth-Century Novel: Experiments in
Epistolary Techniques. " Ph. D. Dissertation, Yale
University, 1973.

Lacy, Kluenter Wesley. "An Essay on Feminine Fiction,
1757-1803. " Ph. D. Dissertation, The University of
Wisconsin, 1972.

West, Anthony. Mortal Wounds. New York: McGraw-
Hill, 1973, pp. 183-221.

CHAUCER, GEOFFREY

Boatner, Janet Williams. "Criseyde's Character in the Major Writers from Benoît through Dryden: The Changes and Their Significance." Ph. D. Dissertation, The University of Wisconsin, 1970.

Brown, Eric Donald. "Archetypes of Transformation: A Jungian Analysis of Chaucer's Wife of Bath's Tale and Clerk's Tale." Ph. D. Dissertation, The Pennsylvania State University, 1972.

Colmer, Dorothy. "Character and Class in The Wife of Bath's Tale." Journal of English and German Philology 72 (July 1973): 329-339.

Delany, Sheila. "Womanliness in the Man of Law's Tale." Chaucer Review 9 (Summer 1974): 63-72.

Frank, Robert Worth, Jr. Chaucer and The Legend of Good Women. Cambridge: Harvard University Press, 1972.

Gordon, Ida L. The Double Sorrow of Troilus. Oxford: Clarendon Press, 1970, pp. 98-102.

Hamilton, Alice. "Heloways and the Burning of Jankyn's Book." Medieval Studies 34 (1972): 196-207.

Hamlin, B. F. "Astrology and The Wife of Bath: A Reinterpretation." Chaucer Review 9 (Fall 1974): 153-165.

Harwood, Britton J. "The Wife and Bath and the Dream of Innocence." Modern Language Quarterly 33 (September 1972): 257-273.

Hoffman, R. L. "Wife of Bath's Uncharitable Offerings." English Language Notes 11 (March 1974): 165-167.

Kelly, Henry A. Love and Marriage in the Age of Chaucer. Ithaca: Cornell University Press, 1975.

Kernan, Anne. The Archwife and the Eunuch." ELH 41 (Spring 1974): 1-25.

Kiessling, Nicolas K. "The Wife of Bath's Tale:

D 878-881." <u>Chaucer Review</u> 7 (Summer 1972): 113-117.

Kloss, Robert J. "Chaucer's <u>The Merchant's Tale</u>: Tender Youth and Stooping Age." <u>American Imago</u> 31 (Spring 1974): 65-79.

Koban, Charles. "Hearing Chaucer Out: The Art of Persuasion in the 'Wife of Bath's Tale.'" <u>Chaucer Review</u> 5 (1971): 225-239.

Mann, Jill. <u>Chaucer and Medieval Estates Satire</u>. Cambridge: Cambridge University Press, 1973, pp. 121-127.

Mitchell, Jerome and William Provost, eds. <u>Chaucer the Love Poet</u>. Athens: University of Georgia Press, 1973.

Murtaugh, Daniel M. "Women and Geoffrey Chaucer." <u>ELH</u> 38 (December 1971): 473-493.

Nichols, Nicholas Pete. "Discretion and Marriage in the <u>Canterbury Tales</u>." Ph. D. Dissertation, Columbia University, 1971.

Olson, Clair C. "The Interludes of the Marriage Group." In <u>Chaucer and Middle English Studies</u>, pp. 164-172. Edited by Beryl Rowland. London: George Allen & Unwin, 1974.

Pitlock, Malcolm. <u>The Prioress's Tale, The Wife of Bath's Tale</u>. Oxford: Basil Blackwell, 1973.

Rajiva, Stanley F. "The Eternal Anti-Feminine." <u>Indian Journal of English Studies</u> 12 (1971): 1-21.

Reed, Gail Helen Vieth. "Chaucer's Women: Commitment and Submission." Ph. D. Dissertation, University of Nebraska-Lincoln, 1973.

Rowland, Beryl. "The Physician's 'Historical Thyng Notable' and the Man of Law." <u>ELH</u> 40 (Summer 1973): 165-178.

_____. "The Wife of Bath's 'Unlawful Philtrum.'" <u>Neophilologus</u> 56 (1972): 201-206.

Smagola, Mary Patricia. "'Spek Wel of Love': The Role of Woman in Chaucer's Legend of Good Women." Ph. D. Dissertation, Case Western Reserve University, 1972.

Szittya, Penn R. "The Green Yeoman as Loathly Lady: The Friar's Parody of the Wife of Bath's Tale." PMLA 90 (May 1975): 386-394.

Tripp, Raymond P., Jr. "The Franklin's Solution to the Marriage Debate." Proceedings of the Society for New Language Study 1 (June 1973): 35-41.

CHEKHOV, ANTON

Clyman, Toby Wainshtroch. "Women in Chekhov's Prose Works." Ph. D. Dissertation, New York University, 1971.

Grishin, N. "The Development of the Female Image in Chekhov's Work." In Australasian Universities Language and Literature Association: Proceedings and Papers of the Thirteenth Congress Held at Monash University 12-18 August 1970, pp. 450-451. Melbourne: AULIA and Monash University, 1971. (Abstract.)

Heilbrun, Carolyn. "Marriage Made on Earth." Ms. 2 (February 1974): 41.

CHESNUTT, CHARLES

Andrews, William L. "Chesnutt's Patesville: The Presence and Influence of the Past in The House Behind the Cedars." CLA Journal 15 (March 1972): 284-294.

Gayle, Addison, Jr. The Way of the New World: The Black Novel in America. Garden City, N.Y.: Doubleday, 1974, pp. 48-50.

Smith, Robert A. "A Pioneer Black Writer and the Problems of Discrimination and Miscegenation." Costerus 9 (1973): 181-185.

CHILD, PHILIP

Jones, D. G. Butterfly on Rock: A Study of Themes

and Images in Canadian Literature. Toronto and
Buffalo: University of Toronto Press, 1970.

CHILDRESS, ALICE

Hatch, James V. "Alice Childress." New York:
Hatch/Billops Collection, 736 Broadway, 1974.
(Available as tape or mimeographed.)

Mobley, Joyce D. "Black Female Voices in the American Theater, 1916-1970." Paper presented for the
Midwest Modern Language Association, Chicago,
3 November 1973. (Mimeographed.)

CHOPIN, KATE

Arner, Robert D. "Music from a Farther Room: A
Study of the Fiction of Kate Chopin." Ph.D. Dissertation, The Pennsylvania State University, 1970.

_____. "Pride and Prejudice: Kate Chopin's
'Desiree's Baby.'" Mississippi Quarterly 25 (1972):
131-140.

Bender, Bert. "Kate Chopin's Lyric Short Stories."
Studies in Short Fiction 11 (Summer 1974): 257-266.

Colwell, Mary. "Kate Chopin, Writer Unknown."
Women: A Journal of Liberation 2 (Fall 1970):
10-11.

Donovan, Josephine. "Feminist Style Criticism." In
Female Studies VI: Closer to the Ground. Edited
by Nancy Hoffman, Cynthia Secor, Adrian Tinsley.
Old Westbury, N.Y.: Feminist Press, 1972.

Earnest, Ernest. The American Eve in Fact and Fiction,
1775-1914. Urbana, Chicago, London: University
of Illinois Press, 1974, pp. 260-263.

Edwards, Lee R. and Arlyn Diamond. "Introduction."
American Voices, American Women. New York:
Avon, 1973.

Fishel, Elizabeth. "Women's Fiction: Who's Afraid of
Virginia Woolf?" Ramparts, June 1973, pp. 45-48.

Forrey, Carolyn. "The New Woman Revisited."

Women's Studies 2 (1974): 37-56.

Fryer, Judith Joy. "The Faces of Eve: A Study of Women in American Life and Literature in the Nineteenth Century." Ph.D. Dissertation, University of Minnesota, 1973.

Koloski, Bernard John. "Kate Chopin and the Search for a Code of Behavior." Ph.D. Dissertation, The University of Arizona, 1972.

_____. "The Structure of Kate Chopin's At Fault." Studies in American Fiction 3 (Spring 1975): 88-95.

_____. "The Swinburne Lines in The Awakening." American Literature 45 (January 1974): 608-610.

Lally, Joan Marie. "Kate Chopin: Four Studies." Ph.D. Dissertation, University of Utah, 1973.

Leary, Lewis. "Kate Chopin, Liberationist?" Southern Literary Journal 3 (Fall 1970): 138-144.

Martin, Richard A. "The Fictive World of Kate Chopin." Ph.D. Dissertation, Northwestern University, 1971.

Milliner, Gladys W. "The Tragic Imperative: The Awakening and The Bell Jar." Mary Wollstonecraft Newsletter 2 (December 1973): 21-27.

Peterson, Peter James. "The Fiction of Kate Chopin." Ph.D. Dissertation, The University of New Mexico, 1972.

Ringe, Donald A. "Romantic Imagery in Kate Chopin's The Awakening." American Literature 43 (January 1972): 580-588.

Rocks, James E. "Kate Chopin's Ironic Vision." Revue de Louisiana/Louisiana Review 1 (1972): 110-120.

Rosen, Kenneth M. "Kate Chopin's The Awakening: Ambiguity as Art." Journal of American Studies (British) 5 (August 1971): 197-199.

Seyersted, Per. Kate Chopin: A Critical Biography. Baton Rouge: Louisiana State University Press, 1970.

Skaggs, Peggy Dechert. "A Woman's Place: The Search for Identity in Kate Chopin's Female Characters." Ph. D. Dissertation, Texas A & M University, 1972.

Snow, Kimberley H. M. S. "Kate Chopin's Masterpiece: The Awakening." Aphra 3 (Spring 1972): 4-15.

Spacks, Patricia M. The Female Imagination, New York: Knopf, 1975.

Sullivan, Ruth and Stewart Smith. "Narrative Stance in Kate Chopin's The Awakening." Studies in American Fiction 1 (Spring 1973): 62-75.

Wheeler, Otis B. "The Five Awakenings of Edna Pontellier." Southern Review 11 (January 1975): 118-128.

Wolff, Cynthia G. "Thanatos and Eros: Kate Chopin's The Awakening." American Quarterly 25 (October 1973): 449-471.

CLAUDEL, PAUL

Bugliani, Ann Camelia. "Women and the Feminine Principle in Claudel's Works." Ph. D. Dissertation, Northwestern University, 1973.

CLEYRE, VOLTAIRINE de

Shulman, Alix. "Viewing Voltairine de Cleyre." Women: A Journal of Liberation 2 (Fall 1970): 5-7.

COHN-VIEBIG, CLARA

Scholtz, Sigrid Gerda. "Images of Womanhood in the Works of German Female Dramatists 1892-1918." Ph. D. Dissertation, Johns Hopkins University, 1971.

COLERIDGE, SAMUEL

Adlard, J. "Quantock Christabel." Philology Quarterly 50 (April 1971): 230-238.

Fleissner, Robert F. "'Kubla Khan' as an Integrationist Poem." Negro American Literature Forum 8 (Fall 1974): 254-256.

O'Hear, Michael Francis. "The Constant Dream: Coleridge's Vision of Woman and Love." Ph.D. Dissertation, University of Maryland, 1970.

Spatz, Jonas. "The Mystery of Eros: Sexual Initiation in Coleridge's 'Christabel.'" PMLA 90 (January 1975): 107-116.

COLETTE

Brée, Germaine. Women Writers in France: Variations on a Theme. New Brunswick, N.J.: Rutgers University Press, 1973, pp. 46-54.

Cottrell, Robert D. Colette. New York: Frederick Ungar, 1974.

Crosland, Margaret. Colette--The Difficulty of Loving: A Biography. Indianapolis: Bobbs-Merrill, 1973.

Heilbrun, Carolyn G. Toward a Recognition of Androgyny. New York: Knopf, 1973, p. 87.

Jong, Erica. "Retrieving Colette." Ms. 2 (April 1974): 31-33.

Moers, Ellen. "Willa Cather and Colette: Mothers of Us All." World, 27 March 1973, pp. 51-53.

Robinson, Lillian S. "Who's Afraid of a Room of One's Own?" In The Politics of Literature, pp. 381, 382, 393. Edited by Louis Kampf and Paul Lauter. New York: Pantheon, 1972.

Ryan, Nancy. Saturday Review, 1 April 1972, p. 74. (Review of The Other Woman.)

Spacks, Patricia Meyer. "Free Women." Hudson Review 24 (Winter 1971-1972): 559-573.

COLLETT, CAMILLA

Berg, Karin Westman. "Looking at Women in Literature." Scandinavian Review 63 (June 1975): 48-55.

COLLINS, WILKIE

Caracciolo, Peter. "Wilkie Collins's 'Divine Comedy':

The Use of Dante in The Woman in White." Nineteenth-Century Fiction 25 (March 1971): 383-403.

Culross, Jack Lewis. "The Prostitute and the Image of
Prostitution in Victorian Fiction." Ph. D. Dissertation, The Louisiana State University and Agricultural
and Mechanical College, 1970.

Heilbrun, Carolyn G. Toward a Recognition of Androgyny.
New York: Knopf, 1973, pp. 70-72.

Marshall, William H. Wilkie Collins. New York:
Twayne, 1970.

CONGREVE, WILLIAM

Corman, Brian. "The Way of the World and Morally
Serious Comedy." University of Toronto Quarterly
44 (Spring 1975): 199-212.

Kaufman, Anthony. "Language and Character in Congreve's The Way of the World." Texas Studies in
Literature 15 (Fall 1973): 411-427.

Lightfoot, John Ewell, Jr. "The Treatment of Women
in Restoration Comedy of Manners." Ph. D. Dissertation, Texas Tech University, 1973.

Morris, Brian, ed. William Congreve. (Mermaid
Critical Commentaries) London: Ernest Benn, 1972;
New Jersey: Rowman & Littlefield, 1972.

Nickles, Mary A. "The Women in Congreve's Comedies:
Characters and Caricatures." Ph. D. Dissertation,
New York University, 1972.

Novak, Maximillian E. "Love, Scandal, and the Moral
Milieu of Congreve's Comedies." In Congreve
Considered (Papers read at a Clark Library Seminar,
December 5, 1970, by Aubrey Williams and Maxi-
millian E. Novak.) University of California, Los
Angeles: William Andrews, Clark Memorial Library,
1971.

Suwannabha, Sumitra. "The Feminine Eye: Augustan
Society as Seen by Selected Women Dramatists of the
Restoration and Early Eighteenth Century." Ph. D.
Dissertation, Indiana University, 1973.

Teyssandier, H. "Congreve's Way of the World: Decorum and Morality." English Studies 52 (April 1971): 124-131.

CONRAD, JOSEPH

Adams, Barbara Block. "Sisters Under Their Skins: The Women in the Lives of Raskolnikov and Razumov." Conradiana 6 (1974): 113-114.

Cash, Joe Lynn. "The Treatment of Women Characters in the Complete Works of Joseph Conrad." Ph. D. Dissertation, Texas Tech University, 1972.

Rose, Charles. "Romance and the Maiden Archetype." Conradiana 6 (1974): 183-188.

Voytovich, Edward R. "The Problem of Identity for Conrad's Women." Essays in Literature (Denver) 2 (March 1974): 51-68.

COOKE, ROSE TERRY

Toth, Susan Allen. "Sarah Orne Jewett and Friends: A Community of Interest." Studies in Short Fiction 9 (Summer 1972): 233-242.

COOPER, JAMES FENIMORE

Baym, Nina. "The Women of Cooper's Leatherstocking Tales." American Quarterly 23 (1971): 698-709. Also in Images of Women in Fiction, pp. 135-154. Edited by Susan Koppelman Cornillon. Bowling Green, Ohio: Bowling Green University Press, 1972.

Carlson, Constance Hedin. "Heroines in Certain American Novels." Ph. D. Dissertation, Brown University, 1971.

Cicardo, Barbara Joan. "The Mystery of the American Eve: Alienation of the Feminine as a Tragic Theme in American Letters." Ph. D. Dissertation, St. Louis University, 1971.

Ginsberg, Elaine. "The Female Initiation Theme in American Fiction." Studies in Fiction 3 (Spring 1975): 27-37.

Graham, Robert John. "Concepts of Women in American Literature, 1813-1871." Ph. D. Dissertation, University of Pennsylvania, 1973.

Montgomery, Judith Howard. "Pygmalion's Image: The Metamorphosis of the American Heroine." Ph. D. Dissertation, Syracuse University, 1971.

Pratt, Linda Ray. "The Abuse of Eve by the New World Adam." In Images of Women in Fiction, pp. 156-160, 169. Edited by Susan Koppelman Cornillon. Bowling Green, Ohio: Bowling Green University Press, 1972.

Slotkin, Richard. Regeneration Through Violence: The Mythology of the American Frontier. Middletown, Conn.: Wesleyan University Press, 1973, pp. 497-506.

CORNEILLE, PIERRE

Allentuch, Harriet R. "Reflections on Women in the Theater of Corneille." Kentucky Romance Quarterly 21 (1974): 97-111.

COSTA, MARIA VELHO da

Ascherson, Neal. New York Review of Books, 20 March 1975, p. 11. (Review of The Three Marias: New Portuguese Letters.)

Barreno, Maria Isabel, Maria Teresa Horta, and Maria Velho da Costa. "The Three Marias: New Portuguese Letters." Ms. 3 (January 1975): 86-87.

de Figueiredo, A. "Portugal's Three Marias: Literary Repression by the Government." Nation, 2 March 1974, pp. 268-269.

Fonesca, Mary Lydon. "The Case of the Three Marias." Ms. 3 (January 1975): 84-85, 108.

Kramer, Jane. New York Times Book Review, 2 February 1975 p. 1. (Review of The Three Marias: New Portuguese Letters.)

Prescott, P. S. Newsweek, 27 January 1975, p. 61. (Review of The Three Marias: New Portuguese Letters.)

CRAIK, DINAH M.

> Showalter, Elaine. "Dinah Mulock Craik and the Tactics of Sentiment: A Case Study in Victorian Female Authorship." Feminist Studies 2, nos. 2/3 (1975): 5-23.

CREELEY, ROBERT

> Hammond, John G. "Solipsism and the Sexual Imagination in Robert Creeley's Fiction." Critique 16, no. 3 (1974-75): 59-69.

CRENNE, HELISENNE de

> Conley, Tom. "Feminism, Ecriture, and the Closed Room: The Angoysses douloureuses qui procedent d'amours." Symposium: A Quarterly Journal in Modern Foreign Literatures 27 (Winter 1973): 322-332.

CUMMINS, MARIA

> Frederick, John T. "Hawthorne's 'Scribbling Women.'" New England Quarterly 48 (June 1975): 231-240.

> Smith, Henry Nash. "The Scribbling Women and the Cosmic Success Story." Critical Inquiry 1 (September 1974): 47-70.

-D-

DANTE ALIGHIERI

> Dronke, Peter. "Francesca and Héloïse." Comparative Literature 27 (Spring 1975): 113-135.

> Paolucci, Anne. "Women in the Political Love-Ethic of the Divine Comedy and the Faerie Queene." Dante Studies with the Annual Report of the Dante Society 90 (1972): 139-153.

DAVIS, REBECCA HARDING

> Duus, Louise. "Neither Saint Nor Sinner: Women in

Late Nineteenth-Century Fiction. " <u>American Literary
Realism 1870-1910</u> 7 (Summer 1974): 276-278.

Kahn, C. "Lost and Found. " <u>Ms.</u> 2 (April 1974): 36.

Olsen, Tillie. "Biographical Interpretation. " In <u>Life in
the Iron Mills</u> by Rebecca Harding Davis. Old
Westbury, N. Y.: Feminist Press, 1974.

DEFOE, DANIEL

Arora, Sudesh Vaid. "The Divided Mind: A Study of
Selected Novels of Defoe and Richardson. " Ph. D.
Dissertation, Kent State University, 1974.

Brooks, Douglas. "Defoe: <u>Moll Flanders</u> and <u>Roxana.</u> "
In <u>Number and Pattern in the Eighteenth-Century
Novel</u>. London and Boston: Routledge & Kegan
Paul, 1973.

Brown, Lloyd W. "Defoe and the Feminine Mystique. "
In <u>Transactions of the Samuel Johnson Society of the
Northwest</u>, vol. 4, pp. 4-18. Edited by Robert H.
Carnie. Calgary, Alberta: Samuel Johnson Society
of the Northwest, 1972.

Ferguson, Moira Campbell. "Declarations of Independence:
The Rebel Heroine, 1684-1800. " Ph. D. Dissertation,
University of Washington, 1973.

Foster, Joan Cavallaro. "Daniel Defoe and the Position
of Women in Eighteenth-Century England: A Study of
<u>Moll Flanders</u> and <u>Roxana.</u> " Ph. D. Dissertation,
The University of New Mexico, 1972.

Hartog, Curt. "Aggression, Femininity, and Irony in
<u>Moll Flanders.</u> " <u>Literature and Psychology</u> 22
(1972): 121-138.

Heilbrun, Carolyn G. <u>Toward a Recognition of Androgyny</u>.
New York: Knopf, 1973, pp. 50, 55-56.

Higdon, David Leon. "The Critical Fortunes and Mis-
fortunes of Defoe's <u>Roxana.</u> " <u>Bucknell Review</u> 20
(Spring 1972): 67-82.

Hume, Robert D. "The Conclusion of Defoe's <u>Roxana</u>:

Fiasco or Tour de Force." Eighteenth-Century Studies 3 (Summer 1970): 475-490.

Jacobson, Margaret Charlotte Kingsland. "Women in the Novels of Defoe, Richardson, and Fielding." Ph.D. Dissertation, The University of Connecticut, 1975.

Jenkins, Ralph E. "The Structure of Roxana." Studies in the Novel 2 (Summer 1970): 145-158.

Kaler, Anne Katherine. "Daniel Defoe's Version of the Picaresque Traditions in His Novel Roxana." Ph.D. Dissertation, Temple University, 1970.

Karl, Frederick R. "Moll's Many-Colored Coat: Veil and Disguise in the Fiction of Defoe." Studies in the Novel 5 (Spring 1973): 86-97.

Kestner, Joseph A., III. "Defoe and Madame de La Fayette: Roxana and La Princess de Monpensier." Papers on Language and Literature 8 (1972): 297-301.

Krier, William John. "Courtesy Which Grants Integrity: A Literal Reading of Moll Flanders." ELH 38 (September 1971): 397-410.

_____. "A Pattern of Limitations: The Heroine's Novel of Mind." Ph.D. Dissertation, Indiana University, 1973.

McGowan, Raymond Edward. "Daniel Defoe's Moll Flanders: Fact into Fiction." Ph.D. Dissertation, Tulane University, 1974.

McMaster, Juliet. "The Equation of Love and Money in Moll Flanders." Studies in the Novel 2 (Summer 1970): 131-144.

Mason, Shirlene Rae. "Daniel Defoe's Paradoxical Stand on the Status of Women." Ph.D. Dissertation, University of Utah, 1974.

Miller, Nancy Kipnis. "Gender and Genre: An Analysis of Literary Femininity in the Eighteenth-Century Novel." Ph.D. Dissertation, Columbia University, 1974.

Moynihan, Robert D.   "Clarissa and the Enlightened
   Woman as Literary Heroine."   Journal of the History
   of Ideas 36 (January-March 1975):   159-166.

Novak, Maximillian E.   "Defoe's 'Indifferent Monitor':
   The Complexity of Moll Flanders."   Eighteenth-Century Studies 3 (Spring 1970):   351-365.

Oda, Minoru.   "Moll's Complacency: Defoe's Use of
   Comic Structure in Moll Flanders."   Studies in English Literature (English Literary Society of Japan)
   48, no. 1 (1971):   31-41.   (In Japanese.)

Preston, John.   "Moll Flanders: 'The Satire of the
   Age.'"   The Created Self.   New York: Barnes &
   Noble, 1970.

Smith, LeRoy W.   "Daniel Defoe: Incipient Pornogra-
   pher."   Literature and Psychology 22 (1972):   165-
   178.

Steeves, Edna L.   "Pre-Feminism in Some Eighteenth-
   Century Novels."   Texas Quarterly 16 (Autumn
   1973):   48-57.

Zimmerman, E.   "Language and Character in Defoe's
   Roxana."   Essays in Criticism 21 (July 1971):   227-
   235.

DE FOREST, JOHN WILLIAM

Davenport, Marguerite Lee.   "Woman in Nineteenth-Century American Fiction: Ideals and Stereotypes in the
   Novels of John William DeForest."   Ph. D. Dissertation, The University of Texas at Austin, 1972.

Earnest, Ernest.   The American Eve in Fact and Fiction,
   1775-1914.   Urbana, Chicago, London: University
   of Illinois Press, 1974, pp. 174-176.

DICKENS, CHARLES

Barickman, Richard Bruce.   "Mind Forg'd Manacles:
   Dickens' Late Heroes and Heroines."   Ph. D. Dissertation, Yale University, 1970.

Basch, Françoise.   Relative Creatures: Victorian Women

in Society and the Novel. New York: Schocken, 1974.

Berndt, David Edward. "'This Hard, Real Life': Self and Society in Five Mid-Victorian Bildungsromane." Ph. D. Dissertation, Cornell University, 1972.

Cassid, Donna. "Dickens: A Feminist View." Women: A Journal of Liberation 2 (Fall 1970): 21-22.

Cazamian, Louis. The Social Novel in England 1830-1850. London and Boston: Routledge & Kegan Paul, 1973.

Colby, Vineta. Yesterday's Woman: Domestic Realism in the English Novel. Princeton, N. J.: Princeton University Press, 1974.

Culross, Jack Lewis. "The Prostitute and the Image of Prostitution in Victorian Fiction." Ph. D. Dissertation, The Louisiana State University and Agricultural and Mechanical College, 1970.

Detter, Howard Montgomery. "The Female Sexual Outlaw in the Victorian Novel: A Study in the Conventions of Fiction." Ph. D. Dissertation, Indiana University, 1971.

Ellis, Katherine. "Paradise Lost: The Limits of Domesticity in the Nineteenth-Century Novel." Feminist Studies 2 nos. 2/3 (1975): 55-63.

Greaves, John. Who's Who in Dickens. London: Elm Tree Books, 1972.

Heilbrun, Carolyn G. Toward a Recognition of Androgyny. New York: Knopf, 1973, pp. 42, 51-54, 55, 79, 89.

Higbie, Robert Griggs. "Characterization in the English Novel: Richardson, Jane Austen, and Dickens." Ph. D. Dissertation, Indiana University, 1973.

Hobsbaum, Philip. A Reader's Guide to Charles Dickens. London: Thames & Hudson, 1972.

Johnson, Pamela Hansford. "The Sexual Life in Dickens' Novels." In Dickens 1970, pp. 173-194. Edited by Michael Slater. London: Chapman & Hall, 1970.

Kennedy, George William. "Domestic Ritual in the Novels of Charles Dickens." Ph. D. Dissertation, State University of New York at Buffalo, 1973.

Kennedy, Veronica M. S. "Mrs. Gamp as the Great Mother: A Dickensian Use of the Archetype." Victorian Newsletter no. 41 (Spring 1972): 1-5.

Kilian, Crawford. "In Defense of Esther Summerson." Dalhousie Review 54 (Summer 1974): 318-328.

Leavis, F. R. and Q. D. Leavis. Dickens the Novelist. London: Chatto & Windus, 1970.

Moers, Ellen. "Bleak House: The Agitating Women." Dickensian 69 (1973): 13-24.

Moore, Katharine. Victorian Wives. New York: St. Martin's Press, 1974.

Osborne, Marianne Muse. "The Hero and Heroine in the British Bildungsroman: David Copperfield and A Portrait of the Artist as a Young Man, Jane Eyre and The Rainbow." Ph. D. Dissertation, Tulane University, 1971.

Petlewski, Paul John. "Order to Disorder: A Study of Four Novels by Charles Dickens." Ph. D. Dissertation, University of Florida, 1973.

Pope, Katherine V. "MLA Seminar 73: Women in Dickens." Dickens Studies Newsletter 5 (March 1974): 4-7.

Steig, Michael and F. A. C. Wilson. "Hortense versus Bucket: The Ambiguity of Order in Bleak House." Modern Language Quarterly 33 (September 1972): 289-298.

Stewart, Garrett. "The 'Golden Bower' of Our Mutual Friend." ELH 40 (Spring 1973): 105-130.

Zwerdling, Alex. "Esther Summerson Rehabilitated." PMLA 88 (May 1973): 429-439.

DICKINSON, EMILY

Cameron, Kenneth Walter. "Emily Dickinson and

Hesperian Depression." American Transcendental Quarterly 14 (Spring 1972): 184-185.

Cody, John. After Great Pain: The Inner Life of Emily Dickinson. Cambridge: Harvard University Press, 1971. [Excerpt in Hartford Studies in Literature 2 (1970): 113-132.]

Feit, Joanne. "'Another Way to See': Dickinson and Her English Romantic Precursors." Ph.D. Dissertation, Yale University, 1974.

Greene, Elsa. "Emily Dickinson Was a Poetess." College English 34 (October 1972): 63-70.

Grolnick, Simon A. "Emily and the Psychobiographer." Literature and Psychology 23 (1973): 68-81. (Review Essay.)

Jong, Erica. "Visionary Anger." Ms. 2 (July 1973): 30-31.

Miller, F. DeWolfe. "Emily Dickinson: Self-Portrait in the Third Person." New England Quarterly 46 (March 1973): 119-124.

Mudge, Jean McClure. Emily Dickinson and the Image of Home. Amherst, Mass.: University of Massachusetts Press, 1975.

Patterson, Rebecca. "The Cardinal Points Symbolism of Emily Dickinson." Midwest Quarterly 14 (July 1973): 293-317; 15 (October 1973): 31-60.

_____. "Emily Dickinson's 'Double' Tim: Masculine Identification." American Imago 28 (Winter 1971): 330-362.

Porter, David. "The Crucial Experience in Dickinson's Poetry." Emerson Society Quarterly 20 (Fourth Quarter 1974): 280-289.

Todd, Emerson J. Emily Dickinson's Use of the Persona. New York: Humanities, 1974.

Walker, Cheryl Lawson. "The Women's Tradition in American Poetry." Ph.D. Dissertation, Brandeis University, 1973.

Walsh, John Evangelist. The Hidden Life of Emily Dickinson: A Biography. New York: Simon & Schuster, 1971.

Yetman, Michael G. "Emily Dickinson and the English Romantic Tradition." Texas Studies in Literature 15 (Spring 1973): 129-147.

DIDION, JOAN

"The Female Angst." Los Angeles: Pacifica Tape Library, 1972. (Anaïs Nin, Joan Didion and Dory Previn.)

Fishel, Elizabeth. "Women's Fiction: Who's Afraid of Virginia Woolf." Ramparts, June 1973, pp. 45-48.

Geherin, David J. "Nothingness and Beyond: Joan Didion's Play It As It Lays." Critique 16, no. 1: 64-78.

Kazin, Alfred. "Cassandras: Porter to Oates." Bright Book of Life: American Novelists and Storytellers from Hemingway to Mailer. Boston, Toronto: Little, Brown, 1973, pp. 189-198.

_____. "Joan Didion's Portrait of a Professional." Harper's, December 1971, pp. 112-122.

Newton, Judith. "Joan Didion, 1972." In Female Studies IV: Closer to the Ground, pp. 110-115. Edited by Nancy Hoffman, Cynthia Secor, Adrian Tinsley. Old Westbury, N.Y.: The Feminist Press, 1972.

Porterfield, Nolan. "The Desolation Game." North American Review 256 (Winter 1971): 70-72. (Review of Play It As It Lays.)

Rock, Gail. Ms. 1 (January 1973): 41. (Review of the film Play It As It Lays.)

Roiphe, A. "Yet Another Mad Housewife." Ms. 2 (January 1974): 38.

Sanderson, Annette. "The Fragmented Heroine." Harvard Advocate 106 (Winter 1973): 65-67.

Stimpson, Catherine. "The Case of Miss Joan Didion." Ms. 1 (January 1973): 36.

DISRAELI, BENJAMIN

Basch, Françoise. Relative Creatures: Victorian Women in Society and the Novel. New York: Schocken, 1974.

Cazamian, Louis. The Social Novel in England 1830-1850. London and Boston: Routledge & Kegan Paul, 1973.

Isaac, Judith. "The Working Class in Early Victorian Novels." Ph. D. Dissertation, The City University of New York, 1973.

DOSTOYEVSKY, FYODOR

Adams, Barbara Block. "Sisters Under Their Skins: The Women in the Lives of Raskolnikov and Razumov." Conradiana 6 (1974): 113-124.

Seeley, F. F. "Aglaja Epančina." Slavic and East European Journal 18 (Spring 1974): 1-10.

Wasiolek, Edward. "Raskolnikov's Motives: Love and Murder." American Imago 31 (Fall 1974): 252-269.

DRABBLE, MARGARET

Apter, T. E. "Margaret Drabble: The Glamour of Seriousness." Human World no. 12 (August 1973): 18-28.

Beards, Virginia K. "Margaret Drabble: Novels of a Cautious Feminist." Critique 15, no. 1: 35-47.

Bergonzi, Bernard. "Margaret Drabble." In Contemporary Novelists. Edited by James Vinson. London: St. James Press, 1972; New York: St. Martin's Press, 1972.

Betsky, Celia B. Harvard Advocate 106 (Winter 1973): 81-82. (Review of The Needle's Eye.)

Fraser, Kennedy. New Yorker, 16 December 1972, p. 146. (Review of The Needle's Eye.)

Greacen, Robert. Books and Bookmen, May 1972, pp.
68, 70.

Hardin, Nancy S. "Drabble's The Millstone: A Fable
for Our Times." Critique 15, no. 1: 22-34.

_____. "An Interview with Margaret Drabble."
Contemporary Literature 14 (Summer 1973): 273-
295.

Klein, Norma. "Real Novels About Real Women." Ms.
1 (September 1972): 7-8.

McDowell, Frederick P. W. "Recent British Fiction:
New or Lesser-Known Writers." Contemporary
Literature 11 (Autumn 1970): 555-557.

Myer, Valerie Grosvenor. Margaret Drabble: Puritanism
and Permissiveness. New York: Barnes & Noble,
1974.

Oates, Joyce Carol. "Bricks and Mortar." Ms. 3
(August 1974): 34-36.

Quinn, Laurie. American Scholar 42 (Winter 1972-73):
173. (Review of The Needle's Eye.)

Rose, Ellen Cronan. "Margaret Drabble: Surviving the
Future." Critique 15, no. 1: 5-21.

_____. Nation, 23 October 1972, p. 379.

Sale, Roger. New York Review of Books, 5 October
1972, pp. 35-36. (Review of The Needle's Eye.)

Schaefer, J. O'Brien. "The Novels of Margaret Drabble."
New Republic, 26 April 1975, pp. 21-23.

Wikborg, Eleanor. "A Comparison of Margaret Drabble's 'The Millstone' with its 'Vecko-Revyn' Adap-
tation, 'Barnet Du Gave Mig' ['The Child You Gave
Me'']." Moderna Språk (Stockholm) 65 (1971): 305-
311.

DREISER, THEODORE

Burgan, M. A. "Sister Carrie and the Pathos of Naturalism." Criticism 15 (Fall 1973): 336-349.

Carlson, Constance Hedin. "Heroines in Certain American Novels." Ph. D. Dissertation, Brown University, 1971.

Dance, Daryl C. "Sentimentalism in Dreiser's Heroines: Carrie and Jennie." CLA Journal 14 (December 1970): 127-142.

Ginsberg, Elaine. "The Female Initiation Theme in American Fiction." Studies in Fiction 3 (Spring 1975): 27-37.

Glicksberg, Charles I. The Sexual Revolution in Modern American Literature. The Hague: Martinus Nijhoff, 1971, pp. 33-46

Herman, Sondra R. "Loving Courtship or The Marriage Market? The Ideal and Its Critics 1871-1911." American Quarterly 25 (May 1973): 235-252.

Lundquist, James. "Dreiser's Women." Theodore Dreiser. New York: Frederick Ungar, 1974, pp. 27-51.

Montgomery, Judith Howard. "Pygmalion's Image: The Metamorphosis of the American Heroine." Ph. D. Dissertation, Syracuse University, 1971.

Weir, Sybil B. "The Image of Women in Dreiser's Fiction." Pacific Coast Philology 7 (1972): 65-71.

DREXLER, ROSALYN

Kempton, Sally. New York Times Book Review, 27 February 1972, p. 5. (Review of To Smithereens.)

Wood, Michael. New York Review of Books, 10 August 1972, p. 14. (Review of To Smithereens.)

DUNCAN, SARA JEANNETTE

Cloutier, Pierre. "The First Exile." Canadian Literature no. 59 (Winter 1974): 30-37.

DURAS, MARGUERITE

Brée, Germaine. "An Interview with Marguerite Duras."

Contemporary Literature 13 (Autumn 1972): 401-422.

_____. Women Writers in France: Variations on a Theme. New Brunswick, N. J.: Rutgers University Press, 1973, pp. 65-67.

Cismaru, Alfred. "Salvation through Drinking in Marguerite Duras' Short Stories." Modern Fiction Studies 19 (Winter 1973-74): 487-498.

Eisinger, E. M. "Crime and Detection in the Novels of Marguerite Duras." Contemporary Literature 15 (Autumn 1974): 503-520.

Guicharnaud, Jacques. "The Terrorist Marivaudage of Marguerite Duras." Yale French Studies no. 46 (1971): 113-124.

Lipton, Virginia Anne. "Women in Today's World: A Study of Five French Women Novelists." Ph. D. Dissertation, The University of Wisconsin, 1972.

Weiss, Victoria L. "Form and Meaning in Marguerite Duras' Moderato Cantabile." Critique 16, no. 1 (1974): 79-87.

-E-

EASMAN, R. S.

Stegeman, Beatrice. "The Divorce Dilemma: The New Woman in Contemporary African Novels." Critique 15, no. 3: 81-93.

EDGEWORTH, MARIA

Butler, Marilyn. Maria Edgeworth: A Literary Biography. Oxford: Clarendon Press, 1972.

_____. "The Uniqueness of Cynthia Kirkpatrick: Elizabeth Gaskell's Wives and Daughters and Maria Edgeworth's Helen." Review of English Studies 23 (August 1972): 278-290.

Colby, Vineta. Yesterday's Woman: Domestic Realism

in the English Novel. Princeton, N.J.: Princeton University Press, 1974.

Colvin, Christina, ed. Maria Edgeworth: Letters from England, 1813-1844. Oxford: Clarendon Press, 1971.

Craig, Charles Robert. "Maria Edgeworth and the Common-Sense School." Ph.D. Dissertation, The University of Nebraska, 1971.

Harden, Oleta Elizabeth McWhorter. Elizabeth Maria Edgeworth's Art of Prose Fiction. New York: Humanities, 1971.

Manley, Seon and Susan Belcher. O, Those Extraordinary Women! or, The Joys of Literary Lib. Philadelphia: Chilton, 1972, pp. 106-107.

Newcomer, James. Maria Edgeworth. Lewisburg: Bucknell University Press, 1973.

Preston, John. "The Lost World of Maria Edgeworth." Essays in Criticism 24 (April 1974): 198-207. (Review Essay.)

Pritchett, V. S. "Across the Irish Sea." New Statesman, 18 August 1972, p. 227.

Rudolf, Jo-Ellen Schwartz. "The Novels that Taught the Ladies: a Study of Popular Fiction Written by Women, 1702-1834." Ph.D. Dissertation, University of California, San Diego, 1972.

Speakman, James Stewart. "Wit, Humor and Sensibility in Evelina, Belinda, and Northanger Abbey." Ph.D. Dissertation, University of California, Davis, 1972.

EDWARDS, ANNIE

Gorsky, Susan. "The Gentle Doubters: Images of Women in Englishwomen's Novels, 1840-1920." In Images of Women in Fiction, p. 41. Edited by Susan Koppelman Cornillon. Bowling Green, Ohio: Bowling Green University Press, 1972.

_____. "Old Maids and New Women: Alternatives

to Marriage in Englishwomen's Novels, 1847-1915. "
Journal of Popular Culture 7 (Summer 1973): 68-85.

ELIOT, GEORGE

Althaus, Donald Charles. "The Love Triangle as a
Structural Principle in the Novels of George Eliot. "
Ph. D. Dissertation, Ohio University, 1971.

Auster, Henry. Local Habitations: Regionalism in the
Early Novels of George Eliot. Cambridge: Harvard
University Press, 1970.

Basch, Françoise. Relative Creatures: Victorian Women
in Society and the Novel. New York: Schocken,
1974.

Bedient, Calvin. Architects of the Self: George Eliot,
D. H. Lawrence, E. M. Forster. Berkeley: University of California Press, 1972.

Berndt, David Edward. "'This Hard, Real Life': Self
and Society in Five Mid-Victorian Bildungsromane. "
Ph. D. Dissertation, Cornell University, 1972.

Birky, Wilbur Joseph. "Marriage as Pattern and Metaphor in the Victorian Novel. " Ph. D. Dissertation,
The University of Iowa, 1970.

Buckler, William E. "Memory, Morality, and the Tragic
Vision in the Early Novels of George Eliot. " In
The English Novel in the Nineteenth Century, pp.
145-163. Edited by George Goodin. Urbana: University of Illinois Press, 1972.

Colby, Vineta. Yesterday's Woman: Domestic Realism
in the English Novel. Princeton, N. J.: Princeton
University Press, 1974.

Coles, Robert. Irony in the Mind's Life: Essays on
Novels by James Agee, Elizabeth Bowen, and George
Eliot. Charlottesville: University Press of Virginia,
1974.

Conway, Richard Henry. "The Difficulty of Being a
Woman: A Study of George Eliot's Heroines. " Ph. D.
Dissertation, University of Denver, 1973.

Creeger, George R. , ed. George Eliot: A Collection of Critical Essays. Englewood Cliffs, N. J.: Prentice-Hall, 1970.

Decavalcante, Frank. "Sexual Politics in Four Victorian Novels." Ph. D. Dissertation, Kent State Univ. , 1974.

DeGroot, Elizabeth M. "Middlemarch and Dorothea Brooke: The Saints Go Marching On. " Christianity and Literature 22, no. 1 (1972): 13-18.

Dignon, Hugh Alexander. "Love and Courtship in the Novels of George Eliot, Thomas Hardy, and D. H. Lawrence. " Ph. D. Dissertation, New York University, 1974.

DiPasquale, P. , Jr. "The Imagery and Structure of Middlemarch. " English Studies 52 (October 1971): 425-441.

Donovan, Josephine. "Feminist Style Criticism. " In Female Studies VI: Closer to the Ground, pp. 139-149. Edited by Nancy Hoffman, Cynthia Secor, Adrian Tinsley. Old Westbury, N. Y.: Feminist Press, 1972. Also in Images of Women in Fiction. Edited by Susan Koppelman Cornillon.

Edwards, Lee R. "Women, Energy, and Middlemarch. " In Woman: An Issue, pp. 223-238. Edited by Lee R. Edwards, Mary Heath and Lisa Baskin. Boston: Little, Brown, 1972.

Edwards, Michael. "A Reading of Adam Bede. " Critical Quarterly 14 (Autumn 1972): 205-218.

Eisner, Greta. "George Eliot: The Problem Novels. " Ph. D. Dissertation, University of California, Irvine, 1974.

Ermarth, Elizabeth. "Maggie Tulliver's Long Suicide. " Studies in English Literature 1500-1900 14 (Autumn 1974): 587-601.

Figes, Eva. Patriarchal Attitudes. New York: Stein & Day, 1970.

Fuermann, Warren Bryan. "The Novels of George Eliot:

A Critical Commentary. " Ph. D. Dissertation, University of Illinois at Urbana-Champaign, 1974.

Fulmer, Constance Marie. "Contrasting Pairs of Heroines in George Eliot's Fiction. " Studies in the Novel 6 (Fall 1974): 288-294.

Godwin, Gail. "If She Hadn't Called Herself George Eliot, Would We Have Heard of Marian Evans?" Ms. 3 (September 1974): 72-75, 88.

Gorsky, Susan. "The Gentle Doubters: Images of Women in Englishwomen's Novels, 1840-1920. " In Images of Women in Fiction, pp. 29, 33, 35, 36, 44, 49. Edited by Susan Koppelman Cornillon. Bowling Green, Ohio: Bowling Green University Press, 1972.

Halperin, John. Egoism and Self-Discovery in the Victorian Novel. New York: Burt Franklin, 1974, pp. 125-192.

_____. The Language of Meditation: Four Studies in Nineteenth-Century Fiction. Devon: Arthur H. Stockwell, 1973.

Hardwick, Elizabeth. Seduction and Betrayal: Women and Literature. New York: Random House, 1974, pp. 186-190.

Heilbrun, Carolyn G. Toward a Recognition of Androgyny. New York: Knopf, 1973, pp. 12, 50, 69, 73-74, 82-86, 90, 103.

Hoffman, Leonore Noll. "A Delicate Balance: The Resolutions to Conflicts of Women in the Fiction of Four Women Writers of the Victorian Period. " Ph. D. Dissertation, Indiana University, 1974.

Hollahan, Eugene. "The Concept of 'Crisis' in Middlemarch. " Nineteenth-Century Fiction 28 (March 1974): 450-457.

Isaac, Judith. "The Working Class in Early Victorian Novels. " Ph. D. Dissertation, The City University of New York, 1973.

Katz, Judith Nina. "Rooms of Their Own: Forms and

Images of Liberation in Five Novels. " Ph. D. Dissertation, The Pennsylvania State University, 1972.

Kenyon, Frank Wilson. The Consuming Flame: The Story of George Eliot. New York: Dodd, Mead, 1970.

Knoepflmacher, U. C. "Middlemarch: An Avuncular View. " Nineteenth-Century Fiction 30 (June 1975): 53-81.

Kraft, Stephanie Barlett. "Women and Society in the Novels of George Eliot and Edith Wharton. " Ph. D. Dissertation, The University of Rochester, 1973.

Kroeber, Karl. Styles in Fictional Structure: The Art of Jane Austen, Charlotte Brontë, George Eliot. Princeton, N. J.: Princeton University Press, 1971.

Laski, Marghanita. George Eliot and Her World. London: Thames & Hudson, 1973.

Manley, Seon and Susan Belcher. O, Those Extraordinary Women! Philadelphia: Chilton, 1972, pp. 193-199.

Martin, Bruce K. "Rescue and Marriage in Adam Bede." Studies in English Literature 1500-1900 12 (Autumn 1972): 745-763.

Mills, Nicolaus. "Nathaniel Hawthorne and George Eliot." American and English Fiction in the Nineteenth Century. Bloomington: Indiana University Press, 1973, pp. 52-73.

Moore, Katharine. Victorian Wives. New York: St. Martin's Press, 1974.

Palko, Albert J. "Latter-Day Saints: George Eliot's New Saint Theresa in Image and Symbol. " Ph. D. Dissertation, University of Notre Dame, 1973.

Pearce, T. S. George Eliot. Totowa, N. J.: Rowman & Littlefield, 1973.

Reisen, Diana Mary Cohart. "Pilgrims of Mortality: The Quest for Identity in the Novels of George Eliot." Ph. D. Dissertation, Columbia University, 1972.

Roberts, Lynne Tidaback. "Perfect Pyramids: The Mill on the Floss." Texas Studies in Literature and Language 13 (Spring 1971): 111-124.

Roberts, Neil. George Eliot: Her Beliefs and Her Art. Pittsburgh: University of Pittsburgh Press, forthcoming.

Sabiston, Elizabeth. "Prison of Womanhood." Comparative Literature 25 (Fall 1973): 336-351.

Sedgley, Anne. "Daniel Deronda." Critical Review no. 13 (1970): 3-19.

Showalter, Elaine Cottler. "The Double Standard: Criticism of Women Writers in England, 1845-1880." Ph. D. Dissertation, University of California, Davis, 1970.

Smalley, Barbara. George Eliot and Flaubert: Pioneers of the Modern Novel. Athens: Ohio University Press, 1974.

Spacks, Patricia M. The Female Imagination. New York: Knopf, 1975.

Stone, Donald D. "Victorian Feminism and the Nineteenth-Century Novel." Women's Studies 1 (1972): 65-92.

Sukenick, Lynn. "Sense and Sensibility in Women's Fiction: Studies in the Novels of George Eliot, Virginia Woolf, Anaïs Nin, and Doris Lessing." Ph. D. Dissertation, The City University of New York, 1974.

Sullivan, W. J. "Music and Musical Allusion in The Mill on the Floss." Criticism 16 (Summer 1974): 232-246.

Swann, Brian. "George Eliot's Ecumenical Jew, or The Novel as Outdoor Temple." Novel 8 (Fall 1974): 39-50.

Swinden, Patrick, ed. George Eliot: Middlemarch: A Casebook. London: Macmillan, 1972.

Warner, Frances Claire. "Toward Middlemarch: The

Heroine's Search for Guidance in the Earlier Novels of George Eliot. " Ph. D. Dissertation, University of Illinois at Urbana-Champaign, 1974.

Wiesenfarth, Joseph. "The Medea in Daniel Deronda. " Die Neueren Sprachen 22 (1973): 103-108.

Wolfe, Thomas Pingrey II. "The Inward Vocation: An Essay on George Eliot's Daniel Deronda. " Ph. D. Dissertation, Rutgers University, The State University of New Jersey, 1973.

Woodcock, John A. "The Moral Dimension of Beauty in George Eliot's Heroines. " Ph. D. Dissertation, State University of New York at Stony Brook, 1971.

Zak, Michele Wender. "Feminism and the New Novel. " Ph. D. Dissertation, Ohio State University, 1973.

Zimmerman, Bonnie Sue. "'Appetite for Submission': The Female Role in the Novels of George Eliot. " Ph. D. Dissertation, State University of New York at Buffalo, 1974.

ESTIENNE, NICOLE

Aronson, Nicole. "Nicole Estienne and Women's Liberation in the XVIth Century. " Foreign Language Teacher 1 (Fall 1971): 22-29.

EURIPIDES

Burnett, Anne Pippin. Catastrophe Survived: Euripides' Plays of Mixed Reversal. Oxford: Clarendon Press, 1971.

Edwards, Duane. "Tess of the d'Urbervilles and Hippolytus. " Midwest Quarterly 15 (July 1974): 392-405.

Goertz, Donald Charles. "The Iphigeneia at Aulis: A Critical Study. " Ph. D. Dissertation, The University of Texas at Austin, 1972.

Hamilton, John Daniel Burgoyne. "The Characterization and Function of Helen in Euripidean Drama. " Ph. D. Dissertation, University of Minnesota, 1973.

Morrow, Lynn Shipman. "Euripides' Treatment of
Women: An Androgynous Answer." Ph. D. Dissertation, The Ohio State University, 1974.

EVANS, MARI

Sedlack, Robert P. "Mari Evans: Consciousness and
Craft." CLA Journal 15 (June 1972): 465-476.

-F-

FAULKNER, WILLIAM

Barnes, Daniel R. "Faulkner's Miss Emily and Hawthorne's Old Maid." Studies in Short Fiction 9
(Fall 1972): 373-378.

Broughton, Panthea Reid. William Faulkner: The Abstract and the Actual. Baton Rouge: Louisiana
State University Press, 1974.

Brown, Calvin S. "Dilsey: From Faulkner to Homer."
In William Faulkner: Prevailing Verities and World
Literature, pp. 57-75. Edited by Wolodymyr T.
Zyla and Wendell M. Aycock. Lubbock, Texas:
Texas Tech University, 1973.

Burns, Mattie Ann. "The Development of Women Characters in the Works of William Faulkner." Ph. D.
Dissertation, Auburn University, 1974.

Carlock, Mary Sue. "Kaleidoscopic Views of Motion."
In William Faulkner: Prevailing Verities and World
Literature, pp. 95-113. Edited by Wolodymyr T.
Zyla and Wendell M. Aycock. Lubbock, Texas:
Texas Tech University, 1973.

Collins, Carvel. "Miss Quentin's Paternity Again."
In The Merrill Studies in The Sound and the Fury,
pp. 80-88. Compiled by James B. Meriwether.
Columbus: Charles E. Merrill, 1970.

Dean, Sharon Welch. "Lost Ladies: The Isolated Heroine in the Fiction of Hawthorne, James, Fitzgerald,

Hemingway and Faulkner. " Ph. D. Dissertation, University of New Hampshire, 1973.

Dunphy, Patricia. "The Case Against Women in Contemporary Literature: Hemingway and Faulkner. " Women: A Journal of Liberation 2 (Fall 1970): 20-21.

Gladstein, Mimi Reisel. "The Indestructible Woman in the Works of Faulkner, Hemingway, and Steinbeck. " Ph. D. Dissertation, University of New Mexico, 1973.

Gregory, Eileen. "Caddy Compson's World. " In The Merrill Studies in The Sound and the Fury, pp. 89-101. Compiled by James B. Meriwether. Columbus: Charles E. Merrill, 1970.

Houghton, Donald E. "Whores and Horses in Faulkner's 'Spotted Horses.'" Midwest Quarterly 11 (July 1970): 361-369.

Inge, M. Thomas, ed. William Faulkner's "A Rose for Emily." Columbus: Charles E. Merrill, 1970.

Jarrett, David W. "Eustacia Vye and Eula Varner, Olympians: The Worlds of Thomas Hardy and William Faulkner. " Novel 6 (1973): 163-174.

Johnston, Walter E. "The Shepherdess in the City. " Comparative Literature 26 (Spring 1974): 124-141.

Kent, George E. "The Black Woman in Faulkner's Works, with the Exclusion of Dilsey. " Phylon 35 (December 1974): 430-441; Part II, 36 (March 1975): 55-67.

Lyons, Anne Ward. "Myth and Agony: The Southern Woman as Belle. " Ph. D. Dissertation, Bowling Green State University, 1974.

McElrath, Joseph R., Jr. "Pylon: The Portrait of a Lady. " Mississippi Quarterly 26 (Summer 1974): 277-290.

Matton, Collin Gilles. "The Role of Women in Three of Faulkner's Families. " Ph. D. Dissertation, Marquette University, 1974.

Page, Sally R. Faulkner's Women: Characterization and Meaning. Deland, Fla.: Everett Edwards, 1972.

Pitavy, François L. "A Forgotten Faulkner Story: 'Miss Zilphia Gant.'" Studies in Short Fiction 9 (Spring 1972): 131-142.

Reirdon, Suzanne Renshaw. "An Application of Script Analysis to Four of William Faulkner's Women Characters." Ed. D. Dissertation, East Texas State University, 1974.

Tucker, E. L. "Faulkner's Drusilla and Ibsen's Hedda." Modern Drama 16 (September 1973): 157-161.

Williams, David Larry. "William Faulkner and the Mythology of Woman." Ph. D. Dissertation, University of Massachusetts, 1973.

FAUSET, JESSIE

Davis, Arthur P. From the Dark Tower. Washington, D. C.: Howard University Press, 1974, pp. 90-94.

Edwards, Lee R. and Arlyn Diamond. "Introduction." American Voices, American Women. New York: Avon, 1973.

Feeney, Joseph J., S. J. "Greek Tragic Patterns in a Black Novel: Jessie Fauset's 'The Chinaberry Tree.'" CLA Journal 18 (December 1974): 211-215.

Gayle, Addison, Jr. The Way of the New World: The Black Novel in America. Garden City, N. Y.: Doubleday, 1975, pp. 115-122.

Sato, Hiroko. "Under the Harlem Shadow: A Study of Jessie Fauset and Nella Larsen." In The Harlem Renaissance Remembered, pp. 63-83. Edited by Arna Bontemps. New York: Dodd, Mead, 1972.

FERN, FANNY

Earnest, Ernest. The American Eve in Fact and Fiction, 1775-1914. Urbana, Chicago, London: University of Illinois Press, 1974, pp. 79-81.

Wood, Ann D. "The 'Scribbling Women' and Fanny Fern:

Why Women Wrote." American Quarterly 23 (Spring 1971): 3-24.

FIELDING, HENRY

Jacobson, Margaret Charlotte Kingsland. "Women in the Novels of Defoe, Richardson, and Fielding." Ph.D. Dissertation, The University of Connecticut, 1975.

FITZGERALD, F. SCOTT

Callahan, John F. The Illusions of a Nation: Myth and History in the Novels of F. Scott Fitzgerald. Urbana, Chicago, and London: University of Illinois Press, 1972.

Carlson, Constance Hedin. "Heroines in Certain American Novels." Ph.D. Dissertation, Brown University, 1971.

Coleman, Tom C., III. "Nicole Warren Diver and Scott Fitzgerald: The Girl and the Egotist." Studies in the Novel 3 (1971): 34-43.

Dean, Sharon Welch. "Lost Ladies: The Isolated Heroine in the Fiction of Hawthorne, James, Fitzgerald, Hemingway, and Faulkner." Ph.D. Dissertation, University of New Hampshire, 1973.

Farley, Pamella. "Form and Function: The Image of Woman in Selected Works of Hemingway and Fitzgerald." Ph.D. Dissertation, The Pennsylvania State University, 1973.

Glicksberg, Charles I. The Sexual Revolution in Modern American Literature. The Hague: Martinus Nijhoff, 1971, pp. 58-67.

Hunt, Jan and John M. Suarez. "The Evasion of Adult Love in Fitzgerald's Fiction." Centennial Review 17 (Spring 1973): 152-169.

Korenman, Joan S. "'Only Her Hairdresser...': Another Look at Daisy Buchanan." American Literature 46 (January 1975): 574-578.

Montgomery, Judith Howard. "Pygmalion's Image: The

Metamorphosis of the American Heroine. " Ph. D.
Dissertation, Syracuse University, 1971.

Moses, Edwin. "F. Scott Fitzgerald and the Quest to
the Ice Palace. " CEA Critic 36 (January 1974):
11-14.

FITZGERALD, ZELDA

Aaron, Daniel. "The Legend of the Golden Couple. "
Virginia Quarterly Review 48 (1972): 157-160.
(Review Essay.)

Hardwick, Elizabeth. Seduction and Betrayal. New
York: Random House, 1974, pp. 87-103.

Heath, Mary. "Marriages: Zelda and Scott, Eleanor
and Franklin. " In Woman: An Issue, pp. 281-288.
Edited by Lee R. Edwards, Mary Heath, and Lisa
Baskin. Boston: Little, Brown, 1972.

Mayfield, Sara. Exiles from Paradise: Zelda and Scott
Fitzgerald. New York: Delacorte Press, 1971.

Milford, Nancy. Zelda: A Biography. New York:
Harper & Row, 1970.

Wertheim, Stanley. "Zelda: A Biography. " Literature
and Psychology 21 (1971): 47-50. (Review Essay.)

FLAUBERT, GUSTAV

Bersani, Leo. "Flaubert and Emma Bovary: The Haz-
ards of Literary Fusion. " Novel 8 (Fall 1974):
16-28.

Cross, Richard K. Flaubert and Joyce: The Rite of
Fiction. Princeton, N. J. : Princeton University
Press, 1971.

Kirton, W. J. S. "Flaubert's Use of Sound in Madame
Bovary. " Forum for Modern Language Studies 11
(January 1975): 36-45.

Lowe, A. M. "Emma Bovary, A Modern Arachne. "
French Studies 26 (January 1972): 30-41.

Sabiston, Elizabeth. "Prison of Womanhood. " Comparative Literature 25 (Fall 1973): 336-351.

Smalley, Barbara. George Eliot and Flaubert: Pioneers of the Modern Novel. Athens: Ohio University Press, 1974.

Wagner, Geoffrey. Five for Freedom. Rutherford, Madison, Teaneck, N. J.: Fairleigh Dickinson University Press, 1972, pp. 30, 31, 33, 34, 53, 55, 56, 59, 91-93, 95, 97, 99, 138-182, 187, 218.

FORD, JOHN

Champion, Larry S. "Ford's 'Tis Pity She's a Whore and the Jacobean Tragic Perspective." PMLA 90 (January 1975): 78-87.

FORSTER, E. M.

Bedient, Calvin. Architects of the Self: George Eliot, D. H. Lawrence, E. M. Forster. Berkeley: University of California Press, 1972.

_____. "Forster's Women: A Room with a View." English Literature in Transition 16 (1973): 275-287.

Finkelstein, Bonnie Blumenthal. Forster's Women: Eternal Differences. New York: Columbia University Press, 1975.

_____. "The Role of Women in the Novels of E. M. Forster with Parallels to the Role of Homosexuals in Maurice." Ph. D. Dissertation, Columbia University, 1972.

Fleishman, Avrom. "Being and Nothing in A Passage to India." Criticism 15 (Spring 1973): 109-125.

Haskell, M. "Howard's End: Margaret and Helen of E. M. Forster's Novel." Mademoiselle 78 (January 1974): 16.

Heilbrun, Carolyn G. Toward a Recognition of Androgyny. New York: Knopf, 1973, pp. 93, 97-101, 134, 135-136.

Levine, June Perry. Creation and Criticism: A Passage

to India. Lincoln: University of Nebraska Press, 1971.

Martin, Richard. The Love that Failed: Ideal and Reality in the Writings of E. M. Forster. The Hague and Paris: Mouton, 1974.

Price, Martin. "People of the Book: Characters in Forster's A Passage to India." Critical Inquiry 1 (March 1975): 605-622.

FREDERIC, HAROLD

Crowley, John W. "The Nude and the Madonna in The Damnation of Theron Ware." American Literature 45 (November 1973): 379-389.

Milne, W. Gordon. "Frederic's 'Free' Woman." American Literary Realism 6 (1973): 258-260.

FREEMAN, MARY E. WILKINS

Anderson, Donald Robert. "Failure and Regeneration in the New England of Sarah Orne Jewett and Mary E. Wilkins Freeman." Ph.D. Dissertation, University of Arizona, 1974.

Diomedi, Claudette Anne. "Mary Wilkins Freeman and the Romance-Novel Tradition." Ph.D. Dissertation, University of Maryland, 1970.

Edwards, Lee R. and Arlyn Diamond. "Introduction." American Voices, American Women. New York: Avon, 1973.

Parker, Jeraldine. "'Uneasy Survivors': Five Women Writers 1896-1923." Ph.D. Dissertation, University of Utah, 1973.

Toth, Susan Allen. "Defiant Light: A Positive View of Mary Wilkins Freeman." New England Quarterly 46 (March 1973): 82-93.

_____. "Sarah Orne Jewett and Friends: A Community of Interest." Studies in Short Fiction 9 (Summer 1972): 233-242.

FUENTES, CARLOS

Gyurko, Lanin A. "The Myths of Ulysses in Fuentes's Zona sagrada." Modern Language Review 69 (April 1974): 316-324.

Siemens, William L. "The Devouring Female in Four Latin American Novels." Essays in Literature (Macomb, Ill.) 1 (Spring 1974): 118-129.

-G-

GAINES, ERNEST

Bryant, J. H. Nation, 5 April 1971, p. 436. (Review of The Autobiography of Miss Jane Pittman.)

Gayle, Addison, Jr. The Way of the New World: The Black Novel in America. Garden City, N.Y.: Doubleday, 1975, pp. 294-301.

Ingram, Forrest and Barbara Steinberg. "On the Verge: An Interview with Ernest J. Gaines." New Orleans Review 3, no. 4 (1973): 339-344.

Major, Clarence. The Dark and Feeling. New York: Third Press, 1974, pp. 57-58.

Stoelting, Winifred L. "Human Dignity and Pride in the Novels of Ernest Gaines." CLA Journal 14 (March 1971): 340-358.

Walker, Alice. New York Times Book Review, 23 May 1971, p. 6. (Review of The Autobiography of Miss Jane Pittman.)

GALDOS, BENITO PEREZ

Armand, Mary Ellen. "Women and Society in the Nineteenth-Century Spanish Novel." Ph.D. Dissertation, Yale University, 1974.

Durand, Frank. "The Reality of Illusion: La desheredada." Modern Language Notes 89 (March 1974): 191-201.

GALSWORTHY, JOHN

Birky, Wilbur Joseph. "Marriage as Pattern and Metaphor in the Victorian Novel." Ph.D. Dissertation, The University of Iowa, 1970.

GARCIA MARQUEZ, GABRIEL

Hall, Linda B. "Labyrinthine Solitude: The Impact of García Marquez." Southwest Review 58 (Summer 1973): 253-262.

Siemens, William L. "The Devouring Female in Four Latin American Novels." Essays in Literature (Macomb, Ill.) 1 (Spring 1974): 118-129.

GARCIA PAVON, FRANCISCO

O'Connor, Patricia W. "Francisco García Pavón's Sexual Politics in the Plinio Novels." Journal of Spanish Studies: Twentieth Century 1 (Spring 1973): 65-81.

Vance, Birgitta. "The Great Clash: Feminist Criticism Meets Up with Spanish Reality." Journal of Spanish Studies: Twentieth Century 2 (Fall 1974): 109-114.

GARLAND, HAMLIN

Carter, Joseph L. "Hamlin Garland's Liberated Women." American Literary Realism 1870-1910 6 (Summer 1973): 255-258.

Culbert, Gary Allen. "Hamlin Garland's Image of Woman: An Allegiance to Ideality." Ph.D. Dissertation, The University of Wisconsin, 1974.

GASKELL, ELIZABETH

Basch, Françoise. Relative Creatures: Victorian Women in Society and the Novel. New York: Schocken, 1974.

Boyle, Patricia M. "Elizabeth C. Gaskell: Her Development and Achievement." Ph.D. Dissertation, University of Pennsylvania, 1970.

Butler, Marilyn. "The Uniqueness of Cynthia Kirkpatrick:

Elizabeth Gaskell's Wives and Daughters and Maria Edgeworth's Helen. " Review of English Studies 23 (August 1972): 278-290.

Cazamian, Louis. The Social Novel in England 1830-1850. London and Boston: Routledge & Kegan Paul, 1973.

Colby, Vineta. Yesterday's Woman: Domestic Realism in the English Novel. Princeton, N. J.: Princeton University Press, 1974.

Craik, W. A. Elizabeth Gaskell and the English Provincial Novel. London: Methuen, 1975.

Culross, Jack Lewis. "The Prostitute and the Image of Prostitution in Victorian Literature." Ph. D. Dissertation, The Louisiana State University and Agricultural and Mechanical College, 1970.

Davis, Marjorie Taylor. "An Annotated Bibliography of Criticism on Elizabeth Cleghorn Gaskell, 1848-1973." Ph. D. Dissertation, The University of Mississippi, 1974.

Detter, Howard Montgomery. "The Female Sexual Outlaw in the Victorian Novel: A Study in the Conventions of Fiction." Ph. D. Dissertation, Indiana University, 1971.

Franko, Patricia. "The Emergence of Harmony: Development in the Novels of Mrs. Gaskell." Ph. D. Dissertation, Temple University, 1973.

Furbank, P. N. "Mendacity in Mrs. Gaskell." Encounter 40 (June 1973): 51-55.

Gorsky, Susan. "The Gentle Doubters: Images of Women in Englishwomen's Novels, 1840-1920. " In Images of Women in Fiction, pp. 29, 33, 42, 46, 47, 49. Edited by Susan Koppelman Cornillon. Bowling Green, Ohio: Bowling Green University Press, 1972.

_____. "Old Maids and New Women: Alternatives to Marriage in Englishwomen's Novels, 1847-1915. " Journal of Popular Culture 7 (Summer 1973): 68-85.

Hopkins, Annette Brown. Elizabeth Gaskell: Her Life and Work. New York: Octagon Books, 1971.

Isaac, Judith. "The Working Class in Early Victorian Novels." Ph. D. Dissertation, The City University of New York: 1973.

Lansbury, Coral. Elizabeth Gaskell: A Study of Woman and Society. New York: Barnes & Noble, forthcoming.

Millett, Kate. Sexual Politics. New York: Avon, 1971, pp. 16-22, 154, 267, 287, 330, 335, 336-361, 362.

Moore, Katharine. Victorian Wives. New York: St. Martin's Press, 1974.

Schwartz, Stephen Lee. "Elizabeth Gaskell: The Novelist as Artist." Ph. D. Dissertation, The University of Rochester, 1971.

Showalter, Elaine Cottler. "The Double Standard: Criticism of Women Writers in England, 1845-1880." Ph. D. Dissertation, University of California, Davis, 1970.

Smith, David. "Mary Barton and Hard Times: Their Social Insights." Mosaic 5 (1972): 97-112.

Spacks, Patricia M. The Female Imagination. New York: Knopf, 1975.

_____. "Taking Care: Some Women Novelists." Novel 6 (Fall 1972): 36-51.

Willens, Susan Popkin. "The Novels of Elizabeth Gaskell: The Comic Vision." Ph. D. Dissertation, The Catholic University of America, 1973.

GIOVANNI, NIKKI

Bailey, P. "Nikki Giovanni: I Am Black, Female, Polite." Ebony (February 1972): 48-50.

Giovanni, Nikki and Margaret Walker. A Poetic Equation: Conversations between Nikki Giovanni and Margaret Walker. Washington, D. C.: Howard University Press, 1974.

Nazer, G. "Lifestyle." Harper's Bazaar, July 1972,
pp. 50-51.

GISSING, GEORGE

Blench, J. W. "George Gissing's Thyrza." Durham
University Journal 33 (March 1972): 85-114.

Coustillas, Pierre. "Introduction." George Gissing:
Essays & Fiction. Baltimore and London: Johns
Hopkins University Press, 1970.

Decavalcante, Frank. "Sexual Politics in Four Victorian
Novels." Ph. D. Dissertation, Kent State University,
1974.

Enzer, Sandra. "Maidens and Matrons: A Collection of
George Gissing's Short Stories of Women." Ph. D.
Dissertation, State University of New York at Stony
Brook, work in progress. (Includes discussion of
Gissing--the context of literary and social history
of the late 19th century.)

Fernando, Lloyd. "Gissing's Studies in 'Vulgarism':
Aspects of His Anti-feminism." Southern Review 4
(1970): 43-52.

Heilbrun, Carolyn G. Toward a Recognition of Androgyny.
New York: Knopf, 1973, pp. 70, 72.

Keating, P. J. The Working Class in Victorian Literature. London: Routledge & Kegan Paul, 1971.

Lacheze, Henri. "England in the Late XIXth Century."
Diliman Review 22 (April 1974): 90-107.

Lindsey, Karen. "The Odd Women." The Second Wave
1, no. 4 (1972): 39-40.

Maglin, Nan Bauer. "Fictional Feminists in The Bostonians and The Odd Women." In Images of Women
in Fiction, pp. 216-236. Edited by Susan Koppelman Cornillon. Bowling Green, Ohio: Bowling
Green University Press, 1972.

Stone, Donald D. "Victorian Feminism and the Nineteenth-
Century Novel." Women's Studies 1 (1972): 65-92.

Tindall, Gillian. Born Exile: George Gissing. London: Temple Smith, 1974.

GLASGOW, ELLEN

Beckham, Beverly Spears. "The Satire of Ellen Glasgow." Ph. D. Dissertation, University of Georgia, 1972.

Carlson, Constance. "Heroines in Certain American Novels." Ph. D. Dissertation, Brown University, 1971.

Forrey, Carolyn. "The New Woman Revisited." Women's Studies 2 (1974): 37-56.

Godbold, E. Stanly, Jr. Ellen Glasgow and the Woman Within. Baton Rouge: Louisiana State University Press, 1972.

Holman, C. Hugh. "April in Queenborough: Ellen Glasgow's Comedies of Manners." Sewanee Review 82 (April-June 1974): 263-283.

Inge, M. Thomas, ed. Ellen Glasgow: Centennial Essays. Charlottesville: University Press of Virginia, forthcoming.

Parker, Jeraldine. "'Uneasy Survivors': Five Women Writers 1896-1923." Ph. D. Dissertation, University of Utah, 1973.

Peck, Ellen Margaret McKee. "Exploring the Feminine: A Study of Janet Lewis, Ellen Glasgow, Anaïs Nin, and Virginia Woolf." Ph. D. Dissertation, Stanford University, 1974.

Pratt, Annis. "Women and Nature in Modern Fiction." Contemporary Literature 13 (Autumn 1972): 476-490.

Raper, J. R. Without Shelter: The Early Career of Ellen Glasgow. Baton Rouge: Louisiana State University, 1971.

Richards, Marion K. Ellen Glasgow's Development as a Novelist. The Hague: Mouton, 1971.

_____. "Glasgow's Concept of the Liberated Women."

Paper presented at the PMLA meeting, New York, December 1974.

Rouse, Blair. "Ellen Glasgow: Manners and Art." Cabellian 4 (1972): 96-98.

Spacks, Patricia M. The Female Imagination. New York: Knopf, 1975.

_____. "Taking Care: Some Women Novelists." Novel 6 (Fall 1972): 36-51.

GODWIN, GAIL

Betts, Doris. "More Like an Onion than a Map." Ms. 3 (March 1975): 41-43. (Review of The Odd Woman.)

Dickstein, Lore. New York Times Book Review, 20 October 1974, p. 4. (Review of The Odd Woman.)

Godwin, Gail. "Towards a Fully Human Heroine: Some Worknotes." Harvard Advocate 106 (Winter 1973): 26-28.

Pritchard, William H. "Novel Sex and Violence." Hudson Review 28 (Spring 1975): 147-160. (Review Essay.)

GOLDONI, CARLO

Judicini, Joseph V. "The Problem of the Arranged Marriage and the Education of Girls in Goldoni's La figlia obbediente and Moratín's El sí de las niñas." Riv. di Letterature Moderne e Comparate (Firenze) 24 (1971): 208-223.

GORDON, CAROLINE

Brown, Jerry Elijah. "The Rhetoric of Form: A Study of the Novels of Caroline Gordon." Ph. D. Dissertation, Vanderbilt University, 1974.

Landess, Thomas N., ed. The Short Fiction of Caroline Gordon: A Critical Symposium. Dallas: University of Dallas Press, 1972.

Rocks, James E. "The Short Fiction of Carolina Gordon."

<u>Tulane Studies in English</u>, vol. 3. New Orleans: Tulane University, 1970.

Stanford, Donald. "Caroline Gordon." In <u>Contemporary Novelists</u>. Edited by James Vinson. London: St. James Press, 1972; New York: St. Martin's Press, 1972.

Stuckey, W. J. <u>Caroline Gordon</u>. New York: Twayne, 1972.

GOUDGE, ELIZABETH

Marsden, Madonna. "Gentle Truths for Gentle Readers: The Fiction of Elizabeth Goudge." In <u>Images of Women in Fiction</u>, pp. 68-78. Edited by Susan Koppelman Cornillon. Bowling Green, Ohio: Bowling Green University Press, 1972.

GOULD, LOIS

Crain, Jane Larkin. "Feminist Fiction." <u>Commentary</u> 58 (December 1974): 58-62; Discussion, 59 (May 1975): 22-24.

Freedman, Richard. <u>Book World</u>, 21 June 1970, p. 5. (Review of <u>Such Good Friends</u>.)

Owens, Iris. <u>New York Times Book Review</u>, 14 April 1974, p. 7. (Review of <u>Final Analysis</u>.)

Peer, Elizabeth. "Sex and the Woman Writer." <u>Newsweek</u>, 5 May 1975, 70-72, 73-77.

<u>Saturday Review</u>, 13 June 1970, p. 43. (Review of <u>Such Good Friends</u>.)

GRAND, MRS.

Gorsky, Susan R. "Old Maids and New Women: Alternatives to Marriage in Englishwomen's Novels, 1847-1915." <u>Journal of Popular Culture</u> 7 (Summer 1973): 68-85.

GRAU, SHIRLEY ANN

Eisinger, Chester E. "Shirley Ann Grau." In <u>Contemporary Novelists</u>. Edited by James Vinson. London:

St. James Press, 1972; New York: St. Martin's
Press, 1972.

Keith, Don L. "A Visit with Shirley Ann Grau." Contempora (Atlanta, Ga.) 2, no. 2 (1972): 10-14.

GURO, ELENA (Eleonora Genrikhovna von Notenberg)

Banjanin, Milica. "The Prose and Poetry of Elena
Guro." Russian Literature Triquarterly no. 9 (Spring
1974): 303-316.

-H-

H. D. (Hilda Doolittle)

Friedman, Susan Stanford. "Mythology, Psychoanalysis
and the Occult in the Late Poetry of H. D." Ph. D.
Dissertation, University of Wisconsin, 1973.

_____. "Who Buried H. D. ? A Poet, Her Critics,
and Her Place in 'The Literary Tradition.'" Paper
presented at the Midwest Modern Language Association meeting, Chicago, 2 November 1973. (Mimeographed.)

HALL, RADCLYFFE

Frye, Jennie Cooper. "Radclyffe Hall: A Study in
Censorship." Ph. D. Dissertation, University of
Missouri, 1972.

HANSBERRY, LORRAINE

Farrison, W. Edward. "Lorraine Hansberry's Last
Dramas." CLA Journal 16 (December 1972): 188-
197.

Mobley, Joyce D. "Black Female Voices in the Ameri-
can Theater, 1916-1970." Paper presented for the
Midwest Modern Language Association, Chicago, 3
November 1973. (Mimeographed.)

Potter, Vilma R. "New Politics, New Mothers." CLA
Journal 16 (December 1972): 247-255.

Willis, Robert J. "Anger and the Contemporary Black Theatre." Negro American Literature Forum 8 (Summer 1974): 213-216.

HARDY, THOMAS

Bhatt, Punita B. "Thomas Hardy's Women: A Study in Relationships." Ph. D. Dissertation, The Catholic University of America, 1972.

Burwell, Rose Marie. "Schopenhauer, Hardy and Lawrence: Toward a New Understanding of Sons and Lovers." Western Humanities Review 28 (Spring 1974): 105-117.

Cunningham, A. R. "The 'New Woman Fiction' of the 1890's." Victorian Studies 17 (December 1973): 177-186.

Detter, Howard Montgomery. "The Female Sexual Outlaw in the Victorian Novel: A Study in the Conventions of Fiction." Ph. D. Dissertation, Indiana University, 1971.

Dignon, Hugh Alexander. "Love and Courtship in the Novels of George Eliot, Thomas Hardy, and D. H. Lawrence: A Comparative Study." Ph. D. Dissertation, New York University, 1974.

Draffan, Robert A. "Hardy's Under the Greenwood Tree." English (London) 22 (Summer 1973): 55-60.

Edwards, Duane. "Tess of the d'Urbervilles and Hippolytus." Midwest Quarterly 15 (July 1974): 392-405.

Egan, Joseph J. "The Fatal Suitor: Early Foreshadowing in Tess of the d'Urbervilles." Tennessee Studies in Literature 15 (1970): 161-164.

Eggenschwiler, David. "Eustacia Vye, Queen of Night and Courtly Pretender." Nineteenth-Century Fiction 25 (March 1971): 444-454.

Halperin, John. Egoism and Self-Discovery in the Victorian Novel. New York: Burt Franklin, 1974, pp. 217-245.

Hardwick, Elizabeth. Seduction and Betrayal: Women and Literature. New York: Random House, 1974, pp. 202-206.

Hornback, Bert G. The Metaphor of Chance. Athens, Ohio: Ohio University Press, 1971.

Jarrett, David W. "Eustacia Vye and Eula Varner, Olympians: The Worlds of Thomas Hardy and William Faulkner." Novel 6 (1973): 163-174.

Kozicki, Henry. "Myths of Redemption in Hardy's Tess of the d'Urbervilles." Papers on Language & Literature 10 (Spring 1974): 150-158.

Luedtke, Luther S. "Sherwood Anderson, Thomas Hardy, and 'Tandy.'" Modern Fiction Studies 20 (Winter 1974-75): 531-540.

May, Charles E. "Hardy's Diabolical Dames: A Generic Consideration." Genre 7 (December 1974): 307-321.

Meisel, Perry. Thomas Hardy: The Return of the Repressed. New Haven: Yale University Press, 1972.

Millett, Kate. Sexual Politics. New York: Avon, 1971, pp. 130-134, 147, 252, 269.

Stone, Donald D. "Victorian Feminism and the Nineteenth-Century Novel." Women's Studies 1 (1972): 65-92.

Tarleck, Robert D. "Existential Failing in Tess of the d'Urbervilles." Colby Library Quarterly 9 (March 1971): 256-259.

Tomlinson, T. B. "Hardy's Universe: Tess of the d'Urbervilles." Critical Review no. 16 (1973): 19-38.

Vigar, Penelope. The Novels of Thomas Hardy: Illusion and Reality. London: University of London, Athlone Press, 1974.

Wagner, Geoffrey. Five for Freedom: A Study of Feminism in Fiction. Rutherford, Madison, Teaneck,

N. J.: Fairleigh Dickinson University Press, 1972, pp. 55, 56, 60, 94, 101, 183-211.

Walczak, Louise. "The Single Green Light and the Splendid and Terrible Spectrum: A Study of the Secular Romance Quest in the Novels of Thomas Hardy and D. H. Lawrence." Ph. D. Dissertation, University of Illinois at Urbana-Champaign, 1973.

Zellefrow, K. "Return of the Native: Hardy's Map and Eustacia's Suicide." Nineteenth-Century Fiction 28 (September 1973): 214-220.

HAWTHORNE, NATHANIEL

Bales, Kent. "The Allegory and the Radical Romantic Ethic of The Blithedale Romance." American Literature 46 (March 1974): 41-53.

Baym, Nina. "Hawthorne's Women: The Tyranny of Social Myths." Centennial Review 15 (Summer 1971): 250-272.

Browning, Preston M. "Hester Prynne as a Secular Saint." Midwest Quarterly 13 (1972): 351-362.

Byers, J. R. "House of Seven Gables and 'The Daughters of Dr. Byles': A Probable Source." PMLA 89 (January 1974): 174-177.

Canaday, Nicholas, Jr. "Hawthorne's The Scarlet Letter." Explicator 28 (January 1970): 28-29.

Carlson, Constance Hedin. "Heroines in Certain American Novels." Ph. D. Dissertation, Brown University, 1971.

Cicardo, Barbara Joan. "The Mystery of the American Eve: Alienation of the Feminine as a Tragic Theme in American Letters." Ph. D. Dissertation, St. Louis University, 1971.

Dean, Sharon Welch. "Lost Ladies: The Isolated Heroine in the Fiction of Hawthorne, James, Fitzgerald, Hemingway and Faulkner." Ph. D. Dissertation, University of New Hampshire, 1973.

Flint, Allen. "The Saving Grace of Marriage in

Hawthorne's Fiction. " Emerson Society Quarterly 19 (2nd Quarter 1973): 112-116.

Fryer, Judith Joy. "The Faces of Eve: A Study of Women in American Life and Literature in the Nineteenth Century. " Ph. D. Dissertation, University of Minnesota, 1973.

Gallagher, Kathleen. "The Art of Snake Handling: Lamia, Elsie Venner, and 'Rappaccini's Daughter. '" Studies in American Fiction 3 (Spring 1975): 51-64.

Hall, S. "Beatrice Cenci: Symbol and Vision in The Marble Faun. " Nineteenth-Century Fiction 25 (June 1970): 85-95.

Hardwick, Elizabeth. Seduction and Betrayal. New York: Random House, 1974, pp. 180-186.

Heilbrun, Carolyn G. Toward a Recognition of Androgyny. New York: Knopf, 1973, pp. 62, 63-67, 104.

Hirsh, John C. "Zenobia as Queen: The Background Sources to Hawthorne's The Blithedale Romance, " National Hawthorne Journal (1971): 182-191.

Justus, James H. "Hawthorne's Coverdale: Character and Art in The Blithedale Romance. " American Literature 47 (March 1975): 21-36.

Krier, William John. "A Pattern of Limitations: The Heroine's Novel of Mind. " Ph. D. Dissertation, Indiana University, 1973.

Kushen, Betty. "Love's Martyrs: The Scarlet Letter as Secular Cross. " Literature and Psychology 22 (1972): 109-120.

Liebman, Sheldon W. "The Forsaken Maiden in Hawthorne's Stories. " American Transcendental Quarterly 19 (1973): 13-19.

Mills, Nicolaus. "Nathaniel Hawthorne and George Eliot. " American and English Fiction in the Nineteenth Century. Bloomington: Indiana University Press, 1973, pp. 52-73.

Montgomery, Judith H. "The American Galatea. "

College English 32 (May 1971): 890-899.

_____. "Pygmalion's Image: The Metamorphosis of the American Heroine." Ph.D. Dissertation, Syracuse University, 1971.

Mottram, Richard Allen. "Hawthorne's Men: Their Dominant Influence." Ph.D. Dissertation, Tulane University, 1974.

Pratt, Linda Ray. "The Abuse of Eve by the New World Adam." In Images of Women in Fiction, pp. 156, 157, 160-165, 169. Edited by Susan Koppelman Cornillon. Bowling Green, Ohio: Bowling Green University Press, 1972.

Shear, Walter. "Characterization in The Scarlet Letter." Midwest Quarterly 12 (July 1971): 437-454.

Spitzer, Michael. "Hawthorne's Women: Female Influences on the Life and Fiction of Nathaniel Hawthorne." Ph.D. Dissertation, New York University, 1974.

Todd, Robert E. "The Magna Mater Archetype in The Scarlet Letter." New England Quarterly 45 (1972): 421-429.

Van Cromphout, Gustaaf. "Blithedale and the Androgyne Myth: Another Look at Zenobia." Emerson Society Quarterly 18 (1972): 141-145.

HAYS, MARY

Luria, Gina M. "Mary Hays: A Critical Autobiography." Ph.D. Dissertation, New York University, 1972.

HAYWOOD, ELIZA

Heinemann, Marcia. "Eliza Haywood's Career in the Theatre." Notes & Queries 20 (1973): 9-13.

Novak, Maximillian E. "Some Notes Toward a History of Fictional Forms: From Aphra Behn to Daniel Defoe." Novel 6 (Winter 1973): 120-133.

Rudolf, Jo-Ellen Schwartz. "The Novels that Taught the Ladies: A Study of Popular Fiction Written by

Women, 1702-1834. " Ph. D. Dissertation, University of California, San Diego, 1972.

Spacks, Patricia Meyer. "'Ev'ry Woman is at Heart a Rake. '" Eighteenth-Century Studies 8 (Fall 1974): 27-64.

Steeves, Edna L. "Pre-Feminism in Some Eighteenth Century Novels. " Texas Quarterly 16 (Autumn 1973): 48-57.

Suwannabha, Sumitra. "The Feminine Eye: Augustan Society as Seen by Selected Women Dramatists of the Restoration and Early Eighteenth Century. " Ph. D. Dissertation, Indiana University, 1973.

HAZZARD, SHIRLEY

Colmer, John. "Patterns and Preoccupations of Love: The Novels of Shirley Hazzard. " Meanjin Quarterly 29 (Summer 1970): 461-467.

HEBERT, ANNE

Atwood, Margaret. "Ice Women vs Earth Mothers. " Survival: A Thematic Guide to Canadian Literature. Toronto: Anansi, 1972, pp. 195-212.

Chaisson, Arthur Paul. "The Tragic Mood in the Works of Anne Hébert. " Ph. D. Dissertation, Tufts University, 1974.

Lennox, John W. "The Past: Themes and Symbols of Confrontation in The Double Hook and 'Le Torrent. '" Journal of Canadian Fiction 2 (Winter 1973): 70-72.

Macri, F. M. "Anne Hébert: Story and Poem. " Canadian Literature no. 58 (Autumn 1973): 9-18.

HELLMAN, LILLIAN

Angermeier, Brother Carrol. "Moral and Social Protest in the Plays of Lillian Hellman. " Ph. D. Dissertation, The University of Texas at Austin, 1970.

Blitgen, Sister Carol. "The Overlooked Hellman. " Ph. D. Dissertation, University of California, Santa Barbara, 1972.

Fremont-Smith, Eliot. "Lillian Hellman: Portrait of a Lady." New York Magazine, 17 September 1973, p. 82.

Haynes, M. Ms. 2 (January 1974): 31-33. (Review of Pentimento.)

Hellman, Lillian. Pentimento. Boston: Little, Brown, 1973.

Johnson, Annette Bergmann. "A Study of Recurrent Character Types in the Plays of Lillian Hellman." Ph.D. Dissertation, University of Massachusetts, 1971.

Lorimer, Cynthia Diane Miller. "A Study of Female Characters in the Eight Plays of Lillian Hellman." Ph.D. Dissertation, Purdue University, 1970.

Moers, Ellen. "Family Theater." Commentary, September 1972, pp. 96-99.

Moody, Richard. Lillian Hellman, Playwright. New York: Pegasus, 1972.

Spacks, Patricia M. The Female Imagination. New York: Knopf, 1975.

_____. "Free Women." Hudson Review 24 (Winter 1971-72): 559-573.

"Women on Women." American Scholar 41 (Fall 1972): 599-622. See also Patricia McLaughlin, "Comment," pp. 622-627.

Yee, Carole Zonis. "Lillian Hellman, Her Attitude about Self and Identity." Paper presented at the PMLA meeting, New York, December 1974.

HEMINGWAY, ERNEST

Bakker, J. Ernest Hemingway: The Artist as Man of Action. Assen (The Netherlands): Van Gorcum, 1972.

Canaday, Nicholas, Jr. "The Motif of the Inner Ring in Hemingway's Fiction." CEA Critic 36 (January 1974): 18-21.

Carlson, Constance Hedin. "Heroines in Certain American Novels." Ph. D. Dissertation, Brown University,
1971.

Dean, Sharon Welch. "Lost Ladies: The Isolated
Heroine in the Fiction of Hawthorne, James, Fitzgerald, Hemingway and Faulkner." Ph. D. Dissertation, University of New Hampshire, 1973.

Dunphy, Patricia. "The Case Against Women in Contemporary Literature: Hemingway and Faulkner."
Women: A Journal of Liberation 2 (Fall 1970):
20-21.

Farley, Pamella. "Form and Function: The Image of
Woman in Selcted Works of Hemingway and Fitz-
gerald." Ph. D. Dissertation, The Pennsylvania
State University, 1973.

Glicksberg, Charles I. The Sexual Revolution in Modern
American Literature. The Hague: Martinus Nijhoff,
1971, pp. 82-95.

Gottschalk, Klaus-Dieter. "Verkehrte Welt in Hemingway's 'The Doctor and the Doctor's Wife.'"
Neureren Sprachen 21 (May 1972): 285-293.

Greco, Anne. "Margot Macomber: 'Bitch Goddess,'
Exonerated." Fitzgerald-Hemingway Annual (1972):
215-226.

Kobler, J. F. "Let's Run Catherine Barkley up the
Flag Pole and See Who Salutes." CEA Critic 36
(January 1974): 4-10.

Presley, John W. "'Hawks Never Share': Women and
Tragedy in Hemingway." Hemingway Notes 3 (Fall
1973): 3-6.

Sharrock, Roger. "Singles and Couples: Hemingway's
A Farewell to Arms and Updike's Couples." Ariel
4, no. 4 (1973): 21-43.

HENDERSON, GEORGE WYLIE

Kane, Patricia and Doris Y. Wilkinson. "Survival
Strategies: Black Women in Ollie Miss and Cotton
Comes to Harlem." Critique 16, no. 1: 101-109.

HERBST, JOSEPHINE

Kempthorne, Dion Quinton. "Josephine Herbst: A
Critical Introduction." Ph.D. Dissertation, The
University of Wisconsin, 1973.

HESSE, HERMANN

Bennett, Veldon J. "The Role of the Female in the
Works of Hermann Hesse." Ph.D. Dissertation,
University of Utah, 1972.

Leuchter, Johanna. "Sex Roles in Three of Hermann
Hesse's Novels." In Images of Women in Fiction,
pp. 175-180. Edited by Susan Koppelman Cornillon.
Bowling Green, Ohio: Bowling Green University
Press, 1972.

HEYWOOD, THOMAS

Johnson, Marilyn Laurine. "Images of Women in the
Works of Thomas Heywood." Ph.D. Dissertation,
Temple University, 1974.

HIMES, CHESTER

Kane, Patricia and Doris Y. Wilkinson. "Survival
Strategies: Black Women in Ollie Miss and Cotton
Comes to Harlem." Critique 16, no. 1: 101-109.

HOBBES, JOHN OLIVER

Colby, Vineta. "The Wrong Paradise: John Oliver
Hobbes." The Singular Anomaly. New York: New
York University Press, 1970, pp. 175-233.

HOLMES, OLIVER WENDELL

Doxey, William Sanford. "Characterization in the Prose
Fiction of Dr. Oliver Wendell Holmes." Ph.D.
Dissertation, University of North Carolina at Chapel
Hill, 1970.

Gallagher, Kathleen. "The Art of Snake Handling: Lamia,
Elsie Venner, and 'Rappaccini's Daughter.'" Studies
in American Fiction 3 (Spring 1975): 51-64.

Parker, Gail Thain. "Sex, Sentiment, and Oliver Wendell

Holmes. " Women's Studies 1 (1972): 47-64.

HOMER

Freiert, William Kendall. "The Motifs of Confrontation with Women in Homer's Odyssey. " Ph. D. Dissertation, University of Minnesota, 1972.

HORTA, MARIA TERESA

Ascherson, Neal. New York Review of Books, 20 March 1975, p. 11. (Review of The Three Marias: New Portuguese Letters.)

Barreno, Marie Isabel, Maria Teresa Horta, and Maria Velho da Costa. "The Three Marias: New Portuguese Letters. " Ms. 3 (January 1975): 86-87.

de Figueiredo, A. "Portugal's Three Marias: Literary Repression by the Government. " Nation, 2 March 1974, pp. 268-269.

Fonesca, Mary Lydon. "The Case of the Three Marias. " Ms. 3 (January 1975): 84-85, 108.

Kramer, Jane. New York Times Book Review, 2 February 1975, p. 1. (Review of The Three Marias: New Portuguese Letters.)

Prescott, P. S. Newsweek, 27 January 1975, p. 61. (Review of The Three Marias: New Portuguese Letters.)

HOWELLS, WILLIAM DEAN

Bremer, Sidney L. H. "Woman in the Works of William Dean Howells. " Ph. D. Dissertation, Stanford University, 1971.

Cohn, Jan. "The Houses of Fiction: Domestic Architecture in Howells and Edith Wharton. " Texas Studies in Literature and Language 15 (Fall 1973): 537-549.

Crowley, John W. "The Oedipal Theme in Howell's Fennel and Rue. " Studies in the Novel 5 (Spring 1973): 104-109.

Earnest, Ernest. The American Eve in Fact and Fiction, 1775-1914. Urbana, Chicago, London: University of Illinois Press, 1974, pp. 145-154.

Greenwald, Fay T. "The Young Girls in the Novels of W. D. Howells and Henry James." Ph. D. Dissertation, New York University, 1974.

Parker, Gail Thain. "William Dean Howells: Realism and Feminism." Harvard English Studies 4: Uses of Literature. Edited by Monroe Engel. Cambridge: Harvard University Press, 1973.

Wright, Dorothea Curtis. "Visions and Revisions of the 'New Woman' in American Realistic Fiction from 1880 to 1920: A Study in Authorial Attitudes." Ph. D. Dissertation, University of North Carolina at Chapel Hill, 1971.

HUCH, RICARDA

Scholtz, Sigrid Gerda. "Images of Womanhood in the Works of German Female Dramatists 1892-1918." Ph. D. Dissertation, Johns Hopkins University, 1971.

HUGHES, LANGSTON

Dandridge, Rita B. "The Black Woman as a Freedom Fighter in Langston Hughes' 'Simple's Uncle Sam.'" CLA Journal 18 (December 1974): 273-283.

Rosenblatt, Roger. Black Fiction. Cambridge: Harvard University Press, 1974.

HUNTER, KRISTIN

Booth, Martha F. "Black Ghetto Life Portrayed in Novels for the Adolescent." Ph. D. Dissertation, The University of Iowa, 1971.

Reilly, John M. "Kristin Hunter." In Contemporary Novelists. Edited by James Vinson. London: St. James Press, 1972; New York: St. Martin's Press, 1972.

HURSTON, ZORA NEALE

Davis, Arthur P. From the Dark Tower. Washington,

D. C.: Howard University Press, 1974, pp. 113-120.

Gayle, Addison, Jr. The Way of the New World: The Black Novel in America. Garden City, N. Y.: Doubleday, 1975, pp. 140-148.

Giles, James. "The Significance of Time in Zora Neale Hurston's Their Eyes Were Watching God." Negro American Literature Forum 6 (Spring 1972): 52.

Kilson, Marion. "The Transformation of Eatonville's Ethnographer." Phylon 33 (Summer 1972): 112-119.

Murray, Marian. Jump at the Sun: The Story of Zora Neale Hurston. New York: Third Press, 1975.

Neal, Larry. "Eatonville's Zora Neale Hurston: A Profile." In Black Review #2. Edited by Mel Watkins. New York: Morrow, 1972.

Rayson, Ann L. "Dust Tracks on the Road: Zora Neale Hurston and the Form of Black Autobiography." Negro American Literature Forum 7 (1973): 39-45.

_____. "The Novels of Zora Neale Hurston." Studies in Black Literature 5 (Winter 1974): 1-10.

Rosenblatt, Roger. Black Fiction. Cambridge: Harvard University Press, 1974.

Southerland, Ellease. "The Novelist-Anthropologist's Life/Works: Zora Neale Hurston." Black World 23 (August 1974): 20-30.

Turner, Darwin T. In a Minor Chord: Three Afro-American Writers and Their Search for Identity. Carbondale and Edwardsville: Southern Illinois University Press, 1971, pp. 89-120.

Walker, Alice. "In Search of Zora Neale Hurston." Ms. 3 (March 1975): 74-79, 85-89.

Walker, S. Jay. "Zora Neale Hurston's Their Eyes Were Watching God: Black Novel of Sexism." Modern Fiction Studies 20 (Winter 1974-75): 519-527.

Washington, Mary Helen. "Zora Neale Hurston: The

Black Woman's Search for Identity." <u>Black World</u> 21 (August 1972): 68-75.

Young, James O. <u>Black Writers of the Thirties</u>. Baton Rouge: Louisiana State University Press, 1973, pp. 219-223.

-I-

IBSEN, HENRIK

Balice, Vincent Joseph. "A Study of the Female as Wife and Mother in Ibsen's Dramas." Ph. D. Dissertation, Purdue University, 1971.

Downs, Brian Westerdale. <u>A Study of Six Plays by Ibsen</u>. New York: Octagon Books, 1972.

Durbach, Errol. "The Apotheosis of Hedda Gabler." <u>Scandinavian Studies</u> 43 (Spring 1971): 143-159.

Forrey, Carolyn. "The New Woman Revisited." <u>Women's Studies</u> 2 (1974): 37-56.

Hardwick, Elizabeth. <u>Seduction and Betrayal</u>. New York: Random House, 1974, pp. 31-83.

Heilbrun, Carolyn G. <u>Toward a Recognition of Androgyny</u>. New York: Knopf, 1973, pp. 49, 69, 90-91, 92, 93, 94.

Holtan, Orley I. <u>Mythic Patterns in Ibsen's Last Plays</u>. Minneapolis: University of Minnesota Press, 1970.

Hurt, James. <u>Catiline's Dream; An Essay on Ibsen's Plays</u>. Urbana: University of Illinois Press, 1972.

Lyons, Charles R. <u>Henrik Ibsen: The Divided Consciousness</u>. Carbondale: Southern Illinois University Press, 1972.

Millett, Kate. <u>Sexual Politics</u>. New York: Avon, 1971, pp. 115, 129, 152, 155-156.

Northam, John Richard. <u>Ibsen: A Critical Study</u>. Cambridge (England): University Press, 1973.

Rogers, Katharine M. "A Woman Appreciates Ibsen."
Centennial Review 18 (Winter 1974): 91-108.

Tucker, E. L. "Faulkner's Drusilla and Ibsen's Hedda."
Modern Drama 16 (September 1973): 157-161.

Wagner, Geoffrey. Five for Freedom. Rutherford,
Madison, Teaneck, N. J.: Fairleigh Dickinson University Press, 1972.

Warner, John R. "The Dichotomy of Ibsen's Mrs.
Linde." Discourse 13 (Winter 1970): 88-97.

Webb, Eugene. "The Radical Irony of Hedda Gabler."
Modern Language Quarterly 31 (March 1970): 53-63.

INCHBALD, ELIZABETH

Steeves, Edna L. "Pre-Feminism in Some Eighteenth-
Century Novels." Texas Quarterly 16 (Autumn 1973):
48-57.

-J-

JACKSON, SHIRLEY

Ames, Carol. "Love Triangles in Fiction: The Underlying Fantasies." Ph. D. Dissertation, State University of New York at Buffalo, 1973.

Friedman, Lenemaja. Shirley Jackson. New York:
Twayne, forthcoming.

JAMES, HENRY

Appignanesi, Lisa. Femininity and the Creative Imagination: A Study of Henry James, Robert Musil, and
Marcel Proust. New York: Barnes & Noble, 1973.

Bell, Millicent. "Style as Subject: Washington Square."
Sewanee Review 83 (January-March 1975): 19-38.

Carlson, Constance Hedin. "Heroines in Certain

American Novels. " Ph. D. Dissertation, Brown University, 1971.

Cicardo, Barbara Joan. "The Mystery of the American Eve: Alienation of the Feminine as a Tragic Theme in American Letters. " Ph. D. Dissertation, St. Louis University, 1971.

Davis, Sara deSaussure. "The Female Protagonist in Henry James's Fiction, 1870-1890. " Ph. D. Dissertation, Tulane University, 1974.

Dean, Sharon Welch. "Lost Ladies: The Isolated Heroine in the Fiction of Hawthorne, James, Fitzgerald, Hemingway, and Faulkner. Ph. D. Dissertation, University of New Hampshire, 1973.

Earnest, Ernest. The American Eve in Fact and Fiction, 1775-1914. Urbana, Chicago, London: University of Illinois Press, 1974, pp. 179-189, 199-202, 204-205.

Fryer, Judith Joy. "The Faces of Eve: A Study of Women in American Life and Literature in the Nineteenth Century. " Ph. D. Dissertation, University of Minnesota, 1973.

Geary, Edward Acord. "A Study of the Androgynous Figure in the Fiction of Henry James. " Ph. D. Dissertation, Stanford University, 1971.

Gillette, Jane Brown. "Medusa /Muse: Women as Images of Chaos and Order in the Writings of Henry Adams and Henry James. " Ph. D. Dissertation, Yale University, 1972.

Girgus, Sam B. "The Other Maisie: Inner Death and Fatalism in What Maisie Knew. " Arizona Quarterly 29 (1973): 115-122.

Grant, William E. "'Daisy Miller': A Study of a Study. " Studies in Short Fiction 11 (Winter 1974): 17-26.

Greene, Mildred S. "Les Liaisons Dangereuses and The Golden Bowl: Maggie's 'Loving Reason. '" Modern Fiction Studies 19 (Winter 1973-74): 531-540.

Greenwald, Fay T. "The Young Girls in the Novels of W. D. Howells and Henry James." Ph. D. Dissertation, New York University, 1974.

Grover, P. R. "Henry James and the Theme of the Adventuress." Revue de Littérature Comparée 47 (1973): 586-596.

Grumman, Joan Mary. "Henry James's Great 'Bad' Heroines." Ph. D. Dissertation, Purdue University, 1972.

Halperin, John. Egoism and Self-Discovery in the Victorian Novel: Studies in the Ordeal of Knowledge in the Nineteenth Century. New York: Burt Franklin, 1974, pp. 247-276.

_____. The Language of Meditation: Four Studies in Nineteenth-Century Fiction. Devon: Arthur H. Stockwell, 1973.

Heilbrun, Carolyn G. Toward a Recognition of Androgyny. New York: Knopf, 1973, pp. 49, 63, 65, 66, 67, 90, 92, 94-97.

Hinz, Evelyn J. "Henry James's Names: Tradition, Theory, and Method." Colby Library Quarterly 9 (September 1972): 557-578.

Johnson, Lee Ann. "James's Mrs. Wix: The Dim, Crooked Reflector." Nineteenth-Century Fiction 29 (September 1974): 164-172.

_____. "The Psychology of Characterization: James's Portraits of Verena Tarrant and Olive Chancellor." Studies in the Novel 6 (Fall 1974): 295-303.

Jones, Granville H. "Henry James's 'Georgina's Reasons': The 'Underside of Washington Square.'" Studies in Short Fiction 11 (Spring 1974): 189-194.

Kerr, Howard. Mediums and Spirit-Rappers, and Roaring Radicals. Urbana: University of Illinois Press, 1972, pp. 190-222.

Kormali, Sema Günisik. "The Treatment of Marriage in Representative Novels of Jane Austen and Henry

James." Ph.D. Dissertation, Texas Tech University, 1974.

Krier, William John. "A Pattern of Limitations: The Heroine's Novel of Mind." Ph.D. Dissertation, Indiana University, 1973.

Liebman, S. W. "Point of View in The Portrait of a Lady." English Studies 52 (April 1971): 136-146.

McMaster, Juliet. "The Portrait of Isabel Archer." American Literature 45 (March 1973): 50-66.

Maglin, Nan Bauer. "Fictional Feminists in The Bostonians and The Odd Women. In Images of Women in Fiction, pp. 216-236. Edited by Susan Koppelman Cornillon. Bowling Green, Ohio: Bowling Green University Press, 1972.

Marks, Sita Patricia Smith. "Character Patterns in Henry James's The Wings of the Dove and The Golden Bowl." Ph.D. Dissertation, Michigan State University, 1970.

Mays, Milton A. "Down-Town with Henry James." Texas Studies in Literature and Language 14 (1972): 107-122.

Miller, Theodore C. "The Muddled Politics of Henry James's The Bostonians." Georgia Review 26 (Fall 1972): 336-346.

Mitchell, Juliet. "What Maisie Knew: Portrait of the Artist as a Young Girl." In The Air of Reality, pp. 168-189. Edited by John Goode. London: Methuen, 1972.

Montgomery, Judith H. "The American Galatea." College English 32 (May 1971): 890-899.

_____. "Pygmalion's Image: The Metamorphosis of the American Heroine." Ph.D. Dissertation, Syracuse University, 1971.

Moore, Katharine. Victorian Wives. New York: St. Martin's Press, 1974.

Morgan, Alice. "Henry James: Money and Morality."

   Texas Studies in Literature and Language 12 (Spring 1970): 75-92.

Mull, Donald L. "Freedom and Judgment: The Antinomy of Action in The Portrait of a Lady." Arizona Quarterly 27 (Summer 1971): 124-132.

_____. Henry James' "Sublime Economy." Middletown: Wesleyan University Press, 1973, pp. 48-116.

Nettels, Elsa. "The Scapegoats and Martyrs of Henry James." Colby Library Quarterly 10 (September 1974): 413-427.

Nicoloff, Philip L. "At the Bottom of Things in Henry James's 'Louisa Pallant.'" Studies in Short Fiction 7 (Summer 1970): 409-420.

Oates, Joyce Carol. New Heaven, New Earth: The Visionary Experience in Literature. New York: Vanguard Press, 1974.

Pearce, Howard D. "Witchcraft Imagery and Allusion in James's Bostonians." Studies in the Novel 6 (Summer 1974): 236-247.

Peterson, M. Jeanne. "The Victorian Governess: Status, Incongruence in Family and Society." Victorian Studies 14 (September 1970): 7-23.

Powers, Lyall H. Henry James and The Naturalist Movement. East Lansing: Michigan State University Press, 1971.

_____. Henry James's Major Novels: Essays in Criticism. East Lansing: Michigan State University Press, 1973.

Pratt, Linda Ray. "The Abuse of Eve by the New World Adam." In Images of Women in Fiction, pp. 155, 156, 162, 165-170. Edited by Susan Koppelman Cornillon. Bowling Green, Ohio: Bowling Green University Press, 1972.

Robinson, Lillian S. "Who's Afraid of a Room of One's Own?" In The Politics of Literature, pp. 359, 377, 381, 388. Edited by Louis Kampf and Paul Lauter. New York: Pantheon Books, 1972.

Rowe, John Carlos. "The Symbolization of Milly Theale: Henry James's The Wings of the Dove." ELH 40 (Spring 1973): 131-164.

Sabiston, Elizabeth. "Prison of Womanhood." Comparative Literature 25 (Fall 1973): 336-351.

Samuels, Charles Thomas. The Ambiguity of Henry James. Urbana, Chicago, London: University of Illinois Press, 1971.

Schultz, Elizabeth. "The Bostonians: The Contagion of Romantic Illusion." Genre 4 (March 1971): 45-59.

Shinn, Thelma J. "A Question of Survival: An Analysis of 'The Treacherous Years' of Henry James." Literature and Psychology 23 (1973): 135-148.

Spacks, Patricia M. The Female Imagination. New York: Knopf, 1975.

Stone, Donald D. Novelists in a Changing World: Meredith, James, and the Transformation of English Fiction in the 1880's. Cambridge: Harvard University Press, 1972.

_____. "Victorian Feminism and the Nineteenth-Century Novel." Women's Studies 1 (1972): 65-92.

Sudrann, Jean. "Hearth and Horizon: Changing Concepts of the 'Domestic' Life of the Heroine." Massachusetts Review 14 (Spring 1973): 235-255.

Vann, J. Don, ed. Critics on Henry James. Coral Gables, Fla.: University of Miami Press, 1972.

Wagner, Geoffrey. Five for Freedom. Rutherford, Madison, Teaneck, N. J.: Fairleigh Dickinson University Press, 1972, pp. 30, 31, 36n, 38, 47, 55, 148.

Wallace, Ronald. "Maggie Verver: Comic Heroine." Genre 6 (December 1973): 404-415.

Walters, Margaret. "Keeping the Place Tidy for the Young Female Mind: The Awkward Age." In The Air of Reality, pp. 190-218. Edited by John Goode. London: Methuen, 1972.

Weinstein, Philip M. Henry James and the Requirements of the Imagination. Cambridge: Harvard University Press, 1971, pp. 31-71, 72-96.

Wilson, Raymond J. "Transactional Analysis and Literature." Ph. D. Dissertation, The University of Nebraska-Lincoln, 1973.

Wright, Dorothea Curtis. "Visions and Revisions of the 'New Woman' in American Realistic Fiction from 1880 to 1920: A Study in Authorial Attitudes." Ph. D. Dissertation, University of North Carolina at Chapel Hill, 1971.

Zak, Michele Wender. "Feminism and the New Novel." Ph. D. Dissertation, Ohio State University, 1973.

_____. "Henry James and the Free Woman." Paper presented at the Midwest PMLA meeting, St. Louis, 1972. (Mimeographed.)

JARRELL, RANDALL

Edgerton, Jean MacLean. "Woman Manquée and Woman Triumphant in the Poetry of Randall Jarrell." Ph. D. Dissertation, University of North Carolina at Chapel Hill, 1970.

JEWETT, SARAH ORNE

Anderson, Donald Robert. "Failure and Regeneration in the New England of Sarah Orne Jewett and Mary E. Wilkins Freeman." Ph. D. Dissertation, University of Arizona, 1974.

Cary, Richard, ed. Appreciation of Sarah Orne Jewett: 29 Interpretive Essays. Waterville, Me.: Colby College Press, 1973.

_____. "The Rise, Decline, and Rise of Sarah Orne Jewett." Colby Library Quarterly 9 (1972): 650-663.

_____. "The Sculptor and the Spinster: Jewett's 'Influence' on Cather." Colby Library Quarterly 10 (September 1973): 168-178.

Forrey, Carolyn. "The New Woman Revisited." Women's

Studies 2 (1974): 37-56.

Horn, Robert L. "The Power of Jewett's Deephaven."
Colby Library Quarterly 9 (1972): 617-631.

Humma, John B. "The Art and Meaning of Sarah Orne
Jewett's 'The Courting of Sister Wisby.'" Studies
in Short Fiction 10 (Winter 1973): 85-91.

Jobes, Katharine T. "From Stowe's Eagle Island to
Jewett's 'A White Heron.'" Colby Library Quarterly
10 (December 1974): 515-520.

Noyes, Sylvia G. "Mrs. Almira Todd, Herbalist-Con-
jurer." Colby Library Quarterly 9 (1972): 643-
649.

Parker, Jeraldine. "'Uneasy Survivors': Five Women
Writers 1896-1923." Ph.D. Dissertation, University
of Utah, 1973.

Pratt, Annis. "Women and Nature in Modern Fiction."
Contemporary Literature 13 (Autumn 1972): 470-480,
488-489.

St. Armand, Barton. "Jewett and Marin: The Inner
Vision." Colby Library Quarterly 9 (1972): 632-
643.

Stevenson, Catherine Barnes. "The Double Consciousness
of the Narrator in Sarah Orne Jewett's Fiction."
Colby Library Quarterly 11 (March 1975): 1-12.

Toth, Susan Allen. "Sarah Orne Jewett and Friends:
A Community of Interest." Studies in Short Fiction
9 (Summer 1972): 233-241.

_____. "The Value of Age in the Fiction of Sarah
Orne Jewett." Studies in Short Fiction 8 (Summer
1971): 433-442.

Vella, Michael W. "Sarah Orne Jewett: A Reading of
the Country of the Pointed Firs." Emerson Society
Quarterly 73 (Fourth Quarter 1973): 275-282.

Willoughby, John. "Sarah Orne Jewett and Her Shelter
Island." Confrontation 8 (Spring 1974): 72-86.

Wood, Ann Douglas. "The Literature of Impoverishment: The Women Local Colorists in America 1865-1914." Women's Studies 1 (1972): 3-46.

JHABVALA, R. PRAWER

Williams, Haydn M. The Fiction of Ruth Prawer Jhabvala. Thompson, Conn.: InterCulture Associates, 1975.

_____. "R. K. Narayan and R. Prawer Jhabvala." Literature East and West 16, no. 4 (General Issue): 1136-1154.

JOHNSON, DIANE

Haynes, Muriel. "What Evil Lurks...." Ms. 3 (November 1974): 37-39. (Review of The Shadow Knows.)

McHale, Tom. New York Times Book Review, 5 September 1971, p. 6. (Review of Burning.)

Peer, Elizabeth. "Sex and the Woman Writer." Newsweek, 5 May 1975, pp. 70-72, 73-77.

Pritchard, William H. "Novel Sex and Violence." Hudson Review 28 (Spring 1975): 147-160. (Review Essay.)

Ryan, Marjorie. "The Novels of Diane Johnson." Critique 16, no. 1: 53-63.

JOHNSON, SAMUEL

Clayton, Philip T. "Samuel Johnson's Irene: 'An Elaborate Curiosity.'" Tennessee Studies in Literature. Knoxville: University of Tennessee Press, 1974, pp. 121-135.

JONG, ERICA

Dobbs, Jeanine. "Not Another Poetess: A Study of Female Experience in Modern American Poetry." Ph.D. Dissertation, University of New Hampshire, 1973.

Francke, L. "Mother Confessor." Newsweek, 16 December 1974, pp. 65-68.

Hoffman, Nancy. "A Feminist Approach to Women Poets: 'We Urge You to Risk Your Life.'" Paper presented at the Midwest Modern Language Association Meeting, Chicago, 2 November 1973. (Mimeographed.)

Meyer, E. H. Nation, 12 January 1974, p. 55. (Review of Fear of Flying.)

Peer, Elizabeth. "Sex and the Woman Writer." Newsweek, 5 May 1975, pp. 70-72, 73-77.

Reuben, Elaine. New Republic, 2 February 1974, p. 27. (Review of Fear of Flying.)

Schulman, G. Ms. 2 (August 1973): 40. (Review of Half-Lives.)

Stone, Carole. "Three Mother-Daughter Poems: The Struggle for Separation." Paper presented at the Fifth International Forum for Psychoanalysis, Zurich, 1-5 September 1974.

Updike, John. New Yorker, 17 December 1973, p. 149. (Review of Fear of Flying.)

Vendler, Helen. New York Times Book Review, 12 August 1973, p. 6. (Review of Half-Lives.)

JONSON, BEN

Angell, Charles Francis. "'The Center Attractive': The Function of Women in Ben Jonson's Comedy." Ph. D. Dissertation, University of Massachusetts, 1974.

Hallett, C. A. "Jonson's Celia: A Reinterpretation of Volpone." Studies in Philology 68 (January 1971): 50-69.

JORDAN, JUNE

Moore, Honor. Ms. 3 (April 1975): 48-49, 113-114. (Review of New Days.)

JOYCE, JAMES

Brandabur, Edward. A Scrupulous Meanness: A Study

of Joyce's Early Work. Urbana: University of Illinois Press, 1971.

Card, James Van Dyck. "'Contradicting': The Word for Joyce's 'Penelope.'" James Joyce Quarterly 11 (Fall 1973): 17-26.

Cross, Richard K. Flaubert and Joyce: The Rite of Fiction. Princeton, N. J.: Princeton University Press, 1971.

Haule, James Mark. "The Theme of Isolation in the Fiction of Dorothy M. Richardson, Virginia Woolf, and James Joyce." Ph. D. Dissertation, Wayne State University, 1974.

Kempf, Andrea Caron. "A Portrait of the Woman as a Non-Artist: James Joyce and Molly Bloom." Women: A Journal of Liberation 2 (Fall 1970): 17-18.

Kenner, Hugh. "Molly's Masterstroke." James Joyce Quarterly 10 (Fall 1972): 19-28.

Little, Sherry Burgus. "The Relationship of the Woman Figure and Views of Reality in Three Works by James Joyce." Ph. D. Dissertation, Arizona State University, 1971.

Loss, Archie K. "The Pre-Raphaelite Woman, The Symbolist Femme-Enfant, and the Girl with Long Flowing Hair in the Earlier Work of Joyce." Journal of Modern Literature 3 (February 1973): 3-23.

Monahan, Mary Joan. "The Position of Molly Bloom in Ulysses." Ph. D. Dissertation, Kent State University, 1971.

Osborne, Marianne Muse. "The Hero and Heroine in the British Bildungsroman: David Copperfield, A Portrait of the Artist as a Young Man, Jane Eyre and The Rainbow." Ph. D. Dissertation, Tulane University, 1971.

Unkeless, Elaine Rapp. "Consciousness and Androgyny in James Joyce's Ulysses." Ph. D. Dissertation, Columbia University, 1974.

Williams, B. "Molly Bloom: Archetype or Stereotype."
Marriage and Family 33 (August 1971): 545-546.

-K-

KAUFMAN, SUE

Crain, Jane Larkin. "Feminist Fiction." Commentary
58 (December 1974): 58-62; Discussion, 59 (May
1975): 22-24.

Dickstein, Lora. New York Times Book Review, 3
February 1974, p. 7. (Review of Falling Bodies.)

Peer, Elizabeth. "Sex and the Woman Writer." Newsweek, 5 May 1975, pp. 70-72, 73-77.

Salamone, V. A. Best Sellers 33 (February 1974): 476.
(Review of Falling Bodies.)

KAWABATA, YASUNARI

Miyoshi, Masao. Accomplices of Silence: The Modern
Japanese Novel. Berkeley, Los Angeles, London:
University of California Press, 1974, pp. 106-107,
114-119.

Schlieman, Dorothy S. "Yasunari Kawabata's 'Narrow
Bridge of Art.'" Literature: East & West 15
(December 1971, March 1972, June 1972): 890-907.

KELLEY, EDITH SUMMERS

Kahn, Coppelia. "Lost and Found." Ms. 2 (April 1974):
36, 117-118. (Review of Weeds.)

KENNEDY, ADRIENNE

Mobley, Joyce D. "Black Female Voices in the American Theater, 1916-1970." Paper presented for the
Midwest Modern Language Association, Chicago,
3 November 1973. (Mimeographed.)

KENNEDY, JOHN PENDLETON

Ruoff, John C. "Frivolity to Consumption: Or, Southern
Womanhood in Antebellum Literature." Civil War
History 18 (September 1972): 213-229.

KESEY, KEN

Sullivan, Ruth. "Big Mama, Big Papa, and Little Sons
in Ken Kesey's One Flew Over the Cuckoo's Nest."
Literature and Psychology 25, no. 1 (1975): 34-44.

KOVALEVSKAYA, SOFYA

Stillman, Beatrice. "Sofya Kovalevskaya: Growing Up
in the Sixties." Russian Literature Triquarterly
no. 9 (Spring 1974): 276-302.

-L-

LACLOS, CHODERLOS De

Blum, Carol. "Styles of Cognition as Moral Options in
La Nouvelle Héloïse and Les Liaisons dangereuses."
PMLA 88 (March 1973): 289-298.

Greene, Mildred S. "Les Liaisons Dangereuses and The
Golden Bowl: Maggie's 'Loving Reason.'" Modern
Fiction Studies 19 (Winter 1973-74): 531-540.

Michael, Colette Verger. "La femme et le mal dans
Les liaisons dangereuses de Choderlos de Laclos."
Ph. D. Dissertation, University of Wisconsin, 1973.

Miller, Nancy Kipnis. "Gender and Genre: An Analysis
of Literary Femininity in the Eighteenth-Century
Novel." Ph. D. Dissertation, Columbia University,
1974.

Simmons, Sarah Tawil. "Attitudes de Hamilton, Marivaux, Crebillon fils et Laclos envers la femme
d'apres leurs oeuvres romanesques." Ph. D. Dissertation, University of Colorado, 1970.

Thody, Philip. Laclos: Les liaisons dangereuses.

London: Edward Arnold, 1970.

Wagner, Geoffrey. Five for Freedom. Rutherford, Madison, Teaneck, N.J.: Fairleigh Dickinson University Press, 1972, pp. 51, 61, 63-102.

LAFAYETTE, MADAME de

Allentuch, Harriet Ray. "The Will to Refuse in the Princess de Cleves." University of Toronto Quarterly 44 (Spring 1975): 185-198.

Backer, Dorothy Anne Liot. Precious Women. New York: Basic Books, 1974.

Bárczay-Miller, Eva. "La Princesse de Clèves and the Tragic Dimension of Classicism." Ph.D. Dissertation, Rutgers University, The State University of New Jersey, 1974.

Betts, C. J. "An Aspect of Mme de Lafayette's narrative technique: correspondences of physical detail in La Princesse de Clèves." Australian Journal of French Studies 10 (May-August 1973): 130-143.

Brée, Germaine. Women Writers in France: Variations on a Theme. New Brunswick, N.J.: Rutgers University Press, 1973, pp. 37-38.

Goode, William O. "A Mother's Goals in La princesse de Clèves: Worldly and Spiritual Distinction." Neophilologus (Groningen) 56 (1972): 398-406.

Haig, Sterling. Madame de Lafayette. New York: Twayne, 1970.

Kestner, Joseph A. III. "Defoe and Madame de La Fayette: Roxana and La Princesse de Monpensier." Papers on Language and Literature 8 (1972): 297-301.

Lipton, Virginia Anne. "Women in Today's World: A Study of Five French Women Novelists." Ph.D. Dissertation, The University of Wisconsin, 1972.

Raitt, Janet. Madame de Lafayette and La Princesse de Clèves. London: Harrap, 1971.

Redhead, Ruth Willard. "Love and Death in the Fictional Works of Madame de Lafayette." Ph.D. Dissertation, University of Minnesota, 1971.

Simmons, Sarah Tawil. "Attitudes de Hamilton, Marivaux, Crebillon fils et Laclos envers la femme d'apres leurs oeuvres romanesques." Ph.D. Dissertation, University of Colorado, 1970.

Tiefenbrun, Susan W. "The Art of Repetition in 'La Princesse de Clèves.'" Modern Language Review 68 (January 1973): 40-50.

_____. "A Structural Stylistic Analysis of La Princesse de Cleves." Ph.D. Dissertation, Columbia University, 1971.

Weisz, Pierre. "Tragédie et vérité romanesque: La princesse de Clèves." L'Esprit Créateur (Lawrence, Kansas) 13 (1973): 229-240.

Woshinsky, Barbara R. La princesse de Clèves: The Tension of Elegance. The Hague: Mouton, 1973.

LAGERKVIST, PÄR

Block, Adèle. "The Mythical Female in the Fictional Works of Pär Lagerkvist." International Fiction Review 1 (January 1974): 48-53.

Scobbie, Irene. "Interpretation of Lagerkvist's Mariamne." Scandinavian Studies 45 (Spring 1973): 128-34.

LAMB, MYRNA

Thurston, Linda. "An Interview with ... Myrna Lamb." The Second Wave 1 (Spring 1971): 12-15.

LARSEN, NELLA

Davis, Arthur P. From the Dark Tower. Washington, D.C.: Howard University Press, 1974, pp. 94-98.

Gayle, Addison, Jr. The Way of the New World: The Black Novel in America. Garden City, N.Y.: Doubleday, 1975, pp. 108-115.

Sato, Hiroko. "Under the Harlem Shadow: A Study of

Jessie Fauset and Nella Larsen. " In The Harlem
Renaissance Remembered, pp. 63-83. Edited by
Arna Bontemps. New York: Dodd, Mead, 1972.

Thornton, Hortense E. "Sexism as Quagmire: Nella
Larsen's Quicksand. " CLA Journal 16 (March
1973): 285-301.

Whitlow, Roger. Black American Literature. Chicago:
Nelson Hall, 1973. pp. 92-96.

Youman, Mary Mabel. "Nella Larsen's 'Passing': A
Study in Irony. " CLA Journal 18 (December 1974):
235-241.

LASHER-SCHÜLER, ELSE

Cohn, Hans W. Else Lasher-Schüler: The Broken
World. London: Cambridge University Press, 1974.

Scholtz, Sigrid Gerda. "Images of Womanhood in the
Works of German Female Dramatists 1892-1918. "
Ph. D. Dissertation, Johns Hopkins University, 1971.

LAURENCE, MARGARET

Atwood, Margaret. "Ice Women vs Earth Mothers. "
Survival: A Thematic Guide to Canadian Literature."
Toronto: Anansi, 1972, pp. 195-212.

Bowering, George. "That Fool of a Fear: Notes on
'A Jest of God. ' Canadian Literature no. 50
(Autumn 1971): 41-56.

Forman, Denyse and Uma Parameswaran. "Echoes and
Refrains in the Canadian Novels of Margaret
Laurence. " Centennial Review 16 (Summer 1972):
233-253.

Gibson, Graeme. Eleven Canadian Novelists. Toronto:
Anansi, 1973.

Good, Jacquelyn Mary. "The Image of Women in Canadian Literature with Particular Reference to Margaret Laurence. " M. A. Thesis, University of New
Brunswick, n. d.

Jones, D. G. Butterfly on Rock: A Study of Themes

and Images in Canadian Literature. Toronto and
Buffalo: University of Toronto Press, 1970.

Kertzer, J. M. "The Stone Angel: Time and Respon-
sibility." Dalhousie Review 54 (Autumn 1974):
499-509.

Lever, Bernice. "Manawaka Magic." Journal of
Canadian Fiction 3, no. 3 (1974): 93-96. (Review
of The Diviners.)

McLay, C. M. "Every Man Is an Island: Isolation in
'A Jest of God.'" Canadian Literature 50 (Autumn
1971): 57-68.

Miner, Valerie. "The Matriarch of Manawaka."
Saturday Night 89 (May 1974): 20.

Mitchell, Sr. Beverley. Journal of Canadian Fiction 2,
no. 4 (1973): 112. (Review of The Firedwellers.)

Moss, John. Patterns of Isolation in English Canadian
Fiction. Toronto: McClelland & Stewart, 1974.

Mugo, Micere. Journal of Canadian Fiction 1, no. 2
(1972): 86. (Review of A Tree for Poverty.)

Pesando, Frank. "In a Nameless Land: The Use of
Apocalyptic Mythology in the Writings of Margaret
Laurence." Journal of Canadian Fiction 2, no. 1
(1973): 53-58.

Pratt, Annis. "Women and Nature in Modern Fiction."
Contemporary Literature 13 (Autumn 1972): 476-490.

Read, S. E. "The Maze of Life: The Work of Margaret
Laurence." In Writers of the Prairies, pp. 132-141.
Edited by Donald G. Stephens. Vancouver: Univer-
sity of British Columbia Press, 1973.

Thomas, Clara, transcriber. "A Conversation about
Literature: An Interview with Margaret Laurence and
Irving Layton." Journal of Canadian Fiction 1, no. 2
(1972): 58-64.

_____. "The Novels of Margaret Laurence." Studies
in the Novel 4 (1972): 154-164.

_____. "The Short Stories of Margaret Laurence."
World Literature Written in English 11, no. 1
(1972): 25-33.

LAWRENCE, D. H.

Brayfield, Peggy L. "Lawrence's 'Male and Female
Principles' and the Symbolism of 'The Fox.'"
Mosaic 4 (1971): 41-51.

Broembsen, F. Von. "Mythic Identification and Spatial
Inscendence: The Cosmic Vision of D. H. Lawrence."
Western Humanities Review 29 (Spring 1975): 137-
154.

Brookesmith, Peter. "The Future of the Individual."
Human World no. 10 (February 1973): 42-65.

Brown, Homer O. "'The Passionate Struggle into
Conscious Being': D. H. Lawrence's The Rainbow."
D. H. Lawrence Review 7 (Fall 1974): 275-290.

Burwell, Rose Marie. "Schopenhauer, Hardy and Lawrence: Toward a New Understanding of Sons and
Lovers." Western Humanities Review 28 (Spring
1974): 105-117.

Chavis, Geraldine G. "Ursula Brangwen: Toward
Self and Selflessness." Thoth 12 (1971): 18-28.

Clupper, Beatrice Blong. "The Male Principal in D. H.
Lawrence's Fiction." Ph.D. Dissertation, University of Illinois at Urbana-Champaign, 1971.

Cohen, Judith Dana. "The Violation or Fulfillment of
Individuality in Marriage, as Seen in Selected Works
of D. H. Lawrence." Ph.D. Dissertation, University
of Pennsylvania, 1970.

Cushman, Keith. "The Making of D. H. Lawrence's
'The White Stocking.'" Studies in Short Fiction 10
(Winter 1973): 51-66.

Davis, Patricia C. "Chicken Queen's Delight: D. H.
Lawrence's The Fox." Modern Fiction Studies 19
(Winter 1973-74): 565-571.

Dignon, Hugh Alexander. "Love and Courtship in the Novels of George Eliot, Thomas Hardy, and D. H. Lawrence: A Comparative Study." Ph. D. Dissertation, New York University, 1974.

Gidley, M. "Antipodes: D. H. Lawrence's 'St. Mawr.'" Ariel 5 (January 1974): 25-41.

Grotte, Margaret Spencer. "The Unsteady Arch: The Place of The Rainbow in the Lawrentian Love-Ethic." Ph. D. Dissertation, Cornell University, 1974.

Gurko, Leo. "D. H. Lawrence's Greatest Collection of Short Stories--What Holds It Together." Modern Fiction Studies 18 (Summer 1972): 173-182.

Hardy, B. N. "Women in D. H. Lawrence's Works." In D. H. Lawrence: Novelist, Poet, Prophet. Edited by S. Spender. New York: Harper, 1973.

Harris, Janice H. "D. H. Lawrence and Kate Millett." Massachusetts Review 15 (Summer 1974): 522-529.

Heilbrun, Carolyn G. Toward a Recognition of Androgyny. New York: Knopf, 1973, pp. 88, 95, 101, 102-110, 112, 115, 124.

Horney, Larry J. "The Emerging Woman of the Twentieth-Century: A Study of Women in D. H. Lawrence's Novels, The Rainbow and Women in Love." Ed. D. Dissertation, Ball State University, 1972.

Jacobson, Sibyl. "The Paradox of Fulfillment: A Discussion of Women in Love." Journal of Narrative Technique 3 (January 1973): 53-65.

Kermode, Frank. D. H. Lawrence. New York: Viking, 1973.

Kleinbard, David J. "D. H. Lawrence and Ontological Insecurity." PMLA 89 (January 1974): 154-163.

Millett, Kate. Sexual Politics. New York: Avon, 1971, pp. 209, 237-293, 296-297, 311, 324, 334, 356, 362.

Osborne, Marianne Muse. "The Hero and Heroine in the British Bildungsroman: David Copperfield, A Portrait of the Artist as a Young Man, Jane Eyre, and The Rainbow." Ph. D. Dissertation, Tulane University, 1971.

Pritchard, R. E. D. H. Lawrence: Body of Darkness. London: Hutchinson University Library, 1971.

Ragussis, Michael. "The False Myth of St. Mawr: Lawrence and the Subterfuge of Art." Papers on Language and Literature 11 (Spring 1975): 186-196.

Remsbury, John. "Women in Love as Novel of Change." D. H. Lawrence Review 6 (Summer 1973): 149-172.

Reuben, Elaine. "Feminist Criticism in the Classroom, or, 'What do you mean we, white man?'" Women's Studies 1 (1973): 315-326.

Sanders, Scott. D. H. Lawrence: The World of the Five Major Novels. New York: Viking, 1973.

Shields, E. F. "Broken Vision in Lawrence's 'The Fox.'" Studies in Short Fiction 9 (Fall 1972): 353-364.

Walczak, Louise. "The Single Green Light and the Splendid and Terrible Spectrum: A Study of the Secular Romance Quest in the Novels of Thomas Hardy and D. H. Lawrence." Ph. D. Dissertation, University of Illinois at Urbana-Champaign, 1973.

Ziebarth, Janet A. "Sexuality and Social Critique in the Novels of D. H. Lawrence, 1915-1922." Ph. D. Dissertation, Rutgers University, The State University of New Jersey, 1974.

LEDUC, VIOLETTE

Beauvoir, Simone de. All Said and Done. New York: G. P. Putnam's, 1974, pp. 47-52.

Lipton, Virginia Anne. "Women in Today's World: A Study of Five French Women Novelists." Ph. D. Dissertation, The University of Wisconsin, 1972.

LEE, VERNON

Colby, Vineta. "The Puritan Aesthete: Vernon Lee."
The Singular Anomaly. Philadelphia: Chilton, 1972,
pp. 235-303.

Ormond, Leonee. "Vernon Lee as a Critic of Aestheti-
cism in Miss Brown." Colby Library Quarterly 9
(September 1970): 131-153.

LE GUIN, URSULA K.

Atherton, Deborah. "Duality and Difference." Woman
Becoming 1 (July 1973): 70-71. (Review of The
Left Hand of Darkness.)

McNelly, Willis E. "Archetypal Patterns in Science
Fiction." CEA Critic 35 (May 1973): 15-19.

Russ, Joanna. "The Image of Women in Science Fic-
tion." In Images of Women in Fiction, pp. 79-94.
Edited by Susan Koppelman Cornillon. Bowling
Green, Ohio: Bowling Green University Press, 1972.
(Reprinted from Red Clay Reader.)

Scholes, Robert. "The Good Witch of the West."
Hollins Critic 11 (April 1974): 1-12.

Sellers, Jill. Spokeswoman, 15 March 1975, pp. 8-9.
(Review of The Dispossessed.)

LEHMANN, ROSAMOND

Gindin, James. "Rosamond Lehmann: A Revaluation."
Contemporary Literature 15 (Spring 1974): 203-211.

Thornton, Lawrence. "Rosamond Lehmann, Henry James
and the Temporal Matrix of Fiction." Virginia
Woolf Quarterly 1 (Spring 1973): 66-75.

Tindall, Gillian. "Rosamond Lehmann." In Contemporary
Novelists. Edited by James Vinson. London: St.
James Press, 1972; New York: St. Martin's Press,
1972.

LENNOX, CHARLOTTE

Miner, Earl, Jr. Stuart and Georgian Moments.

Berkeley: University of California Press, 1972, p. 288.

LESSING, DORIS

Alcorn, Noeline E. "Vision and Nightmare: A Study of Doris Lessing's Novels." Ph. D. Dissertation, University of California, Irvine, 1971.

Barnouw, Dagmar. "Disorderly Company: From The Golden Notebook to The Four-Gated City." Contemporary Literature 14 (Autumn 1973): 74-97.

Bolling, Douglass. "Structure and Theme in Briefing for a Descent into Hell." Contemporary Literature 14 (Autumn 1973): 133-147.

Brooks, Ellen W. "Fragmentation and Integration: A Study of Doris Lessing's Fiction." Ph. D. Dissertation, New York University, 1971.

_____. "The Image of Woman in Lessing's The Golden Notebook." Critique 15, no. 1 (1973): 101-109.

Burkom, Selma R. "A Reconciliation of Opposites: A Study of the Works of Doris Lessing." Ph. D. Dissertation, University of Minnesota, 1970.

Carey, John L. "Art and Reality in The Golden Notebook." Contemporary Literature 14 (Autumn 1973): 437-456.

Craig, Joanne. "The Golden Notebook: The Novelist as Heroine." University of Windsor Review 10 (Fall-Winter 1974): 55-66.

Didion, Joan. New York Times Book Review, 14 March 1971, pp. 1, 38-39.

Gindin, James. "Lessing Criticism." Contemporary Literature 14 (Autumn 1974): 586-589.

Godwin, Gail. "The Personal Matter of Doris Lessing." North American Review 256 (Summer 1971): 66-70.

Halliday, Patricia Ann Young. "The Pursuit of Wholeness

in the Work of Doris Lessing: Dualities, Multiplicities, and the Resolution of Patterns in Illumination." Ph. D. Dissertation, University of Minnesota, 1973.

Hardin, Nancy Shields. "Doris Lessing and the Sufi Way." Contemporary Literature 14 (Autumn 1973): 565-581.

Hardwick, Elizabeth. New York Times Book Review, 13 May 1973, pp. 1-2. (Review of The Summer Before the Dark.)

Hendin, Josephine. Harper's, June 1973, pp. 82-86. (Review of The Summer Before the Dark.)

Hinz, Evelyn J. and John J. Teunissen. "The Pietà as Icon in The Golden Notebook." Contemporary Literature 14 (Autumn 1973): 457-470.

Howe, Florence. "A Conversation with Doris Lessing (1966)." Contemporary Literature 14 (Autumn 1973): 418-436.

Hynes, Joseph. "The Construction of The Golden Notebook." Iowa Review 4 (Summer 1973): 100-113.

Jong, Erica. "Everywoman Out of Love?" Partisan Review 40, no. 3 (1973): 500-503.

Kaplan, Sydney Janet. "Doris Lessing." Contemporary Literature 14 (Autumn 1973): 536-549.

Karl, Frederick R. "Doris Lessing in the Sixties: The New Anatomy of Melancholy." Contemporary Literature 13 (1972): 15-33.

Krouse, Agate Nesaule. "The Feminism of Doris Lessing." Ph. D. Dissertation, The University of Wisconsin, 1972.

Lessing, Doris. "On The Golden Notebook." Partisan Review 40 (Winter 1973): 14-30.

_____. A Small Personal Voice: Essays, Reviews, Interviews. Edited and Introduction by Paul Schlueter. New York: Knopf, 1974.

McDowell, Margaret B.   "Reflections on the New Feminism. " Midwest Quarterly 12 (April 1971):   309-333.

Marchino, Lois Annett.   "The Search for Self in the
Novels of Doris Lessing. " Ph. D. Dissertation, The
University of New Mexico, 1972.

Markow, Alice Bradley.   "The Pathology of Feminine
Failure in the Fiction of Doris Lessing. " Critique
16, no. 1:   88-100.

Morgan, Ellen.   "Alienation of the Woman Writer in
The Golden Notebook. " Contemporary Literature 14
(Autumn 1973):   471-480.

Mulkeen, Anne M.   "Twentieth-Century Realism: The
'Grid' Structure of The Golden Notebook. " Studies
in the Novel 4 (1972):   262-274.

Mutti, Giuliana.   "Female Roles and the Function of Art
in The Golden Notebook. " Massachusetts Studies
in English 3 (Spring 1972):   78-83.

Naumer, Mary Ann Singleton.   "The City and the Veld:
A Study of the Fiction of Doris Lessing. " Ph. D.
Dissertation, University of Oregon, 1973.

Oates, Joyce Carol.   "A Visit with Doris Lessing. "
Southern Review 9 (October 1973):   873-882.

Porter, Dennis.   "Realism and Failure in The Golden
Notebook. " Modern Language Quarterly 35 (March
1974):   56-65.

Porter, Nancy M.   "A Way of Looking at Doris Lessing."
In Female Studies VI: Closer to the Ground, pp.
123-139.   Edited by Nancy Hoffman, Cynthia Secor,
Adrian Tinsley.   Old Westbury, N. Y. :   Feminist
Press, 1972.

Pratt, Annis.   "Archetypal Approaches to the New
Feminist Criticism. " Bucknell Review 12 (Spring
1973):   3-14.

_____.   "Women and Nature in Modern Fiction. "
Contemporary Literature 13 (Autumn 1972):   487,
490.

_____ and L. S. Dembo, eds. Doris Lessing: Critical Studies. Madison: University of Wisconsin
Press, 1974. (Essays from the Autumn 1973 issue
of Contemporary Literature.)

Robinson, Lillian S. "Who's Afraid of a Room of One's
Own?" In The Politics of Literature, pp. 375, 381,
390. Edited by Louis Kampf and Paul Lauter. New
York: Pantheon Books, 1972.

Sanderson, Annette. "The Fragmented Heroine." Harvard
Advocate 106 (Winter 1973): 65-67.

Schlueter, Paul. The Novels of Doris Lessing. Carbondale: Southern Illinois University Press, 1973.

Shapiro, S. Crawdaddy, November 1973, p. 89. (Review
of The Summer Before the Dark.)

Smith, Diane E. S. "A Thematic Study of Doris Lessing's Children of Violence." Ph.D. Dissertation,
Loyola University of Chicago, 1971.

Spacks, Patricia M. The Female Imagination. New
York: Knopf, 1975.

_____. "Free Women." Hudson Review 24 (Winter
1971-72): 559-573.

Spencer, Sharon. "'Femininity' and The Woman Writer:
Doris Lessing's The Golden Notebook and The Diary
of Anaïs Nin." Women's Studies 1 (1973): 247-258.

Stein, Karen F. "Reflections in a Jagged Mirror:
Some Metaphors of Madness." Aphra 6 (Spring
1975): 2-11.

Sudrann, Jean. "Hearth and Horizon: Changing Concepts of the 'Domestic' Life of the Heroine."
Massachusetts Review 14 (Spring 1973): 235-255.

Sukenick, Lynn. "Feeling and Reason in Doris Lessing's Fiction." Contemporary Literature 14 (Autumn
1973): 98-118.

_____. "Sense and Sensibility in Women's Fiction:
Studies in the Novels of George Eliot, Virginia

Woolf, Anaïs Nin, and Doris Lessing." Ph. D. Dissertation, The City University of New York, 1974.

Thorpe, Michael. Doris Lessing. Harlow, England: Published for the British Council by Longman Group, 1973.

Tindall, Gillian. "Doris Lessing." In Contemporary Novelists. Edited by James Vinson. London: St. James Press, 1972; New York: St. Martin's Press, 1972.

Widmann, R. L. "Lessing's The Summer Before the Dark." Contemporary Literature 14 (Autumn 1973): 582-585.

Zak, Michele Wender. "Feminism and the New Novel." Ph. D. Dissertation, Ohio State University, 1973.

_____. "The Grass Is Singing: A Little Novel about the Emotions." Contemporary Literature 14 (Autumn 1973): 481-490.

LEVERTOV, DENISE

Dobbs, Jeanine. "Not Another Poetess: A Study of Female Experience in Modern American Poetry." Ph. D. Dissertation, University of New Hampshire, 1973.

Heyen, William. "Fourteen Poets: A Chronicle." Southern Review 6 (Spring 1970): 539-550.

Kyle, Carol A. "Every Step an Arrival: Six Variations and the Musical Structure of Denise Levertov's Poetry." Centennial Review 17 (Summer 1973): 281-296.

Malkoff, Karl. Crowell's Handbook of Contemporary American Poetry. New York: Thomas Y. Crowell, 1973, pp. 172-178.

Molesworth, Charles. "Denise Levertov." Deland, Fla.: Everett/Edwards, n. d. (Cassette.)

Reid, Ivan. "'Everyman's Land': Ivan Reid Interviews Denise Levertov." Southern Review (Adelaide) 5 (September 1972): 231-236.

Walker, Cheryl Lawson. "The Women's Tradition in
American Poetry." Ph.D. Dissertation, Brandeis
University, 1973.

LEVI-STRAUSS, CLAUDE

McNelly, Cleo. "Natives, Women and Claude Lévi-
Strauss." Massachusetts Review 16 (Winter 1975):
7-29.

LEWIS, JANET

Hofheins, Roger and Dan Tooker. "A Conversation with
Janet Lewis." Southern Review 10 (April 1974):
329-341.

Killoh, Ellen. "Patriarchal Women: A Study of Three
Novels by Janet Lewis." Southern Review 10 (April
1974): 342-364.

Peck, Ellen Margaret McKee. "Exploring the Feminine:
A Study of Janet Lewis, Ellen Glasgow, Anaïs Nin,
and Virginia Woolf." Ph.D. Dissertation, Stanford
University, 1974.

LEWIS, SINCLAIR

Carlson, Constance Hedin. "Heroines in Certain American Novels." Ph.D. Dissertation, Brown University,
1971.

Hopkins, Elaine. "From 'Freedom' to 'Slavery'--Carol
Kennicott in Main Street." Paper presented at the
Midwest MLA meeting, St. Louis, November 1972.
(Mimeographed.)

Maglin, Nan Bauer. "Women in Three Sinclair Lewis
Novels." Massachusetts Review 14 (Autumn 1973):
783-801.

LICHNOWSKY, MECHTILD

Scholtz, Sigrid Gerda. "Images of Womanhood in the
Works of German Female Dramatists 1892-1918."
Ph.D. Dissertation, Johns Hopkins University, 1971.

LINTON, ELIZA LYNN

Colby, Vineta. "Wild Women, Revolting Daughters, and the Shrieking Sisterhood: Mrs. Eliza Lynn Linton." The Singular Anomaly. New York: New York University Press, 1970, pp. 15-45.

Showalter, Elaine Cottler. "The Double Standard: Criticism of Women Writers in England, 1845-1880." Ph. D. Dissertation, University of California, Davis, 1970.

Stone, Donald D. "Victorian Feminism and the Nineteenth-Century Novel." Women's Studies 1 (1972): 65-92.

LISPECTOR, CLARICE

Boring, Phyllis Zatlin. "The Brazilian Novel in the 1960s." Papers on Language & Literature 11 (Winter 1975): 95-111.

LIVESAY, DOROTHY

Mitchell, Beverley. "'How Silence Sings' in the Poetry of Dorothy Livesay 1926-1973." Dalhousie Review 54 (Autumn 1974): 510-528.

O'Donnell, Kathleen. "Dorothy Livesay and Simone Routier: A Parallel Study." Humanities Association Bulletin 23 (Fall 1972): 28-37.

Stevens, Peter. "Dorothy Livesay: The Love Poetry." In Poets and Critics. Toronto: Oxford University Press, 1974, pp. 33-52.

_____. "Out of the Silence and Across the Distance: The Poetry of Dorothy Livesay." Queen's Quarterly 78 (1971): 579-591.

Zimmerman, S. "Livesay's Houses." Canadian Literature no. 61 (Summer 1974): 32-45.

LOKHVITSKAYA, MIRRA

Cioran, Sam. "The Russian Sappho: Mirra Lokhvitskaya." Russian Literature Triquarterly no. 9 (Spring 1974): 317-335.

LORDE, AUDRE

Larkin, Joan. Ms. 3 (September 1974): 38-40. (Review of From a Land Where Other People Live.)

LOWELL, AMY

Manley, Seon and Susan Belcher. O, Those Extraordinary Women! Philadelphia: Chilton, 1972, pp. 257-258.

Ruihley, Glenn R. The Thorn of a Rose: Amy Lowell Reconsidered. Hamden, Conn.: Shoestring, 1974.

LUCE, CLARE BOOTHE

Lester, Elenore. "Older But Not Wiser." Ms. 2 (August 1973): 42-44. (Review of The Women.)

Weintraub, Rodelle. "The Gift of Imagination: An Interview with Clare Boothe Luce." Shaw Review 17 (January 1974): 53-59.

LURIE, ALISON

Breslin, J. B. America, 10 August 1974, p. 58. (Review of The War Between the Tates.)

Cowan, Rachel B. Ms. 3 (January 1975): 41-42. (Review of The War Between the Tates.)

Kazin, Alfred. "Cassandras: Porter to Oates." Bright Book of Life: American Novelists and Storytellers from Hemingway to Mailer. Boston: Toronto: Little, Brown, 1973.

Leonard, John. New Republic 171 (August 10/17 1974): 24. (Review of The War Between the Tates.)

Pritchard, William H. "Novel Sex and Violence." Hudson Review 28 (Spring 1975): 147-160. (Review Essay.)

Sale, R. New York Review of Books, 8 August 1974, p. 32. (Review of The War Between the Tates.)

Sanborn, Sara. New York Times Book Review, 28 July

1974, p. 1. (Review of The War Between the Tates.)

Times Literary Supplement, 21 June 1974, p. 657. (Review of The War Between the Tates.)

Wolff, G. New Times, 26 July 1974, p. 62. (Review of The War Between the Tates.)

LYDGATE, JOHN

Edward, A. S. G. "John Lydgate, Medieval Antifeminism and Harley 2251." Annuale Mediavale 13 (1972): 32-44.

_____. "Lydgate's Attitudes to Women." English Studies 51 (October 1970): 436-437.

McRobbie, Kenneth. "Women and Love: Some Aspects of Competition in Late Medieval Society." Mosaic 5, no. 2 (1972): 139-168.

Stoltz, Linda. "Satire and Defense: Antifeminism in the Poetry of Hoccleve and Lydgate." Paper presented at the Midwest MLA Meeting, St. Louis, November 1972. (Mimeographed.)

LYTLE, ANDREW

Joyner, N. "Myth of the Matriarch in Andrew Lytle's Fiction." Southern Literary Journal 7 (Fall 1974): 67-77.

-M-

McCARTHY, MARY

Glicksberg, Charles I.. The Sexual Revolution in Modern American Literature. The Hague: Martinus Nijhoff, 1971, pp. 187-196.

Hoerchner, Susan Jane. "'I Have to Keep the Two Things Separate'; Polarity in Women in the Contemporary American Novel." Ph.D. Dissertation, Emory University, 1973.

Kazin, Alfred. "Cassandras: Porter to Oates." Bright Book of Life: American Novelists and Storytellers from Hemingway to Mailer. Boston, Toronto: Little, Brown, 1973.

Moore, Harry T. "Mary McCarthy." In Contemporary Novelists. Edited by James Vinson. London: St. James Press, 1972; New York: St. Martin's Press, 1972.

Robinson, Lillian S. "Who's Afraid of a Room of One's Own?" In The Politics of Literature, pp. 375, 387, 390. Edited by Louis Kampf and Paul Lauter. New York: Pantheon Books, 1972.

Showalter, Elaine. "Killing the Angel in the House: The Autonomy of Women Writers." Antioch Review 32, no. 3 (1973): 339-353.

Spacks, Patricia M. The Female Imagination. New York: Knopf, 1975.

Spender, Stephen. "American Redemption." Love-Hate Relations: English and American Sensibilities. New York: Random House, 1974, pp. 126-130.

McCULLERS, CARSON

Buchen, Irving H. "Carson McCullers, A Case of Convergence." Bucknell Review 21 (Spring 1973): 15-28.

Ginsberg, Elaine. "The Female Initiation Theme in American Fiction." Studies in Fiction 3 (Spring 1975): 27-37.

Joyce, Edward Thomas. "Race and Sex: Opposition and Identity in the Fiction of Carson McCullers." Ph. D. Dissertation, State University of New York at Stony Brook, 1973.

Lyons, Anne Ward. "Myth and Agony: The Southern Woman as Belle." Ph. D. Dissertation, Bowling Green State University, 1974.

Millichap, Joseph R. "Carson McCullers' Literary Ballad." Georgia Review 27 (Fall 1973): 329-339.

Nelson, Doris Lowene. "The Contemporary American
Family Novel: A Study in Metaphor." Ph. D. Dissertation, University of Southern California, 1970.

Presley, Delma Eugene. "Carson McCullers and the
South." Georgia Review 28 (Spring 1974): 19-32.

White, Barbara Anne. "Growing Up Female: Adolescent
Girlhood in American Literature." Ph. D. Dissertation, The University of Wisconsin-Madison, 1974.

McCULLOUGH, COLLEEN

Ferrari, Margaret. America, 10 August 1974, p. 59.
(Review of Tim; a Novel.)

MAILER, NORMAN

Hoerchner, Susan Jane. "'I Have to Keep the Two
Things Separate'; Polarity in Women in the Con-
temporary American Novel." Ph. D. Dissertation,
Emory University, 1973.

Millett, Kate. Sexual Politics. New York: Avon, 1971,
pp. 10-16, 129, 238, 314-335, 337, 356, 362.

Oates, Joyce Carol. "Out of the Machine." In Will the
Real Norman Mailer Please Stand Up, pp. 216-223.
Edited by L. Adams. Port Washington, N. Y.:
Kennikat Press, 1974.

Silverstein, Howard. "Norman Mailer and the Quest
for Manhood." Ph. D. Dissertation, New York University, 1972.

MALLARME, STEPHANE

Revard, Stella. "Yeats, Mallarmé, and the Archetypal
Feminine." Papers on Language and Literature 8
(Supplement, Fall 1972): 112-127.

MALLET-JORIS, FRANÇOISE

Lipton, Virginia Anne. "Women in Today's World: A
Study of Five French Women Novelists." Ph. D.
Dissertation, The University of Wisconsin, 1972.

Somer, Carol. "... And Other Feminists." The Second
Wave 1 (Spring 1971): 31-32. (Review of The
Witches.)

MANLEY, MARY DE LA RIVIERE

Köster, Patricia. "Humanism, Feminism, Sensationalism:
Mrs. Manley vs. Society." In Transactions of the
Samuel Johnson Society of the Northwest, vol. 4,
pp. 42-53. Edited by Robert H. Carnie. Calgary,
Alberta: Samuel Johnson Society of the Northwest,
1972.

Miner, Earl, ed. Stuart and Georgian Moments. Berkeley: University of California Press, 1972, pp. 272,
273.

Novak, Maximillian E. "Some Notes Toward a History
of Fictional Forms: From Aphra Behn to Daniel
Defoe." Novel 6 (Winter 1973): 120-133.

Spacks, Patricia Meyer. "'Ev'ry Woman is at Heart a
Rake.'" Eighteenth Century Studies 8 (Fall 1974):
27-46.

Steeves, Edna L. "Pre-Feminism in Some Eighteenth-
Century Novels." Texas Quarterly 16 (Autumn
1973): 48-57.

MANN, THOMAS

Ezergailis, Inta Miske. "Male and Female Principles:
Thomas Mann's Image of Schiller and Goethe."
Mosaic 6 (Winter 1973): 37-53.

Wagner, Geoffrey. Five for Freedom. Rutherford,
Madison, Teaneck, N.J.: Fairleigh Dickinson University Press, 1972, pp. 19, 72, 139, 144, 176,
178, 212-229.

MANSFIELD, KATHERINE

Hayman, Ronald. Literature and Living: A Consideration of Katherine Mansfield and Virginia Woolf.
London: Covent Garden Press, 1972.

Justus, James H. "Katherine Mansfield: The Triumph

of Egoism. " Mosaic 6 (Spring 1973): 13-22.

Magalaner, Marvin. The Fiction of Katherine Mansfield.
Carbondale: Southern Illinois University Press, 1971.

Moore, Leslie. Katherine Mansfield; The Memories of
LM. New York: Taplinger, 1972.

Nebeker, Helen E. "The Pear Tree: Sexual Implications
in Katherine Mansfield's 'Bliss.'" Modern Fiction
Studies 18 (Winter 1972-73): 545-551.

Zinman, Toby Silverman. "The Snail under the Leaf:
Katherine Mansfield's Ironic Vision." Ph. D. Dissertation, Temple University, 1973.

MARIE DE FRANCE

Mickel, Emanuel J., Jr. Marie de France. New York:
Twayne, 1974.

_____. "Marie de France's Use of Irony as a Stylistic
and Narrative Device." Studies in Philology 71
(July 1974): 265-290.

Moore, John C. Love in Twelfth-Century France.
Philadelphia: University of Pennsylvania Press,
1972, pp. 92-94.

Schulman, Grace. "Women the Inventors." Nation, 11
December 1972, pp. 594-596.

MARIVAUX, PIERRE CARLET DE CHAMBLAIN DE

Kavaliunas, Jolita Elijana Jurate. "Passions and the
Search for Happiness: The Concepts of Passions
and Guilts in Their Relationship to Happiness, as
Manifold in Certain French Novels of the Eighteenth
Century." Ph. D. Dissertation, Case Western Re-
serve University, 1972.

Larson, Jeffry Kurt. "Pride and Préciosité: A Study of
Emulative Feminine Consciousness in Marivaux's
La Vie de Marianne." Ph. D. Dissertation, Yale
University, 1970.

Simmons, Sarah Tawil. "Attitudes de Hamilton, Marivaux, Crebillon fils et Laclos envers la femme

d'apres leurs oeuvres romanesques." Ph. D. Dissertation, University of Colorado, 1970.

Sturzer, Felicia. "Levels of Meaning in the Novels of
Marivaux." Ph. D. Dissertation, State University
of New York at Buffalo, 1973.

Zylawy, Roman Ihor. "Aspects of Women's Ideology
and the Rise of the Feminine Ethics from the XVIIth
to the XVIIIth Century as Reflected in the Works of
Marivaux and Prévost." Ph. D. Dissertation, University of Colorado, 1973.

MARKANDAYA, KAMALA

Argyle, Barry. "Kamala Markandaya's Nectar in a
Sieve." Ariel: A Review of International English
Literature 4, no. 1 (1973): 35-45.

Rubenstein, Roberta. "Kamala Markandaya's Two Vir-
gins." World Literature Written in English 13
(November 1974): 225-230.

MARSHALL, PAULE

Braithwaite, Edward. "Rehabilitation." Critical
Quarterly 13 (Summer 1971): 175-183.

_____. "West Indian History and Society in the Art
of Paule Marshall's Novel." Journal of Black
Studies 1 (December 1970): 225-238.

Brown, Lloyd W. "The Rhythms of Power in Paule
Marshall's Fiction." Novel 7 (Winter 1974): 159-
167.

Kapai, Leela. "Dominant Themes and Technique in
Paule Marshall's Fiction." CLA Journal 16 (September 1972): 49-59.

Marshall, Paule. "Shaping the World of My Art."
New Letters 40 (October 1973): 97-112.

Nazareth, Peter. "Paule Marshall's Timeless People."
New Letters 40 (Autumn 1973): 113-131.

Stoelting, Winifred L. "Time Past and Time Present:

The Search for Viable Links in The Chosen Place, the Timeless People. " CLA Journal 16 (September 1972): 60-71.

Washington, Mary Helen. "Black Women Image Makers." Black World 23 (August 1974): 10-18.

Whitlow, Roger. Black American Literature: A Critical History. Chicago: Nelson Hall, 1973.

MARTINEAU, HARRIET

Basch, Françoise. Relative Creatures: Victorian Women in Society and the Novel. New York: Schocken, 1974.

Cazamian, Louis. The Social Novel in England 1830-1850. London and Boston: Routledge & Kegan Paul, 1973.

Colby, Vineta. Yesterday's Woman: Domestic Realism in the English Novel. Princeton, N. J.: Princeton University Press, 1974.

Showalter, Elaine Cottler. "The Double Standard: Criticism of Women Writers in England, 1845-1880. " Ph. D. Dissertation, University of California, Davis, 1970.

MASSINGER, PHILIP

Winston, Florence T. "The Significance of Women in the Plays of Philip Massinger." Ph. D. Dissertation, University of Kansas, 1972.

MAURIAC, FRANÇOIS

Wildgen, Kathryn E. "Dieu et Maman: Women in the Novels of François Mauriac. " Renascence 27 (Autumn 1974): 15-22.

MELVILLE, HERMAN

Hennelly, M. "Ishmael's Nightmare and The American Eve. " American Imago 30 (Fall 1973): 274-293.

MEREDITH, GEORGE

Baker, Robert S. "The Ordeal of Richard Feverel: A Psychological Approach to Structure." Studies in the Novel 6 (Summer 1974): 200-217.

_____. "Sir Willoughby Patterne's 'Inner Temple': Psychology and 'Sentimentalism' in The Egoist." Texas Studies in Literature and Language 16 (Winter 1975): 691-703.

Beer, Gillian. Meredith: A Change of Masks. London: The Athlone Press, 1970.

Conrow, Margaret. "Coming to Terms with George Meredith's Fiction." In The English Novel in the Nineteenth Century, pp. 176-195. Edited by George Goodin. Urbana: University of Illinois Press, 1972.

Decavalcante, Frank. "Sexual Politics in Four Victorian Novels." Ph.D. Dissertation, Kent State University, 1974.

DeGraaff, Robert Mark. "The 'Implied Author': A Study of Point of View in Selected Novels by George Meredith." Ph.D. Dissertation, Duke University, 1972.

Detter, Howard Montgomery. "The Female Sexual Outlaw in the Victorian Novel: A Study in the Conventions of Fiction." Ph.D. Dissertation, Indiana University, 1971.

Fowler, Lois J. "Diana of the Crossways: A Prophecy for Feminism." In In Honor of Austin Wright. Edited by Joseph Baim, Ann L. Hayes, and Robert J. Gangewere. Pittsburgh: Carnegie-Mellon University, 1972.

Golden, Arline. "'The Game of Sentiment': Tradition and Innovation in Meredith's Modern Love." ELH 40 (Summer 1973): 264-284.

Halperin, John. The Language of Meditation: Four Studies in Nineteenth-Century Fiction. Devon: Arthur H. Stockwell, 1973.

Hartley, Susan Rebecca. "The Later Novels of George

Meredith: Women's Struggle for Emancipation."
Ph. D. Dissertation, Florida State University, 1973.

Heilbrun, Carolyn G. Toward a Recognition of Androgyny.
New York: Knopf, 1973, pp. 70-72.

Johnson, Diane. Lesser Lives. New York: Knopf,
1972.

Moore, Katharine. Victorian Wives. New York: St.
Martin's Press, 1974.

Peters, Sister Mary Isabel. "The Concept of Relationship in the Novels of George Meredith." Ph. D.
Dissertation, St. Louis University, 1970.

Roby, Norman Stanley. "The Secret Self of George
Meredith: A Study of His Heroes." Ph. D. Dissertation, University of California, Davis, 1972.

Rudman, Carol. "Meredith, Wilde, Shaw: The Uses of
Irony." Ph. D. Dissertation, University of New
York at Stony Brook, work in progress.

Sönmez, Emel. The Novelist George Meredith: Woman's
Champion. Ankara: Hacettepe University, 1973.

Stevenson, Richard C. "Laetitia Dale and the Comic
Spirit in The Egoist." Nineteenth-Century Fiction
26 (March 1972): 406-418.

Stimpson, C. "Just Outside the Limelight." Ms. 2
(May 1974): 36-39. (Review of Lesser Lives.)

Stone, Donald D. Novelists in a Changing World: Meredith, James, and the Transformation of English
Fiction in the 1880's. Cambridge: Harvard University Press, 1972.

_____. "Victorian Feminism and the Nineteenth
Century Novel." Women's Studies 1 (1972): 65-
92.

Tucker, Cynthia Grant. "Meredith's Broken Laurel:
Modern Love and the Renaissance Sonnet Tradition."
Victorian Poetry 10 (Winter 1972): 351-365.

Wilson, Phillip E. "Affective Coherence, A Principle

of Abated Action, and Meredith's <u>Modern Love</u>."
<u>Modern Philology</u> 72 (November 1974): 151-171.

MIHURA, MIGUEL

Ward, Marilynn Italiano. "Themes of Submission,
Dominance, Independence, and Romantic Love: The
Female Figure in the Post-'Avant Garde' Plays of
Miguel Mihura." Ph. D. Dissertation, University
of Colorado, 1974.

MILLAY, EDNA ST. VINCENT

Cheney, Anne. <u>Millay in Greenwich Village</u>. University:
University of Alabama Press, forthcoming.

Cheney, Martha Anne. "Millay in the Village." Ph. D.
Dissertation, Florida State University, 1971.

Dash, Joan. <u>A Life of One's Own: Three Gifted Women
and the Men They Married</u>. New York: Harper &
Row, 1973.

Dobbs, Jeanine. "Not Another Poetess: Study of Female
Experience in Modern American Poetry." Ph. D.
Dissertation, University of New Hampshire, 1973.

Gassman, Janet. "Edna St. Vincent Millay: 'Nobody's
Own.'" <u>Colby Library Quarterly</u> 9 (June 1971):
297-310.

Manley, Seon and Susan Belcher. <u>O, Those Extraordinary Women!</u> Philadelphia: Chilton, 1972, pp.
291-297.

Minot, Walter S. "Millay's 'Ungrafted Tree': The
Problem of the Artist as Woman." <u>New England
Quarterly</u> 48 (June 1975): 260-269.

Walker, Cheryl Lawson. "The Woman's Tradition in
American Poetry." Ph. D. Dissertation, Brandeis
University, 1973.

MILLER, ARTHUR

Jacobson, Irving. "Family Dreams in <u>Death of a Sales-
man</u>." <u>American Literature</u> 47 (May 1975): 247-
258.

MILLER, HENRY

Millett, Kate. <u>Sexual Politics</u>. New York: Avon, 1971, pp. 3-9, 238, 294-313, 356.

MILTON, JOHN

Cockelreas, Joanne Lewis. "Much Deceiv'd, Much Failing, Hapless Eve: Iconography and Eve in Milton's <u>Paradise Lost</u>." Ph. D. Dissertation, University of New Mexico, 1973.

Doyle, Charles Clay. "Nature's Fair Defect: Milton and William Cartwright on the Paradox of Woman." <u>English Language Notes</u> 11 (December 1973): 107-110.

Figes, Eva. <u>Patriarchal Attitudes</u>. New York: Stein & Day, 1970.

Fisher, Stephanie Ann. "Circean Fatal Women in Milton's Poetry: Milton's Concept of the Renaissance Woman." Ph. D. Dissertation, University of Minnesota, 1971.

Keplinger, Ann. "Milton: Polemics, Epic, and the Woman Problem, Again." <u>Cithara</u> 10 (1971): 40-52.

Landy, Marcia. "Kinship and the Role of Women in <u>Paradise Lost</u>." <u>Milton Studies</u> 4 (1972): 3-18.

McColley, Diane Kelsey. "'Daughter of God and Man': The Callings of Eve in <u>Paradise Lost</u>." Ph. D. Dissertation, University of Illinois at Urbana-Champaign, 1974.

_____. "Free Will and Obedience in the Separation Scene of <u>Paradise Lost</u>." <u>Studies in English Literature 1500-1900</u> 12 (Winter 1972): 103-120.

McMaster, Belle Miller. "'Accomplisht Eve': The Interrelation of Character, Tradition, and Structure in Milton's <u>Paradise Lost</u>." Ph. D. Dissertation, University of Louisville, 1974.

Mollenkott, Virginia R. "Milton and Women's Liberation:

A Note on Teaching Method." Milton Quarterly 7 (December 1973): 99-103.

Norford, Don Parry. "'My Other Half': The Coincidence of Opposites in Paradise Lost." Modern Language Quarterly 36 (March 1975): 21-53.

Rauber, D. F. "The Metamorphoses of Eve." Lock Haven Review 12 (1971): 54-70.

Seigel, C. F. "Reconciliation in Book X of Paradise Lost." Modern Language Review 68 (April 1973): 260-263.

Tayler, Irene. "The Woman Scaly." Bulletin of the Midwest Modern Language Association 6 (Spring 1973): 74-87.

Vessels, Elizabeth Jane. "A Mythic Light on Eve: The Function of Mythological Allusion in Defining Her Character and Role in the Epic Action of Paradise Lost." Ph.D. Dissertation, Fordham University, 1972.

Weinkauf, Mary S. "Dalila: The Worst of All Possible Wives." Studies in English Literature 13 (Winter 1973): 135-147.

MONTAGU, LADY MARY WORTLEY

Miner, Earl, ed. Stuart and Georgian Moments. Berkeley: University of California Press, 1972, pp. 250-251, 255, 260, 264, 271-291.

Spacks, Patricia M. The Female Imagination. New York: Knopf, 1975.

MOORE, BRIAN

Foster, John Wilson. "Passage Through Limbo: Brian Moore's North American Novels." Critique 13 (1971): 5-18.

McKenna, Isobel. "Women in Canadian Literature." Canadian Literature no. 62 (Autumn 1974): 69-78.

MOORE, GEORGE

Birky, Wilbur Joseph. "Marriage as Pattern and Metaphor in the Victorian Novel." Ph.D. Dissertation, The University of Iowa, 1970.

Carstens, John Alden. "The Anti-Romances of George Moore." Ph.D. Dissertation, University of Oregon, 1973.

Detter, Howard Montgomery. "The Female Sexual Outlaw in the Victorian Novel: A Study in the Conventions of Fiction." Ph.D. Dissertation, Indiana University, 1971.

Dunleavy, Janet Egleson. George Moore: The Artist's Vision, The Storyteller's Art. Lewisburg: Bucknell University Press, 1973.

Furst, Lilian R. "George Moore, Zola, and the Question of Influence." Canadian Review of Comparative Literature 1 (Spring 1974): 138-155.

Morton, D. E. "Lyrical Form and the World of Esther Waters." Studies in English Literature 13 (Autumn 1973): 688-700.

Ohmann, Carol. "George Moore's Esther Waters." Nineteenth-Century Fiction 25 (September 1970): 174-187.

Sherer, Raymond. "Psychological and Mythic Patterns in the Novels of George Moore." Ph.D. Dissertation, State University of New York at Buffalo, 1974.

Sporn, Paul. "Marriage and Class Conflict: The Subversive Link in George Moore's A Drama in Muslin." CLIO: An Interdisciplinary Journal of Literature, History and the Philosophy of History 3 (October 1973): 7-20.

Stone, Donald D. "Victorian Feminism and the Nineteenth-Century Novel." Women's Studies 1 (1972): 65-92.

MORE, HANNAH

Miner, Earl, Jr., ed. Stuart and Georgian Moments. Berkeley: University of California Press, 1972, pp. 286-287.

MORGAN, ROBIN

Hoffman, Nancy. "A Feminist Approach to Women Poets. 'We Urge You to Risk Your Life.'" Paper presented at the Midwest Modern Language Association Meeting, Chicago, 2 November 1973. (Mimeographed.)

Lehman, David. Poetry 123 (December 1973): 173. (Review of Monster; Poems.)

Rich, Adrienne. Ms. 2 (August 1973): 41-42. (Review of Monster; Poems.)

Swenson, May. New York Times Book Review, 19 November 1972, p. 7. (Review of Monster; Poems.)

Zinnes, Harriet. "Seven Women Poets." Carleton Miscellany 14 (Spring-Summer 1974): 122-126.

MORRISON, TONI

Blackburn, Sara. New York Times Book Review, 30 December 1973, p. 3. (Review of Sula.)

Frankel, Haskel. New York Times Book Review, 1 November 1970, p. 46. (Review of The Bluest Eye.)

Playboy 21 (March 1974): 22. (Review of Sula.)

Sissman, L. E. New Yorker, 23 January 1971, p. 92. (Review of The Bluest Eye.)

Wilder, Charles M. CLA Journal 15 (December 1971): 253-255. (Review of The Bluest Eye.)

MORTIMER, PENELOPE

Ehrenpreis, I. New York Review of Books, 12 December 1974, p. 42. (Review of Long Distance.)

Geng, Veronica. Ms. 3 (January 1975): 40-41. (Review of Long Distance.)

Grumbach, Doris. New Republic, 28 September 1974, p. 23. (Review of Long Distance.)

Simmons, Judith Cooke. "Penelope Mortimer." In
Contemporary Novelists. Edited by James Vinson.
London: St. James Press, 1972; New York: St.
Martin's Press, 1972.

Times Literary Supplement, 24 September 1971, p. 1137.
(Review of The Home.)

MUNRO, ALICE

Dahlie, Hallvard. "Alice Munro." In Contemporary
Novelists. Edited by James Vinson. London: St.
James Press, 1972; New York: St. Martin's Press,
1972.

_____. "Unconsummated Relationships: Isolation and
Rejection in Alice Munro's Stories." World Literature Written in English 11, no. 1 (1972): 43-48.

Ferrari, Margaret. America, 24 February 1973, p. 168.
(Review of Lives of Girls and Women.)

Gardiner, Jill Marjorie. "The Early Short Stories of
Alice Munro." M.A. Thesis, University of New
Brunswick, 1973.

Garis, Leslie. Ms. 3 (January 1975): 42-43. (Review
of Something I've Been Meaning to Tell You.)

Gibson, Graeme. Eleven Canadian Novelists. Toronto:
Anansi, 1973.

Klein, N. Ms. 2 (August 1973): 30. (Review of Lives
of Girls and Women.)

Metcalf, John. "A Conversation with Alice Munro."
Journal of Canadian Fiction 1, no. 4 (1972): 54-62.

Pritchard, William H. "Novel Sex and Violence." Hudson Review 28 (Spring 1975): 147-160. (Review
Essay.)

Thomas, Clara. Journal of Canadian Fiction 1, no. 4
(1972): 96. (Review of Lives of Girls and Women.)

Wolff, Geoffrey. Time, 15 January 1973, p. 79. (Review of Lives of Girls and Women.)

MURDOCH, IRIS

Anderson, Thayle Kermit. "Concepts of Love in the Novels of Iris Murdoch. " Ph. D. Dissertation, Purdue University, 1970.

Borklund, Elmer. "Iris Murdoch. " In Contemporary Novelists. Edited by James Vinson. London: St. James Press, 1972; New York: St. Martin's Press, 1972.

Fast, Lawrence Edgar. "Self-Discovery in the Novels of Iris Murdoch. " Ph. D. Dissertation, University of Oregon, 1970.

Goshgarian, Gary. "From Fable to Flesh: A Study of the Female Characters in the Novels of Iris Murdoch. " Ph. D. Dissertation, The University of Wisconsin, 1972.

MURFREE, MARY NOAILLES

Lanier, Doris. "Mary Noailles Murfree: An Interview." Tennessee Historical Quarterly 31 (1972): 276-278.

Nilles, Mary. "Craddock's Girls: A Look at Some Unliberated Women. " Markham Review 3 (1972): 74-77.

MUSIL, ROBERT

Appignanesi, Lisa. Femininity and the Creative Imagination: A Study of Henry James, Robert Musil, and Marcel Proust. New York: Barnes & Noble, 1973.

-N-

NATSUME SŌSEKI

Miyoshi, Masao. Accomplices of Silence: The Modern Japanese Novel. Berkeley, Los Angeles, London: University of California Press, 1974.

NEERA (Anna Radius Zuccari)

Pacifici, Sergio. "Women Writers: Neera and Aleramo." The Modern Italian Novel from Capuana to Tozzi. Carbondale and Edwardsville: Southern Illinois University Press, 1973.

NIN, ANAÏS

Baldeshwiler, Eileen. "Nathalie Sarraute and Anaïs Nin as Theorists of the Novel: Feminine Sensibility?" Paper presented at the Midwest MLA meeting, St. Louis, November 1972. (Mimeographed.)

"A Conversation with Anaïs Nin." Second Wave 1 (Summer 1971): 10-16.

Durand, Régis. Anaïs Nin et le 'language des nerfo.'" Langues Modernes 64 (July-August 1970): 73-80.

"The Female Angst." Los Angeles: Pacifica Tape Library, 1972. (Anaïs Nin, Joan Didion and Dory Previn.)

Fowlie, Wallace. New York Times Book Review, 9 September 1973, p. 26. (Review of Anaïs Nin Reader.)

Freeman, Barbara. "A Dialogue with Anaïs Nin." Chicago Review 24 (1972): 29-35.

Goyen, William. New York Times Book Review, 14 April 1974, p. 4. (Review of The Diary of Anaïs Nin.)

Hoffman, Nancy. New Republic, 15 June 1974, p. 31. (Review of The Diary of Anaïs Nin.)

Killoh, Ellen Peck. "The Woman Writer and the Element of Destruction." College English 34 (October 1972): 31-38.

Kuntz, Paul Grimley. "Art as Public Dream: The Practice and Theory of Anaïs Nin." Journal of Aesthetics and Art Criticism 32 (Summer 1974): 525-537.

Moore, Harry T. "Anaïs Nin." In Contemporary Novelists. Edited by James Vinson. London: St.

James Press, 1972; New York: St. Martin's Press,
1972.

Nin, Anaïs   "An Evening with Anaïs Nin." Los Angeles:
Pacifica Tape Library, 1972.

_____. "From the Fourth Journal." Boston Univer-
sity Journal 19 (1971): 7-10.

_____. "Introduction." Rising Tides: 20th Century
American Women Poets, xxix-xxxi. Edited by Laura
Chester and Sharon Barba. New York: Washington
Square Press, 1973.

_____. "Notes on Feminism." In Woman: An Issue,
pp. 25-28. Edited by Lee R. Edwards, Mary Heath
and Lisa Baskin. Boston: Little, Brown, 1972.

_____. "On Feminism and Creation." Michigan
Quarterly Review 13 (Winter 1974): 4-13.

Owen, Peter. "Anaïs Nin." Times Literary Supplement, 19 May 1972, p. 577.

Peck, Ellen Margaret McKee. "Exploring the Feminine:
A Study of Janet Lewis, Ellen Glasgow, Anaïs Nin,
and Virginia Woolf." Ph.D. Dissertation, Stanford
University, 1974.

Robinson, Lillian S. "Who's Afraid of a Room of One's
Own?" In The Politics of Literature, pp. 389-390.
Edited by Louis Kampf and Paul Lauter. New York:
Pantheon Books, 1972.

Schneider, Duance. "The Art of Anaïs Nin." Southern
Review 6 (Spring 1970): 506-514.

Sellers, Jill. The Spokeswoman, 15 July 1974, pp. 7-8.
(Review of The Diary of Anaïs Nin.)

Snitrow, Ann. "Women's Private Writings: Anaïs Nin."
In Notes From the Third World: Women's Liberation. New York: Box AA, Old Chelsea Station,
1971.

Spacks, Patricia M. The Female Imagination. New
York: Knopf, 1975.

_____. "Free Women." Hudson Review 24 (Winter 1971-72): 559-573.

Spencer, Sharon. "'Femininity' and the Woman Writer: Doris Lessing's The Golden Notebook and The Diary of Anaïs Nin." Women's Studies 1 (1973): 247-258.

Stern, Daniel. Nation, 29 November 1971, p. 570. (Review of The Diary of Anaïs Nin.)

Stone, Douglas. "Henry Miller and the Villa Seurat Circle, 1930 to 1940." Ph.D. Dissertation, University of California, Irvine, 1973.

Sukenick, Lynn. "Sense and Sensibility in Women's Fiction: Studies in the Novels of George Eliot, Virginia Woolf, Anaïs Nin, and Doris Lessing." Ph.D. Dissertation, The City University of New York, 1974.

Zee, Nancy. "Anaïs Nin: Beyond the Mask." Ph.D. Dissertation, Brown University, 1973.

_____. "Towards a Definition of the Woman Artist: Notes on the Diaries of Anaïs Nin." Oyez Review (Roosevelt University) 8 (Winter 1973): 49-55.

Zinnes, Harriet. "Reading Anaïs Nin." Carleton Miscellany 14 (Fall-Winter 1973-74): 124-126. (Review Essay.)

NOAILLES, ANNA DE

Allard, Harry Grover, Jr. "Anna de Noailles, Nun of Passion: A Study of the Novels of Anna de Noailles." Ph.D. Dissertation, Yale University, 1973.

NORRIS, FRANK

Bauer, Walter John. "The Man-Woman Relationship in the Novels of Frank Norris." Ph.D. Dissertation, New York University, 1973.

NWAPA, FLORA

Conde, Maryse. "Three Female Writers in Modern Africa." Présence Africaine no. 82 (April-June 1972): 132-143.

Nandakumar, Prema. "An Image of African Womanhood: A Study of Flora Nwapa's 'Efuru'" Africa Quarterly 11 (1971): 136-146. (New Delhi.)

Scheub, H. "Two African Women. " Revue des langues vivantes (Brussels) 37 (1971): 545-558.

-O-

OATES, JOYCE CAROL

Allen, Mary Inez. "The Necessary Blankness: Women in Major American Fiction of the Sixties. " Ph. D. Dissertation, University of Maryland, 1973.

Bellamy, Joe David. "The Dark Lady of the American Letters: An Interview with Joyce Carol Oates. " Atlantic Monthly 229 (February 1972): 63-67.

_____. The New Fiction: Interviews with Innovative American Writers. Urbana, Chicago, London: University of Illinois Press, 1974, pp. 19-31.

Clemons, Walter. "Joyce Carol Oates: Love and Violence. " Newsweek 80 (11 December 1972): 72-74, 77.

Denne, C. A. "Joyce Carol Oates' Women. " Nation, 7 December 1974, pp. 597-599.

Ellman, Mary. "Nolo Contendere. " Book World--The Washington Post, 24 January 1974, pp. 36-37.

Kazin, Alfred. "Cassandras: Porter to Oates. " Bright Book of Life: American Novelists and Storytellers from Hemingway to Mailer, pp. 198-205. Boston and Toronto: Little, Brown, 1973.

Mazzaro, Jerome. "Feeling One's Oates. " Modern Poetry Studies 2, no. 3 (1971): 133-137.

Oates, Joyce Carol. "Transformations of Self: An Interview with Joyce Carol Oates. " Ohio Review 15 (Fall 1973): 51-61.

Silva, Fred. "Joyce Carol Oates." In Contemporary Novelists. Edited by James Vinson. London: St. James Press, 1972; New York: St. Martin's Press, 1972.

Stanbrough, Jane. "Joyce Carol Oates' Carnal Transcendentalism." Denver Quarterly 9 (Spring 1974): 84-89. (Review Essay.)

Sullivan, Walter. "The Artificial Demon: Joyce Carol Oates and the Dimensions of the Real." The Hollins Critic 9 (December 1972): 1-12.

Sweeney, W. Ms. 2 (November 1973): 39-43. (Review of Do with Me What You Will.)

Waller, G. F. "Joyce Carol Oates' Wonderland: An Introduction." Dalhousie Review 54 (Autumn 1974): 480-490.

Wegs, Joyce Markert. "The Grotesque in Some American Novels of the Nineteen-Sixties: Ken Kesey, Joyce Carol Oates, Sylvia Plath." Ph.D. Dissertation, University of Illinois at Urbana-Champaign, 1973.

O'BRIEN, EDNA

Haynes, Muriel. "Trickles of Love." Ms. 3 (February 1975): 42-44. (Review of A Scandalous Woman and Other Stories.)

Kauffmann, Stanley. "Women of World Apart." World, 30 January 1973, pp. 76-79.

New York Times, 2 January 1973, p. 1.

O'Faolain, Julia. New York Times Book Review, 22 September 1974, p. 3. (Review of A Scandalous Woman, and Other Stories.)

Times Literary Supplement, 6 September 74, p. 945. (Review of A Scandalous Woman and Other Stories.)

O'CASEY, SEAN

Bailie, Sister Ellen, O.P. "Women for Liberation in

the Plays of Sean O'Casey. " Ph. D. Dissertation, Indiana University, 1974.

O'CONNOR, FLANNERY

Abbot, Louise Hardeman. "Remembering Flannery O'Connor. " Southern Literary Journal 2 (Spring 1970): 3-25.

Browning, Preston M., Jr. Flannery O'Connor. Carbondale and Edwardsville: Southern Illinois University Press, 1974.

Driskell, Leon V. The Eternal Crossroads: The Art of Flannery O'Connor. Lexington: University Press of Kentucky, 1971.

Eggenschwiler, David. The Christian Humanism of Flannery O'Connor. Detroit: Wayne State University Press, 1972.

Feeley, Kathleen. Flannery O'Connor: Voice of the Peacock. New Brunswick, N.J.: Rutgers University Press, 1972.

Hendin, Josephine. The World of Flannery O'Connor. Bloomington: Indiana University Press, 1970.

Katz, Claire. "Flannery O'Connor: A Rage of Vision. " Ph. D. Dissertation, University of California, Berkeley, 1975.

_____. "Flannery O'Connor's Rage of Vision. " American Literature 46 (March 1974): 54-67.

Kazin, Alfred. "Cassandras. " Bright Book of Life: American Novelists and Storytellers from Hemingway to Mailer. Boston and Toronto: Little, Brown, 1973, pp. 54-60, 173-174.

Muller, Gilbert H. Nightmares and Visions: Flannery O'Connor and the Catholic Grotesque. Athens: University of Georgia Press, 1972.

Orvell, Miles. Invisible Parade: The Fiction of Flannery O'Connor. Philadelphia: Temple University Press, 1972.

Stephens, Martha. The Question of Flannery O'Connor. Baton Rouge: Louisiana State University Press, 1973.

Walters, Dorothy. Flannery O'Connor. New York: Twayne, 1973.

OGALI A. OGALI (Snr)

Roscoe, Adrian A. Mother Is Gold: A Study in West African Literature. Cambridge: University Press, 1971, pp. 148-149.

OGOT, GRACE

Conde, Maryse. "Three Female Writers in Modern Africa." Présence Africaine no. 82 (April-June 1972): 132-143.

Mohr, Norma. "The Many Windows of Grace Ogot." Africa Report 17, no. 7 (1972): 21-22.

OLSEN, TILLIE

Boucher, Sandy. "Tillie Olsen: The Weight of Things Unsaid." Ms. 3 (September 1974): 26-30.

Fishel, Elizabeth. "Women's Fiction: Who's Afraid of Virginia Woolf." Ramparts, June 1973, pp. 45-48.

Gottlieb, Annie. New York Times Book Review, 31 March 1974, p. 5. (Review of Yonnondio: From the Thirties.)

Olsen, Tillie. "Women Who Are Writers in Our Century: One Out of Twelve." College English 34 (October 1972): 6-17.

_____. "Silences: When Writers Don't Write." In Images of Women in Fiction, pp. 97-112. Edited by Susan Koppelman Cornillon. Bowling Green, Ohio: Bowling Green University Press, 1972.

Stone, Elizabeth. Crawdaddy, September 1974, pp. 88-89. (Review of Yonnondio: From the Thirties.)

O'NEILL, EUGENE

Glicksberg, Charles I. The Sexual Revolution in Modern American Literature. The Hague: Martinus Nijhoff, 1971, pp. 68-82.

Josephs, Lois S. "The Women of Eugene O'Neill: Sex Role Stereotype." Ball State University Forum 14 (Summer 1973): 308.

Pampel, Brigitte C. G. "The Relationship of the Sexes in the Works of Strindberg, Wedekind, and O'Neill." Ph. D. Dissertation, Northwestern University, 1972.

-P-

PALEY, GRACE

Bendow, Burton. Nation, 11 May 1974, p. 597. (Review of Enormous Changes at the Last Minute.)

Shapiro, Harriet. "Grace Paley: 'Art is on the Side of the Underdog.'" Ms. 2 (May 1974): 43-45.

Wood, M. New York Review of Books, 21 March 1974, p. 19. (Review of Enormous Changes at the Last Minute.)

PANAEVA, ARDOTYA

Ledkovsky, Marina. "Ardotya Panaeva: Her Salon and Her Life." Russian Literature Triquarterly no. 9 (Spring 1974): 423-432.

PARRA, TERESA DE LA

Norris, Nélida Galovic. "A Critical Appraisal of Teresa de la Parra." Ph. D. Dissertation, University of California, Los Angeles, 1970.

PASTERNAK, BORIS

Harris, Jane Gary. "Pasternak's Vision of Life: The History of Feminine Image." Russian Literature

Triquarterly no. 9 (Spring 1974): 389-421.

Pasternak, Josephine. "Patior." Russian Literature Triquarterly no. 9 (Spring 1974): 371-388.

PAVLOVA, KAROLINA

Monter, Barbara Heldt. "From an Introduction to Pavlova's A Double Life." Russian Literature Triquarterly no. 9 (Spring 1974): 337-353.

Sendich, Munir. "Karolina Pavlova: A Survey of Her Poetry." Russian Literature Triquarterly no. 3 (Spring 1972): 229-248.

PEACOCK, THOMAS LOVE

Crabbe, John Kenyon. "The Noblest Gift: Women in the Fiction of Thomas Love Peacock." Ph.D. Dissertation, University of Oregon, 1973.

Fay, Janet Ann. "The Serious Satire of Thomas Love Peacock: A Critical Study of His Moral, Intellectual, and Aesthetic Opinions." Ph.D. Dissertation, New York University, 1973.

Mise, Raymond Winfield. "The Gothic Heroine and the Nature of the Gothic Novel." Ph.D. Dissertation, University of Washington, 1970.

PETRY, ANN

Emanuel, James A. "Ann Petry." In Contemporary Novelists. Edited by James Vinson. London: St. James Press, 1972; New York: St. Martin's Press, 1972.

Gayle, Addison, Jr. The Way of the New World: The Black Novel in America. Garden City, N.Y.: Doubleday, 1975, pp. 192-196.

Rosenblatt, Roger. Black Fiction. Cambridge: Harvard University Press, 1974.

Shinn, Thelma J. "Women in the Novels of Ann Petry." Critique 16, no. 1, pp. 110-120.

PIERCY, MARGE

Beis, Patricia Sharon. "Cold Fire: Some Contemporary
American Women Poets." Ph.D. Dissertation,
Saint Louis University, 1972.

Blackburn, Sara. New York Times Book Review, 12
August 1973, p. 2. (Review of Small Changes.)

Dobbs, Jeanine. "Not Another Poetess: A Study of
Female Experience in Modern American Poetry."
Ph.D. Dissertation, University of New Hampshire,
1973.

Ferrari, Margaret. America, 29 December 1973, p.
507. (Review of To Be of Use.)

Harris, Marie. Parnassus 3 (Fall/Winter 1974): 154-
158. (Review of To Be of Use.)

Kuehl, Linda. Commonweal, 2 April 1971, pp. 92-94.

Piercy, Marge. "Through the Cracks." Partisan Review 41 (1974): 202-216.

Rosenthal, L. Ms. 2 (September 1973): 29. (Review
of Small Changes.)

Schulder, Diane. "Two Women." New Republic, 27
October 1973, 30-31.

Todd, Richard. Atlantic 232 (September 1973): 105.
(Review of Small Changes.)

PISAN, CHRISTINE de

Brée, Germaine. Women Writers in France: Variations
on a Theme. New Brunswick, N.J.: Rutgers University Press, 1973, pp. ix, 16-22.

Davis, Judith M. "Christine de Pisan and Chauvinist
Diplomacy." In Female Studies VI: Closer to the
Ground, pp. 116-122. Edited by Nancy Hoffman,
Cynthia Secor, Adrian Tinsley. Old Westbury, N.Y.:
Feminist Press, 1972.

Finkel, Helen Ruth. "The Portrait of the Woman in the

Works of Christine de Pisan. " Ph. D. Dissertation, Rice University, 1972.

Lipton, Virginia Anne. "Women in Today's World: A Study of Five French Women Novelists. " Ph. D. Dissertation, The University of Wisconsin, 1972.

Reno, Christine McArdle. "Self and Society in L'Avision-Christine of Christine de Pisan. " Ph. D. Dissertation, Yale University, 1972.

PLATH, SYLVIA

Aird, Eileen. Sylvia Plath: Her Life and Work. New York: Harper & Row, 1975.

Allen, Mary Inez. "The Necessary Blankness: Women in Major American Fiction of the Sixties. " Ph. D. Dissertation, University of Maryland, 1973.

Alvarez, A. The Savage God: A Study of Suicide. New York: Random House, 1972.

Balitas, Vincent Daniel. "Sylvia Plath, Poet. " Ph. D. Dissertation, Indiana University of Pennsylvania, 1973.

Barnard, Caroline King. "God's Lioness: The Poetry of Sylvia Plath. " Ph. D. Dissertation, Brown University, 1973.

Bierman, Larry. "The Vivid Tulips Eat My Oxygen: An Essay on Sylvia Plath's Ariel. " Windless Orchard (Fort Wayne) 4 (February 1971): 44-46.

Boyers, Robert. "On Sylvia Plath. " Salmagundi 21 (1973): 96-104.

Burnham, Richard E. "Sylvia Plath's 'Lady Lazarus. '" Contemporary Poetry 1 (Winter 1973): 42-46.

Chesler, Phyllis. Women and Madness. New York: Avon, 1972, pp. 29-30, 34-38, 52-53.

Cooley, Peter. "Autism, Autoeroticism, Auto-da-fe: The Tragic Poetry of Sylvia Plath. " The Hollins Critic 10 (February 1973): 1-16.

Corrigan, Sylvia Robinson. "Sylvia Plath: A New Feminist Approach." Aphra 1 (Spring 1970): 16-23.

De Feo, Ronald. Modern Occasions, Fall 1971, pp. 624-625.

Dobbs, Jeanine. "Not Another Poetess: A Study of Female Experience in Modern American Poetry." Ph. D. Dissertation, University of New Hampshire, 1973.

Donovan, Josephine. "Sexual Politics in Sylvia Plath's Short Stories." Minnesota Review 4 (1973): 150-157.

Duffy, Martha. "The Triumph of a Tormented Poet." Life, 12 November 1971, pp. 38A-38B.

Evans, Nancy Burr. "The Value and Peril for Women of Reading Women Writers." In Images of Women in Fiction, pp. 306-312. Edited by Susan Koppelman Cornillon. Bowling Green, Ohio: Bowling Green University Press, 1972.

Gabelnick, Faith. "Making Connections: American Women Poets on Love." Ph. D. Dissertation, American University, 1974.

Hardwick, Elizabeth. New York Review of Books, 12 August 1971, p. 3. (Review of Crossing the Water.)

_____. Seduction and Betrayal. New York: Random House, 1974, pp. 104-124.

Hill, Robert W. "Sylvia Plath." (Modern American Poetry Criticism Series) Deland, Fla.: Everett/Edwards, n. d. (Cassette.)

Himelick, Raymond. "Notes on the Care and Feeding of Nightmares: Burton, Erasmus, and Sylvia Plath." Western Humanities Review 28 (Autumn 1974): 313-326.

Hoffman, Nancy Jo. "Reading Women's Poetry: The Meaning and Our Lives." College English 34 (October 1972): 48-62.

Howe, Irving. "Sylvia Plath: A Partial Disagreement." Harper's, January 1972, pp. 88-91.

Hughes, Ted. "Sylvia Plath's Crossing the Water: Some Reflections." Critical Quarterly 13 (Summer 1971): 165.

Kazin, Alfred. "Cassandras: Porter to Oates." Bright Book of Life: American Novelists and Storytellers from Hemingway to Mailer. Boston and Toronto: Little, Brown, 1973, pp. 184-186.

Lane, Gary Martin. "Sylvia Plath's 'The Hanging Man': A Further Note." Contemporary Poetry 2 (Spring 1975): 40-43.

Leib, Mark E. "Into the Maelstrom." Harvard Advocate 106 (Winter 1973): 45-47. (Review Essay.)

Levy, Laurie. "Outside the Bell Jar." Ohio Review 14 (Spring 1973): 67-73.

Libby, Anthony. "God's Lioness and the Priest of Sycorax." Contemporary Literature 15 (Summer 1974): 386-405.

_____. "Roethke, Water Father." American Literature 46 (November 1974): 268-288.

McKay, D. F. "Aspects of Energy in the Poetry of Dylan Thomas and Sylvia Plath." Critical Quarterly 16 (Spring 1974): 53-67.

Malkoff, Karl. Crowell's Handbook of Contemporary American Poetry. New York: Thomas Y. Crowell, 1973.

Martin, Wendy. "God's Lioness"--Sylvia Plath, Her Prose and Poetry." Women's Studies 1 (1973): 191-198.

Meissner, William. "The Rise of the Angel: Life Through Death in the Poetry of Sylvia Plath." Massachusetts Studies in English 3 (1971): 34-39.

Melander, Ingrid. "'The Disquieting Muses': A Note on a Poem by Sylvia Plath." Research Studies

(Washington State University) 39 (1971): 53-54.

_____. "The Poetry of Sylvia Plath: A Study of Themes." Doctoral Dissertation, University of Gothenburg, 1971.

_____. "'Watercolour of Grantchester Meadows': An Early Poem by Sylvia Plath." Modern Språk 65 (1971): 1-5.

Milliner, Gladys W. "The Tragic Imperative: The Awakening and The Bell Jar." Mary Wollstonecraft Newsletter 2 (December 1973): 21-27.

Newlin, Margaret. "The Suicide Bandwagon." Critical Quarterly 14 (1972): 367-378.

Newman, Charles Hamilton, ed. The Art of Sylvia Plath: A Symposium. Bloomington: Indiana University Press, 1970.

Oates, Joyce Carol. "The Death Throes of Romanticism: The Poems of Sylvia Plath." Southern Review 9 (July 1973): 501-522.

_____. New Heaven, New Earth; The Visionary Experience in Literature. New York: Vanguard Press, 1974.

Perloff, Marjorie. "Angst and Animism in the Poetry of Sylvia Plath." Journal of Modern Literature 1 (1970): 57-74.

_____. "On the Road to Ariel: The 'Transitional' Poetry of Sylvia Plath." Iowa Review 4 (Spring 1973): 94-110.

_____. "'A Ritual for Being Born Twice': Sylvia Plath's The Bell Jar." Contemporary Literature 13 (Autumn 1972): 507-522.

Rabenold, Diana. The Second Wave 1, no. 3 (1971): 37-38. (Review of The Bell Jar.)

Romano, J. "Sylvia Plath Reconsidered." Commentary 57 (April 1974): 47-52.

Rosenstein, Harriet. "Reconsidering Sylvia Plath." Ms. 1 (September 1972): 44-51. Also in The First Ms. Reader. New York: Warner Paperback Library, 1973.

Smith, Pamela. "Architectonics: Sylvia Plath's 'Colossus.'" Ariel: A Review of International English Literature 4, no. 1 (1973): 4-21.

Smith, Pamela A. "The Unitive Urge in the Poetry of Sylvia Plath." New England Quarterly 45 (September 1972): 323-339.

Spacks, Patricia M. The Female Imagination. New York: Knopf, 1975.

Stagg, Mary Ellen. "'Perfection Is Terrible': A Study of Sylvia Plath's Poetry." Ph.D. Dissertation, University of Wisconsin, 1973.

Stein, Karen F. "Reflections in a Jagged Mirror: Some Metaphors of Madness." Aphra 6 (Spring 1975): 2-11.

Steiner, Nancy Hunter. A Closer Look at Ariel: A Memory of Sylvia Plath. New York: Harper's Magazine Press, 1973.

Stone, Carole. "Three Mother-Daughter Poems: The Struggle for Separation." Paper presented at the Fifth International Forum for Psychoanalysis, Zurich, 1-5 September 1974.

Taylor, Andrew. "Sylvia Plath's Mirror and Beehive." Meanjin Quarterly 33 (September 1974): 256-265.

Uroff, Margaret D. "Sylvia Plath on Motherhood." Midwest Quarterly 15 (October 1973): 70-90.

Vendler, Helen. New York Times Book Review, 10 October 1971, p. 4. (Review of Crossing the Water.)

Walker, Cheryl Lawson. "The Women's Tradition in American Poetry." Ph.D. Dissertation, Brandeis University, 1973.

Wegs, Joyce Markert. "The Grotesque in Some American

Novels of the Nineteen-Sixties: Ken Kesey, Joyce Carol Oates, Sylvia Plath. " Ph. D. Dissertation, University of Illinois at Urbana-Champaign, 1973.

Zatlin, Linda G. "'This Holocaust I Walk In': The Poetic Vision of Sylvia Plath. " Papers on Women's Studies 1 (October 1974): 158-173.

POPE, ALEXANDER

Braudy, Leo. "Penetration and Impenetrability in Clarissa. " In New Approaches to Eighteenth-Century Literature, pp. 177-206. Edited by Phillip Harth. New York: Columbia University Press, 1974.

Cornelia, Maria. "The Rape of the Lock and the Romance Tradition. " Connecticut Review 8 (October 1974): 84-89.

Hooven, Evelyn. "Racine and Pope's Eloisa. " Essays in Criticism 24 (October 1974): 368-374.

Landa, Louis A. "Of Silkworms and Farthingales and the Will of God. " In Studies in the Eighteenth Century, vol. 2, pp. 269. Edited by R. F. Brissenden. Toronto: University of Toronto Press, 1973.

_____. "Pope's Belinda, the General Emporic of the World, and the Wondrous Worm. " South Atlantic Quarterly 70 (Spring 1971): 215-235.

Morris, D. B. "'The Visionary Maid': Tragic Passion and Redemptive Sympathy in Pope's 'Eloisa to Abelard. '" Modern Language Quarterly 34 (September 1973): 247-271.

Trimble, John. "Clarissa's Role in The Rape of the Lock. " Texas Studies in Literature and Language 15 (Winter 1974): 673-691.

Wimsatt, W. K. "Belinda Ludens: Strife and Play in The Rape of the Lock. " New Literary History (University of Virginia) 4 (Winter 1973): 357-374.

PORTER, KATHERINE ANNE

Ginsberg, Elaine. "The Female Initiation Theme in American Fiction." Studies in Fiction 3 (Spring 1975): 27-37.

Hardy, John Edward. Katherine Anne Porter. New York: Frederick Ungar, 1973.

Hoefer, Jacqueline. "Katherine Anne Porter." In Contemporary Novelists. London: St. James Press, 1972: New York: St. Martin's Press, 1972.

Kazin, Alfred. "Cassandras: Porter to Oates." Bright Book of Life: American Novelists and Storytellers from Hemingway to Mailer. Boston and Toronto: Little, Brown, 1972, pp. 165-173.

Krishnamurthi, Matighatta Gundappa. Katherine Anne Porter: A Study. Mysore: Rao & Raghavan, 1971.

Liberman, Myron M. Katherine Anne Porter's Fiction. Detroit: Wayne State University Press, 1971.

Madden, David. "The Charged Image in Katherine Anne Porter's 'Flowering Judas.'" Studies in Short Fiction 7 (Spring 1970): 277-289.

Miles, Lee Robert. "Unused Possibilities: A Study of Katherine Anne Porter." Ph.D. Dissertation, University of California, Los Angeles, 1973.

Spence, Jon. "Looking-glass Reflections in Ship of Fools." Sewanee Review 82 (April-June 1974): 316-330.

POWELL, DAWN

Josephson, Matthew. "Dawn Powell: A Woman of Esprit." Southern Review (January 1973): 18-52.

PRELLWITZ, GERTRUD

Scholtz, Sigrid Gerda. "Images of Womanhood in the Works of German Female Dramatists 1892-1918." Ph.D. Dissertation, Johns Hopkins University, 1971.

PRICE, REYNOLDS

Shepherd, Alan. "Love (and Marriage) in A Long and Happy Life." Twentieth Century Literature 17 (January 1971): 29-36.

PRICHARD, KATHARINE

Williams, Margaret. "Natural Sexuality: Katharine Prichard's Brumby Innes." Meanjin Quarterly 32 (1973): 91-93.

-R-

RACINE, JEAN

Hooven, Evelyn. "Racine and Pope's Eloisa." Essays in Criticism 24 (October 1974): 368-374.

Mould, William A. "The 'Innocent Stratagème' of Racine's Andromaque." French Review 48 (February 1975): 557-565.

Mueller, Martin. "The Truest Daughter of Dido: Racine's Bérénice." Canadian Review of Comparative Literature 1 (Autumn 1974): 201-217.

Turnell, Martin. Jean Racine: Dramatist. New York: New Directions, 1972.

Whatley, Janet. "L'Orient désert: Bérénice and Antony and Cleopatra." University of Toronto Quarterly 44 (Winter 1975): 96-114.

RADCLIFFE, ANN

Kiely, Robert. The Romantic Novel in England. Cambridge: Harvard University Press, 1972, pp. 65-80.

Mise, Raymond Winfield. "The Gothic Heroine and the Nature of the Gothic Novel." Ph.D. Dissertation, University of Washington, 1970.

Murray, Eugene Bernard. Ann Radcliffe. New York: Twayne, 1972.

Pratt, Annis. "Archetypal Approaches to the New
Feminist Criticism." Bucknell Review 21 (Spring
1973): 3-14.

Ranieri, Marietta R. "The Self Behind the Self: The
Americanization of the Gothic." Ph. D. Dissertation,
The Pennsylvania State University, 1973.

Smith, Nelson C. "Sense, Sensibility and Ann Radcliffe."
Studies in English Literature 1500-1900 13 (Autumn
1973): 577-590.

RADEMACHER, HANNA

Scholtz, Sigrid Gerda. "Images of Womanhood in the
Works of German Female Dramatists 1892-1918."
Ph. D. Dissertation, Johns Hopkins University, 1971.

RALPH, JAMES

Landa, Louis A. "Of Silkworms and Farthingales and
The Will of God." In Studies in the Eighteenth
Century, vol. 2, pp. 259-260. Edited by R. F.
Brissenden. Toronto: University of Toronto Press,
1973.

RAO, RAJA

Shepherd, Ron. "Symbolic Organization in The Serpent
and the Rope." Southern Review (Adelaide) 6 (June
1973): 93-107.

Venkatachari, K. "The Feminine Principle in Raja
Rao's The Serpent and the Rope." Osmania Journal
of English Studies 8, no. 2 (1971): 113-120.

REAGE, PAULINE

Cosman, Carol. "Story of O." Women's Studies 2
(1974): 25-36.

Dworkin, Andrea. "Woman as Victim: Story of O."
Feminist Studies 2, no. 1 (1974): 107-111.

Robinson, Lillian S. "Who's Afraid of a Room of One's
Own?" In The Politics of Literature, pp. 392-394.
Edited by Louis Kampf and Paul Lauter. New

York: Pantheon Books, 1972.

REDMON, ANNE

Garis, Leslie. "Remote Control." Ms. 3 (June 1975):
41-44. (Review of Emily Stone.)

Mesic, Penelope. Book World (Chicago Tribune) sec. 7,
p. 2, 16 February 1975. (Review of Emily Stone.)

RHYS, JEAN

Mellown, Elgin W. "Character and Themes in the
Novels of Jean Rhys." Contemporary Literature
13 (Autumn 1972): 458-475.

Naipaul, V. S. New York Review of Books, 18 May
1972, p. 29-31. (Review of After Leaving Mr.
MacKenzie.)

RICCOBONI, MARIE-JEANNE

Cragg, Olga Browzin. "The Novels of Mme Riccoboni."
Ph. D. Dissertation, Bryn Mawr College, 1970.

Godenne, René. "Mme Riccoboni et le genre trouba-
dour." Australian Journal of French Studies 10
(September-December 1973): 317-325.

Lacy, Kluenter Wesley. "An Essay on Feminine Fiction,
1757-1803." Ph. D. Dissertation, The University
of Wisconsin, 1972.

Stewart, Joan Hinde. "The Novels of Mme Riccoboni."
Ph. D. Dissertation, Yale University, 1970.

RICH, ADRIENNE

Atwood, Margaret. New York Times Book Review, 30
December 1973, p. 1. (Review of Diving into the
Wreck.)

Auden, W. H. "Foreword to A Change of World." In
Adrienne Rich's Poetry, pp. 125-127. Edited by
Gelpi and Gelpi. (See below.)

Boyers, Robert. "On Adrienne Rich: Intelligence and

Will." Salmagundi 22-23 (Spring-Summer 1973):
132-148. Also in Gelpi and Gelpi, Adrienne Rich's
Poetry, pp. 148-160. (See below.)

Flynn, Gale. "The Radicalization of Adrienne Rich."
The Hollins Critic 11 (October 1974): 1-15.

Gabelnick, Faith. "Making Connections: American
Women Poets on Love." Ph.D. Dissertation, American University, 1974.

Gelpi, Albert. "Adrienne Rich: The Poetics of Change."
In American Poetry Since 1960, pp. 132-133.
Edited by Robert B. Shaw. Cheadle, Cheshire:
Carcanet Press Ltd., 1973. Excerpt in Gelpi and
Gelpi, Adrienne Rich's Poetry, p. 89. (See below.)

Gelpi, Barbara Charlesworth and Albert Gelpi, eds.
Adrienne Rich's Poetry. New York: W. W. Norton,
1975.

Hoffman, Nancy. "A Feminist Approach to Women
Poets: 'We Urge You to Risk Your Life.'" Paper
presented at the Midwest Modern Language Association Meeting, Chicago, 2 November 1973. (Mimeographed.)

Howard, Richard. Harper's 247 (December 1973): 120.
(Review of Diving into the Wreck.)

Jarrell, Randall. Review of The Diamond Cutters and
Other Poems. In Adrienne Rich's Poetry, pp. 127-
129. Edited by Gelpi and Gelpi. (See above.)

Jong, Erica. Ms. 2 (July 1973): 30-34. (Review of
Diving into the Wreck: Poems 1971-72.) Also in
Gelpi and Gelpi, Adrienne Rich's Poetry, pp. 171-
174. (See above.)

Kalstone, David. New York Times Book Review, 23
May 1971, p. 31. (Review of The Will to Change.)

Malkoff, Karl. Crowell's Handbook of Contemporary
American Poetry. New York: Thomas Y. Crowell,
1973.

Martin, Wendy. "From Patriarchy to the Female

Principle: A Chronological Reading of Adrienne Rich's Poems." In Adrienne Rich's Poetry, pp. 175-189. Edited by Gelpi and Gelpi. (See above.)

Milford, Nancy. "This Woman's Movement." In Adrienne Rich's Poetry, pp. 189-202. Edited by Gelpi and Gelpi. (See above.)

Rich, Adrienne. "Three Conversations." In Adrienne Rich's Poetry, pp. 105-122. Edited by Gelpi and Gelpi. (See above.)

_____. "When We Dead Awaken: Writing as Re-Vision." College English 34 (October 1972): 18-30. Also in Gelpi and Gelpi, Adrienne Rich's Poetry, pp. 90-98. (See above.)

Tonks, Rosemary. New York Review of Books, 4 October 1973, p. 8. (Review of Diving into the Wreck.)

Vendler, Helen. "Ghostlier Demarcations, Keener Sounds." Parnassus: Poetry in Review 2, no. 1 (Fall-Winter 1973): 5-10, 15-16, 18-24. Excerpts in Gelpi and Gelpi, Adrienne Rich's Poetry, pp. 160-171.

Walker, Cheryl Lawson. "The Women's Tradition in American Poetry." Ph.D. Dissertation, Brandeis University, 1973.

Walker, C. Nation, 8 October 1973, pp. 346-349. (Review of Diving into the Wreck.)

RICHARDSON, DOROTHY

Donovan, Josephine. "Feminist Style Criticism." In Female Studies VI: Closer to the Ground, pp. 139-149. Edited by Nancy Hoffman, Cynthia Secor, Adrian Tinsley. Old Westbury, N.Y.: Feminist Press, 1972.

Haule, James Mark. "The Theme of Isolation in the Fiction of Dorothy M. Richardson, Virginia Woolf, and James Joyce." Ph.D. Dissertation, Wayne State University, 1974.

Kaplan, Sydney. "'Featureless Freedom' or Ironic

Submission: Dorothy Richardson and May Sinclair. "
College English 32 (May 1971): 914-917.

Pratt, Annis. "Archetypal Approaches to the New
Feminist Criticism. " Bucknell Review 21 (Spring
1973): 3-14.

_____. "Women and Nature in Modern Fiction. "
Contemporary Literature 13 (1972): 476-490.

Rose, Shirley. "Dorothy Richardson: The First Hun-
dred Years: A Retrospective Review. " Dalhousie
Review 53 (1973): 92-96.

_____. "Dorothy Richardson's Focus on Time. " Eng-
lish Literature in Transition 17 (1974): 163-172.

Rosenberg, John. Dorothy Richardson: The Genius
They Forgot: A Critical Biography. London: Duckworth; New York: Knopf, 1973.

RICHARDSON, SAMUEL

Arora, Sudesh Vaid. "The Divided Mind: A Study of
Selected Novels of Defoe and Richardson. " Ph. D.
Dissertation, Kent State University, 1974.

Ball, Donald L. Samuel Richardson's Theory of Fiction.
The Hague: Mouton, 1971.

Bell, M. D. "Pamela's Wedding and the Marriage of the
Lamb. " Philological Quarterly 49 (January 1970):
100-112.

Braudy, Leo. "Penetration and Impenetrability in
Clarissa. " In New Approaches to Eighteenth-Century
Literature, pp. 177-206. Edited by Phillip Harth.
New York: Columbia University Press, 1974.

Brophy, Elizabeth Bergen. Samuel Richardson; The
Triumph of Craft. Knoxville: University of Tennessee Press, 1974.

Costa, Richard Hauer. "The Epistolary Monitor in
Pamela. " Modern Language Quarterly 31 (March
1970): 38-47.

Ferguson, Moira Campbell. "Declarations of Independence: The Rebel Heroine, 1684-1800." Ph. D. Dissertation, University of Washington, 1973.

Folkenflick, R. "A Room of Pamela's Own." ELH 39 (December 1972): 585-596.

Freeman, Carol Marie Creanza. "Richardson and the Uses of Romance: A Study of Art, Morality, and Ambiguity in Clarissa." Ph. D. Dissertation, Yale University, 1971.

Geeter, Joan Trooboff. "Richardson's Clarissa: Five Views of an Epistolary Novel." Ph. D. Dissertation, The University of Connecticut, 1972.

Hardwick, Elizabeth. Seduction and Betrayal. New York: Random House, 1974, pp. 196-202.

Heilbrun, Carolyn G. Toward a Recognition of Androgyny. New York: Knopf, 1973, pp. 50, 53, 55, 56, 57-65.

Higbie, Robert Griggs. "Characterization in the English Novel: Richardson, Jane Austen, and Dickens." Ph. D. Dissertation, Indiana University, 1973.

Kinkead-Weekes, Mark. Samuel Richardson: Dramatic Novelist. Ithaca: Cornell University Press, 1973.

Krier, William John. "A Pattern of Limitations: The Heroine's Novel of Mind." Ph. D. Dissertation, Indiana University, 1973.

Levin, Gerald. "Richardson's Pamela: 'Conflicting Trends.'" American Imago 28 (Winter 1971): 319-329.

Miller, Nancy Kipnis. "Gender and Genre: An Analysis of Literary Femininity in the Eighteenth-Century Novel." Ph. D. Dissertation, Columbia University, 1974.

Morton, Donald E. "Theme and Structure in Pamela." Studies in the Novel (Fall 1971): 242-257.

Moynihan, Robert D. "Clarissa and the Enlightened Woman as Literary Heroine." Journal of the History of Ideas 36 (January-March 1975): 159-166.

Needham, Gwendolyn B. "Richardson's Characterization
of Mr. B. and Double Person in Pamela. " Eighteenth-Century Studies 3 (Summer 1970): 433-474.

Roussel, Roy. "Reflections on the Letter: The Reconciliation of Distance and Presence in Pamela. "
ELH 41 (Fall 1974): 375-399.

Spacks, Patricia Meyer. "Early Fiction and the
Frightened Male. " Novel 8 (Fall 1974): 5-15.

Staskiel, Sister M. Pacelli, C.S.B. "The Divine
Clarissa: Secular Sanctity in the Eighteenth Century."
Ph. D. Dissertation, Duquesne University, 1972.

Stein, William Bysshe. "Pamela: The Narrator as
Unself-Conscious Hack. " Bucknell Review 20 (Spring
1972): 39-66.

Temple, Euan R. A. "The Somber World of Clarissa. "
Ph. D. Dissertation, University of Arkansas, 1970.

Wilson, Stuart. "Richardson's Pamela: An Interpretation. " PMLA 88 (January 1973): 79-91.

Wolff, Cynthia Griffin. The Psychological Fiction of
Samuel Richardson. Hamden, Conn.: Shoe String
Press, 1972.

Wolff, Renate. "Pamela as Myth and Dream. " Costerus
7 (1973): 223-235.

ROBERTS, ELIZABETH MADOX

Hawley, Isabel Lockwood. "Elizabeth Madox Roberts:
Her Development as Self-Conscious Narrative Artist."
Ph. D. Dissertation, University of North Carolina at
Chapel Hill, 1970.

Nilles, Mary Elizabeth. "The Rise and Decline of a
Literary Reputation: Vagaries in the Career of
Elizabeth Madox Roberts. " Ph. D. Dissertation, New
York University, 1972.

ROBINS, ELIZABETH

Marcus, Jane Connor. "Elizabeth Robins." Ph.D. Dissertation, Northwestern University, 1973.

ROSSETTI, DANTE GABRIEL

Gelpi, Barbara Charlesworth. "The Image of the Anima in the Work of Dante Gabriel Rossetti." Victorian Newsletter no. 45 (Spring 1974): 1-7.

Keane, Robert N. "Rossetti's 'Jenny': Moral Ambiguity and the 'Inner Standing Point.'" Papers on Language and Literature 9 (Summer 1973): 271-280.

Miller, John Raymond. "Dante Gabriel Rossetti from the Grotesque to the Fin de Siecle: Sources, Characteristics and Influences of the femme fatale." Ph.D. Dissertation, University of Georgia, 1974.

Nelson, James G. "The Rejected Harlot: A Reading of Rossetti's 'A Last Confession' and 'Jenny.'" Victorian Poetry 10 (Summer 1972): 123-129.

Sonstroem, David. Rossetti and the Fair Lady. Middletown, Conn.: Wesleyan University Press, 1970.

ROSS, SINCLAIR

Atwood, Margaret. "Ice Women vs Earth Mothers." Survival: A Thematic Guide to Canadian Literature. Toronto: Anansi, 1972, pp. 195-212.

Djwa, Sandra. "Sinclair Ross." Canadian Literature no. 47 (Winter 1971): 49-66.

Jones, D. G. Butterfly on Rock: A Study of Themes and Images in Canadian Literature. Toronto and Buffalo: University of Toronto Press, 1970.

Moss, John. Patterns of Isolation in English Canadian Fiction. Toronto: McClelland & Stewart, 1974.

ROSSNER, JUDITH

Blackburn, S. "Real Dropout Novel." Ms. 1 (January 1973): 35-36. (Review of Any Minute I Can Split.)

ROUSSEAU, JEAN-JACQUES

Alves, Dora Lilian. "Love and the Resources of Style in Julie's Letters in Rousseau's Nouvelle Héloïse." Ph. D. Dissertation, The Catholic University of America, 1974.

Blum, Carol. "Styles of Cognition as Moral Options in La Nouvelle Héloise and Les Liaisons dangereuses." PMLA 88 (March 1973): 289-298.

Figes, Eva. Patriarchal Attitudes. New York: Stein & Day, 1970.

Gutwirth, Madelyn. "Madame de Staël, Rousseau, and the Woman Question." PMLA 86 (1971): 100-109.

Miller, Nancy Kipnis. "Gender and Genre: An Analysis of Literary Femininity in the Eighteenth-Century Novel." Ph. D. Dissertation, Columbia University, 1974.

ROWE, NICHOLAS

Dammers, Richard Herman. "Female Characters and Feminine Morality in the Tragedies of Nicholas Rowe." Ph. D. Dissertation, University of Notre Dame, 1971.

Klinger, George Charles. "English She-Tragedy, 1680-1715; Its Characteristics and Its Relationship to the Sentimental Tradition." Ph. D. Dissertation, Columbia University, 1970.

ROWSON, SUSANNA

Brandt, Ellen Barbara. "Susanna Haswell Rowson: a Critical Biography." Ph. D. Dissertation, University of Pennsylvania, 1974.

Ginsberg, Elaine. "The Female Initiation Theme in American Fiction." Studies in Fiction 3 (Spring 1975): 27-37.

Graham, Robert John. "Concepts of Women in American Literature, 1813-1871." Ph. D. Dissertation, University of Pennsylvania, 1973.

McGrath, Kathleen Conway. "Popular Literature as

Social Reinforcement: The Case of Charlotte Temple." In Images of Women in Fiction, pp. 21-27. Edited by Susan Koppelman Cornillon. Bowling Green, Ohio: Bowling Green University Press, 1972.

Martin, Wendy. "Profile: Susanna Rowson, Early American Novelist." Women's Studies 2 (1974): 1-8.

Spacks, Patricia Meyer. "'Ev'ry Woman is at Heart a Rake.'" Eighteenth Century Studies 8 (Fall 1974): 27-46.

Stein, Roger B. "Pulled Out of the Bag: American Fiction in the Eighteenth Century." Studies in American Fiction 2 (Spring 1974): 13-36.

Weil, Dorothy Louise. "Susanna Rowson, The Young Lady's Friend." Ph.D. Dissertation, University of Cincinnati, 1974.

ROY, GABRIELLE

Primeau, Marguerite A. "Gabrielle Roy et la prairie canadienne." In Writers of the Prairies, pp. 115-128. Edited by Donald G. Stephens. Vancouver: University of British Columbia Press, 1973.

Urbas, Jeanette. "Equations and Flutes." Journal of Canadian Fiction 1 (Spring 1972): 69-73.

RUMBOLD, ZOË AKINS

Mielech, Ronald Albert. "The Plays of Zoë Akins Rumbold." Ph.D. Dissertation, The Ohio State University, 1974.

-S-

SACKVILLE-WEST, VICTORIA

Heilbrun, Carolyn. "A Marriage Made on Earth." Ms. 2 (February 1974): 39-42. (Review of Portrait of a Marriage.)

MacKnight, Nancy Margaret. "Vita: A Portrait of V. Sackville-West." Ph. D. Dissertation, Columbia University, 1972.

Naremore, James. The World Without a Self: Virginia Woolf and the Novel. New Haven: Yale University Press, 1973, pp. 190, 191, 195, 196, 197, 201-208.

Nicolson, Nigel. Portrait of a Marriage. New York: Atheneum, 1973.

Stevens, Michael. V. Sackville-West: A Critical Biography. London: Michael Joseph, 1973.

Tooker, Stephen Michael. "A World of One's Own: The Novels of V. Sackville-West." Ph. D. Dissertation, Boston University Graduate School, 1973.

Trautman, Joanne. The Jessamy Brides: The Friendship of Virginia Woolf and V. Sackville-West. University Park: The Pennsylvania State University, 1973.

_____. "A Talk with Nigel Nicolson." Virginia Woolf Quarterly 1 (Fall 1972): 38-44.

SANCHEZ, SONIA

Mobley, Joyce D. "Black Female Voices in the American Theater, 1916-1970." Paper presented for the Midwest Modern Language Association, Chicago, 3 November 1973. (Mimeographed.)

Williams, D. H. Library Journal 99 (August 1974): 1960.

SAND, GEORGE (Mme. Dudevant)

Barry, Joseph. "Letters of a Lioness." World (16 January 1973): 61-62. (Review of Correspondence: George Sand.)

Brée, Germaine. Women Writers in France: Variations on a Theme. New Brunswick, N. J.: Rutgers University Press, 1973.

Cate, Curtis. George Sand. Boston: Houghton Mifflin, forthcoming.

Edwards, Samuel. George Sand: A Biography of the First Modern, Liberated Woman. New York: McKay, 1972. Also published under the name, Noel Gerson, London: Hale, 1973.

Figes, Eva. Patriarchal Attitudes. New York: Stein & Day, 1970.

Gerson, Noel Bartram. George Sand: A Biography of the First Modern, Liberated Woman. (see Edwards, Samuel, above)

Lipton, Virginia Anne. "Women in Today's World: A Study of Five French Women Novelists." Ph. D. Dissertation, The University of Wisconsin, 1972.

Lubin, Georges. "George Sand et la révolte des femmes contre les institutions." In Roman et Société: Colloque, 6 November 1971, pp. 42-51. Paris: Armand Collin, 1973.

Pappas, Dee Ann. "George Sand: A Life of Conflict." Women: A Journal of Liberation 2 (Fall 1970): 12-16.

Perry, Anne Castelain. "George Sand Feuilletoniste: 1844-1848." Ph. D. Dissertation, Washington University, 1973.

Thomson, Patricia. "Elizabeth Barrett and George Sand." Durham University Journal 33 (June 1972): 205-219.

West, Anthony. "George Sand." Mortal Wounds. New York: McGraw-Hill, 1973, pp. 225-307.

SARRAUTE, NATHALIE

Baldeshwiler, Eileen. "Nathalie Sarraute and Anaïs Nin as Theorists of the Novel: Feminine Sensibility." Paper presented at the Midwest MLA, St. Louis, November 1972. (Mimeographed.)

Brée, Germaine. "Interviews with Two French Novelists: Nathalie Sarraute and Célia Bertin." Contemporary Literature 14 (Spring 1973): 137-146.

_____. Women Writers in France: Variations on a Theme. New Brunswick, N. J.: Rutgers University Press, 1973.

Madison, Elizabeth Christen. "Reality and Imagery in the Novels of Virginia Woolf and Nathalie Sarraute." Ph. D. Dissertation, Indiana University, 1974.

SARTON, MAY

Anderson, Dawn Holt. "May Sarton's Women." In Images of Women in Fiction, pp. 243-250. Edited by Susan Koppelman Cornillon. Bowling Green, Ohio: Bowling Green University Press, 1972.

Douglas, Ellen. New York Times Book Review, 4 November 1973, p. 77. (Review of As We Are Now.)

Gabelnick, Faith. "Making Connections: American Women Poets on Love." Ph. D. Dissertation, American University, 1974.

Heilbrun, Carolyn G. "Introduction." Mrs. Stevens Hears the Mermaids Singing by May Sarton. New York: W. W. Norton, 1975.

Putney, Paula G. "Sister of the Mirage and Echo: An Interview with May Sarton." Contempora (Atlanta, Georgia) 2 (1972): 1-6.

Sarton, May. Journal of Solitude. New York: W. W. Norton, 1973.

Sibley, Agnes Marie. May Sarton. New York: Twayne, 1972.

_____. "May Sarton." In Contemporary Novelists. Edited by James Vinson. London: St. James Press, 1972; New York: St. Martin's Press, 1972.

SAYERS, DOROTHY L.

Harrison, Barbara Grizutti. "Dorothy L. Sayers and the Tidy Art of Detective Fiction." Ms. 3 (November 1974): 66-69, 84-89.

Peters, Margot and Agate Nesaule Krouse. "Women and

Crime: Sexism in Allingham, Sayers, and Christie."
Southwest Review 59 (Spring 1974): 144-152.

Soloway, Sara Lee. "Dorothy Sayers: Novelist." Ph. D.
Dissertation, University of Kentucky, 1971.

Watson, Colin. "Girls Who Kept Cool." Snobbery with
Violence: Crime Stories and Their Audience. New
York: St. Martin's Press, 1971.

SCARBOROUGH, DOROTHY

Neatherlin, James William. "Dorothy Scarborough:
Form and Milieu in the Work of a Texas Writer."
Ph. D. Dissertation, The University of Iowa, 1973.

SCHAEFFER, SUSAN FROMBERG

Booth, W. C. New York Times Book Review, 20 May
1973, p. 56. (Review of Falling.)

Karp, Lila. Ms. 2 (August 1973): 34. (Review of
Falling.)

Thurman, Judith. "Unchanged by Suffering?" Ms. 3
(March 1975): 46-47. (Review of Anya.)

SCHREINER, OLIVE

Beeton, Ridley. "In Search of Olive Schreiner in
Texas." Texas Quarterly 17 (Autumn 1974): 105-
154.

_____. "Two Notes on Olive Schreiner's Letters."
Research in African Literature 3 (Fall 1972): 180-
189.

Colby, Vineta. "The Imperative Impulse: Olive
Schreiner." The Singular Anomaly. New York:
New York University Press, 1970, pp. 47-109.

Forrey, Carolyn. "The New Woman Revisited." Wom-
en's Studies 2 (1974): 37-56.

Gorsky, Susan R. "Old Maids and New Women: Alternatives to Marriage in Englishwomen's Novels, 1847-
1915." Journal of Popular Culture 7 (Summer 1973):
68-85.

Hoffman, Leonore Noll. "A Delicate Balance: The Resolutions to Conflicts of Women in the Fiction of Four Women Writers of the Victorian Period." Ph. D. Dissertation, Indiana University, 1974.

Rive, Richard M. "An Infinite Compassion: A Critical Comparison of Olive Schreiner's Novels." Contrast (Cape Town) 29 (1972): 25-43.

Walsh, William. A Manifold Voice: Studies in Commonwealth Literature. New York: Barnes & Noble, 1970.

Wilson, Elaine. "Pervasive Symbolism in The Story of an African Farm." English Studies in Africa 14 (1971): 179-186.

SCUDERY, MADELEINE De

Backer, Dorothy Anne Liot. Precious Women. New York: Basic Books, 1974, pp. 16, 62, 85, 146, 187-201, 212, 218, 226, 227, 229, 242, 251, 270, 271, 285, 286.

Keating, Rebecca Tingle. "The Literary Portraits in the Novel of Mlle de Scudéry." Ph. D. Dissertation, Yale University, 1970.

Lipton, Virginia Anne. "Women in Today's World: A Study of Five French Women Novelists." Ph. D. Dissertation, The University of Wisconsin, 1972.

Simmons, Sarah Tawil. "Attitudes de Hamilton, Marivaux, Crebillon fils et Laclos envers la femme d'apres leurs oeuvres romanesques." Ph. D. Dissertation, University of Colorado, 1970.

SEDGWICK, CATHARINE

Bell, Michael Davitt. "History and Romance Convention in Catharine Sedgwick's Hope Leslie." American Quarterly 22 (Summer 1970): 211-221.

Foster, Edward Halsey. Catharine Maria Sedgwick. New York: Twayne, 1974.

Riley, Glenda Gates. "The Subtle Subversion: Changes

in the Traditional Images of the American Woman."
The Historian 32 (February 1970): 210-227.

Slotkin, Richard. Regeneration Through Violence: The
Mythology of the American Frontier. Middletown,
Conn.: Wesleyan University Press, 1973, pp. 451-
454.

Wood, Ann D. "The 'Scribbling Women' and Fanny
Fern: Why Women Wrote." American Quarterly 23
(Spring 1971): 3-24.

SEWELL, ELIZABETH MISSING

Frerichs, Sarah Cutts. "Elizabeth Missing Sewell: A
Minor Novelist's Search for the Via Media in the
Education of Women in the Victorian Era." Ph. D.
Dissertation, Brown University, 1974.

SEXTON, ANNE

Beis, Patricia Sharon. "Cold Fire: Some Contemporary
American Women Poets." Ph. D. Dissertation, Saint
Louis University, 1972.

Dobbs, Jeanine. "Not Another Poetess: A Study of
Female Experience in Modern American Poetry."
Ph. D. Dissertation, University of New Hampshire,
1973.

Ferrari, M. "Anne Sexton: Between Death and God."
America, 9 November 1974, pp. 281-283.

Gabelnick, Faith. "Making Connections: American
Women Poets on Love." Ph. D. Dissertation, American University, 1974.

Gilbert, S. M. Nation, 14 September 1974, p. 214.
(Review of The Death Notebooks.)

Hoffman, Nancy Jo. "Reading Women's Poetry: The
Meaning and Our Lives." College English 34 (October 1972): 48-62.

Levertov, D. "Anne Sexton: Light Up the Cave."
Ramparts 13 (December 1974): 61-63.

McClatchy, J. D. "Anne Sexton: Somehow to Endure."
Centennial Review 19 (Spring 1975): 1-36.

Malkoff, Karl. Crowell's Handbook of Contemporary
American Poetry. New York: Thomas Y. Crowell,
1973, pp. 279-287.

Meinke, Peter. New Republic, 22 June 1974, p. 27.
(Review of The Death Notebooks.)

Mood, John J. "'A Bird Full of Bones': Anne Sexton--
A Visit and a Reading." Chicago Review 23 (1972):
107-123.

Newlin, Margaret. "The Suicide Bandwagon." Critical
Quarterly 14 (Winter 1972): 367-378.

Root, William Pitt. Poetry 123 (October 1973): 48-51.

Samuelson, David A. "Mothers, Lovers, and Significant
Others in Some Contemporary Metafictions." Paper
presented at the Midwest MLA Meeting, St. Louis,
November 1972. (Mimeographed.)

Shor, Ira. "Anne Sexton's 'For My Lover ...': Feminism in the Classroom." College English 34 (May
1973): 1082-1093. Also in Female Studies VI:
Closer to the Ground, pp. 57-67. Edited by Nancy
Hoffman, Cynthia Secor, Adrian Tinsley. Old Westbury, N.Y.: The Feminist Press, 1972.

Stone, Carole. "Three Mother-Daughter Poems: The
Struggle for Separation." Paper presented at the
Fifth International Forum for Psychoanalysis, Zurich,
1-5 September 1974.

Swenson, May. New York Times Book Review, 19 November 1972, p. 7. (Review of The Book of Folly.)

Van Duyn, Mona. "Seven Women." Poetry (March 1970):
430-439.

Walker, Cheryl Lawson. "The Women's Tradition in
American Poetry." Ph.D. Dissertation, Brandeis
University, 1973.

SHAKESPEARE, WILLIAM

Bean, John C. "Passion Versus Friendship in the Tudor Matrimonial Handbooks and Some Shakespearean Implications." Wascana Review 9 (Spring 1974): 231-240.

Bligh, John. "The Women in the Hamlet Story." Dalhousie Review 53 (Summer 1973): 275-285.

Boatner, Janet Williams. "Criseyde's Character in the Major Writers from Benoît through Dryden: The Changes and Their Significance." Ph.D. Dissertation, The University of Wisconsin, 1970.

Bryant, J. A., Jr. "The Merchant of Venice and the Common Flaw." Sewanee Review 81 (Summer 1973): 606-622.

Burton, Philip. The Sole Voice: Character Portraits from Shakespeare. New York: Dial, 1970.

Cornett, Patricia L. "The Shrew in Shakespearean Comedy." Shakespeare Newsletter 23 (1973): 4.

Davidson, Clifford. "Shakespeare's Cleopatra." Paper presented at the Midwest MLA Meeting, St. Louis, November 1972. (Mimeographed.)

Davis, Arthur G. The Royalty of Lear. New York: St. John's University Press, 1974.

Dias, Walter. Shakespeare: His Tragic World. New Delhi: S. Chand, 1972.

Dickes, Robert. "Desdemona: An Innocent Victim?" American Imago 27 (Fall 1970): 279-297.

Faber, M. D. "Othello: Symbolic Action, Ritual and Myth." American Imago 31 (Summer 1974): 159-205.

Feil, Doris. "The Female Page in Renaissance Drama." Ph.D. Dissertation, Arizona State University, 1971.

Friedman, Simon. "Some Shakespearian Characterizations of Women and Their Traditions." Ph.D. Dissertation, Yale University, 1973.

Goldberg, S. L. An Essay on King Lear. London: Cambridge University Press, 1974.

Goldstien, Neal L. "Love's Labour's Lost and the Renaissance Vision of Love." Shakespeare Quarterly 25 (Summer 1974): 335-350.

Harrison, Ruth Howard. "The Spirited Lady Through Nicolete to Rosalind." Ph. D. Dissertation, University of Oregon, 1974.

Heilbrun, Carolyn G. Towards a Recognition of Androgyny. New York: Knopf, 1973, pp. 28-34, 36-37, 66, 95.

Humphreys, A. R. The Merchant of Venice. Oxford: Basil Blackwell, 1973.

Hyman, Lawrence W. "The Unity of Measure for Measure." Modern Language Quarterly 36 (March 1975): 3-20.

Kelly, Thomas. "Shakespeare's Romantic Heroes: Orlando Reconsidered." Shakespeare Quarterly 24 (Winter 1973): 12-24.

Magee, William H. "Helena, A Female 'Hamlet.'" English Miscellany 22 (1971): 31-46.

Martz, William J. Shakespeare's Universe of Comedy. New York: David Lewis, 1971.

Mason, H. A. Shakespeare's Tragedies of Love: An Examination of the Possibilities of Common Readings of "Romeo and Juliet," "Othello," "King Lear," and "Antony and Cleopatra." London: Chatto & Windus, 1970; New York: Barnes & Noble, 1970.

Moody, JoAnn. "Britomart, Imogen, Perdita, The Duchess of Malfi: A Study of Women in English Renaissance Literature." Ph. D. Dissertation, University of Minnesota, 1971.

Morris, Helen. Romeo & Juliet. Oxford: Basil Blackwell, 1970.

Muir, Kenneth. "Much Ado About the Shrew." Trivium 7 (1972): 1-4.

Onuska, John T., Jr. "Oh Mom, Poor Mom, Shakespeare's Hung You in the Tiring-House and I'm Feelin' So Sad." Paper presented at the Midwest MLA Meeting, St. Louis, November 1972. (Mimeographed.)

O'Sullivan, James Paul. "The Disguised Heroine in Six Shakespearean Comedies." Ph.D. Dissertation, The University of Connecticut, 1970.

Park, Clara Claiborne. "As We Like It: How a Girl Can Be Smart and Still Popular." American Scholar 42 (Spring 1973): 262-278.

Pederson, Lise. "Shakespeare's The Taming of the Shrew vs. Shaw's Pygmalion: Male Chauvinism vs. Women's Lib." Shaw Review 17 (January 1974): 32-39.

Reid, Stephen. "Desdemona's Guilt." American Imago 27 (Fall 1970): 245-262.

_____. "In Defense of Goneril and Regan." American Imago 27 (Fall 1970): 226-244.

Richmond, Velma B. "Lady Macbeth: Feminine Sensibility Gone Wrong." CEA Critic 35, no. 3 (1973): 20-24.

Salingar, Leo. "Medieval Stage Heroines." Shakespeare and the Traditions of Comedy. London: Cambridge University Press, 1974.

Sawyer, Lynn Blechman. "The Function of Female Characters in Shakespeare's Political Plays." Ph.D. Dissertation, University of North Carolina at Chapel Hill, 1971.

Schäfer, Jürgen. "'When They Marry, They Get Wenches.'" Shakespeare Quarterly 22 (1971): 203-211.

Schork, R. J. "Allusion, Theme, and Characterization in Cymbeline." Studies in Philology 69 (1972): 210-216.

Schweikart, Patsy. "A Feminist Critique of Measure for

Measure." Papers on Women's Studies 1 (October 1974): 147-157.

Swinden, Patrick. An Introduction to Shakespeare's Comedies. New York: Macmillan, 1973.

Traci, Philip J. The Love Play of Antony and Cleopatra. The Hague and Paris: Mouton, 1970.

Tzipporah. "Othello and Sexism." Women: A Journal of Liberation 2 (Fall 1970): 18-19.

Wagenknecht, Edward. The Personality of Shakespeare. Norman: University of Oklahoma Press, 1972.

Wheeler, Richard P. "The King and the Physician's Daughter: All's Well That Ends Well and the Late Romances." Comparative Drama 8 (Winter 1974-75): 311-327.

Wild, Henry Douglas. "The Revolutionary Role of the Heroines." Shakespeare: Prophet for Our Time. Wheaton, Ill.: Theosophical Publishing House, 1971.

Williams, Edith W. "In Defense of Lady Macbeth." Shakespeare Quarterly 24 (1973): 221-223.

Williams, Gwyn. "Suffolk and Margaret." Shakespeare Quarterly 25 (Summer 1974): 310-322.

Windt, Judith Hanna. "Not Cast in Other Women's Mold: Strong Women Characters in Shakespeare's Henry VI Trilogy, Drayton's Englands Heroicall Epistles and Jonson's Poems to Ladies." Ph.D. Dissertation, Stanford University, 1974.

SHAW, GEORGE BERNARD

Adams, Elsie. "Feminism and Female Stereotypes in Shaw." Shaw Review 17 (January 1974): 17-22.

Braby, Maud Churton. "G.B.S. and a Suffragist." Independent Shavian 12 (Fall 1973): 1-3.

Crane, Gladys M. "Shaw and Women's Lib." Shaw Review 17 (January 1974): 23-31.

_____. "Shaw's Misalliance: The Comic Journey

from Rebellious Daughter to Conventional Woman-hood." Educational Theatre Journal 25 (1973): 480-489.

Dukore, Bernard F. Bernard Shaw, Playwright: Aspects of Shavian Drama. Columbia: University of Missouri Press, 1973.

Greiner, Norbert. "Mill, Marx and Bebel: Early Influences on Shaw's Characterization of Women." Shaw Review 18 (January 1975): 10-17.

Heilbrun, Carolyn G. Toward a Recognition of Androgyny. New York: Knopf, 1973, pp. 15, 77, 100, 110-111.

Hugo, Leon. Bernard Shaw: Playwright and Preacher. London: Methuen, 1971.

Jordan, Robert J. "Theme and Character in Major Barbara." Texas Studies in Literature 12 (Spring 1970): 471-480.

Kester, Dolores Ann. "Shaw and the Victorian 'Problem' Genre: The Woman Side." Ph.D. Dissertation, The University of Wisconsin, 1973.

Khanna, Savitri. "Shaw's Image of Woman." The Shavian 4 (Summer 1973): 253-259.

Lorichs, Sonja. "The Unwomanly Woman." The Shavian 4 (Summer 1973): 250-252.

_____. The Unwomanly Woman in Bernard Shaw's Drama and Her Social and Political Background. Uppsala: Universitetsiblioteket, 1973; New York: Humanities, 1973.

McCauley, Janie Caves. "Kipling on Women: A New Source for Shaw." Shaw Review 17 (January 1974): 40-44.

Nathan, Rhoda B. "The Shavian Sphinx." Shaw Review 17 (January 1974): 45-52.

Nelson, Raymond S. "Mrs. Warren's Profession and English Prostitution." Journal of Modern Literature 2 (1972): 357-366.

Pedersen, Lise. "Shakespeare's The Taming of the Shrew vs. Shaw's Pygmalion: Male Chauvinism vs. Women's Lib." Shaw Review 17 (January 1974): 32-39.

Rudman, Carol. "Meredith, Wilde, Shaw: The Uses of Irony." Ph. D. Dissertation, University of New York at Stony Brook, work in progress.

Sidnell, Michael J. "Misalliance: Sex, Socialism and the Collectivist Poet." Modern Drama 17 (June 1974): 125-139.

Watson, Barbara Bellow. "Introduction to the Norton Library Edition." A Shavian Guide to the Intelligent Woman. New York: Norton, 1972.

_____. "The New Woman and the New Comedy." Shaw Review 17 (January 1974): 2-16.

Weintraub, Rodelle. "The Gift of Imagination: An Interview with Clare Boothe Luce." Shaw Review 17 (January 1974): 53-59.

Wisenthal, J. L. The Marriage of Contraries: Bernard Shaw's Middle Plays. Cambridge: Harvard University Press, 1974.

SHELLEY, MARY

Ellis, Katherine. "Paradise Lost: The Limits of Domesticity in the Nineteenth-Century Novel." Feminist Studies 2, nos. 2/3 (1975): 55-63.

Feldman, Paula Renée. "The Journals of Mary Wollstonecraft Shelley: An Annotated Edition." Ph. D. Dissertation, Northwestern University, 1974.

Gerson, Noel B. Daughter of Earth and Water: A Biography of Mary Wollstonecraft Shelley. New York: William Morrow, 1973.

Kmetz, Gail. "Mary Shelley: In the Shadow of 'Frankenstein.'" Ms. 3 (February 1975): 12-16.

Manley, Seon and Susan Belcher. "Frankenstein's Mother." O, Those Extraordinary Women!

Philadelphia: Chilton, 1972, pp. 31-56.

Neumann, Bonnie Rayford. "Mary Shelley." Ph. D. Dissertation, The University of New Mexico, 1972.

Ozolins, Aija. "The Novels of Mary Shelley: From Frankenstein to Falkner." Ph. D. Dissertation, University of Maryland, 1972.

Walling, William A. Mary Shelley. New York: Twayne, 1972.

SHIRLEY, JAMES

Kalmar, Elaine Bush. "Misery of Birth and State: Essays on the Tragedies of James Shirley." Ph. D. Dissertation, The University of New Mexico, 1971.

Zimmer, Ruth Kachel. "A Study of the Heroines in the Dramatic Pieces of James Shirley." Ph. D. Dissertation, University of Kentucky, 1971.

SHULMAN, ALIX KATES

Bender, Marylin. New York Times Book Review, 23 April 1972, p. 34. (Review of Memoirs of an Ex-Prom Queen.)

Fishel, Elizabeth. "Women's Fiction: Who's Afraid of Virginia Woolf." Ramparts, June 1973, pp. 45-48.

Morgan, Ellen. "Humanbecoming: Form and Focus in the Neo-Feminist Novel," In Images of Women in Fiction, pp. 197-204. Edited by Susan Koppelman Cornillon. Bowling Green, Ohio: Bowling Green University Press, 1972.

SIMMS, WILLIAM GILMORE

Ruoff, John C. "Frivolity to Consumption: Or, Southern Womanhood in Antebellum Literature." Civil War History 18 (September 1972): 213-229.

Steinhagen, Carol Therese. "Plantation and Wilderness: Themes of Aggression and Regression in the Border Romances of William Gilmore Simms." Ph. D. Dissertation, University of Illinois at Urbana-Champaign, 1974.

SIMON, CLAUDE

Fletcher, John. "Women in Crisis: Louise and Mrs. Eliot." Critical Quarterly 15 (Summer 1973): 157-170.

SINCLAIR, MAY

Boll, Theophilus E. M. Miss May Sinclair: Novelist. Rutherford, N. J.: Fairleigh Dickinson University Press, 1973.

Gorsky, Susan. "The Gentle Doubters: Images of Women in Englishwomen's Novels, 1840-1920." In Images of Women in Fiction, pp. 35, 42, 47. Edited by Susan Koppelman Cornillon. Bowling Green, Ohio: Bowling Green University Press, 1972.

Kaplan, Sydney. "'Featureless Freedom' or Ironic Submission: Dorothy Richardson and May Sinclair." College English 32 (May 1971): 914-917.

Pratt, Annis. "Women and Nature in Modern Fiction." Contemporary Literature 13 (Autumn 1972): 481-482.

Robb, Kenneth A. "May Sinclair: An Annotated Bibliography." English Literature in Transition 16 (1973): 177-231.

Zegger, Hrisey Dimitrakis. "May Sinclair's Psychological Novels." Ph. D. Dissertation, New York University, 1970.

SMITH, CHARLOTTE

Fry, Carrol Lee. "Charlotte Smith, Popular Novelist." Ph. D. Dissertation, The University of Nebraska, 1970.

Pratt, Annis. "Archetypal Approaches to the New Feminist Criticism." Bucknell Review 21 (Spring 1973): 3-14.

SMITH, LILLIAN

Blackwell, Louise and Frances Clay. "Lillian Smith, Novelist." CLA Journal 15 (June 1972): 452-458.

Sugg, Redding S., Jr. "Lillian Smith and the Condition of Woman." South Atlantic Quarterly 71 (1972): [155]-164.

SMOLLETT, TOBIAS

Spacks, Patricia Meyer. "Early Fiction and the Frightened Male." Novel 8 (Fall 1974): 5-15.

SOPHOCLES

Heilbrun, Carolyn G. Toward a Recognition of Androgyny. New York: Knopf, 1973, pp. 9-14, 13, 93.

Rosenstein, Harriet. "On Androgyny." Ms. 1 (May 1973): 38-43.

SPARK, MURIEL

Holloway, John. "Narrative Structure and Text Structure: Isherwood's A Meeting by the River, and Muriel Spark's The Prime of Miss Jean Brodie." Critical Inquiry 1 (March 1975): 581-604.

Kemp, Peter. Muriel Spark. London: Paul Elek, 1974.

Laffin, Garry S. "Muriel Spark's Portrait of the Artist as a Young Girl." Renascence 24 (1972): 213-223.

McLeod, Patrick Gould. "Vision and Moral Encounter: A Reading of Muriel Spark's Novels." Ph.D. Dissertation, Rice University, 1973.

Mansfield, Joseph Gerard. "Another World Than This: The Gothic and the Catholic in the Novels of Muriel Spark." Ph.D. Dissertation, University of Iowa, 1973.

Richmond, Velma Bourgeois. "The Darkening Vision of Muriel Spark." Critique 15 no. 1 (1973-74): 71-85.

Stanford, Derek. "Muriel Spark." In Contemporary Novelists. Edited by James Vinson. London: St. James Press, 1972; New York: St. Martin's Press, 1972.

Stubbs, Patricia. Muriel Spark. Harlow: Longman for the British Council, 1973.

Sudrann, Jean. "Hearth and Horizon: Changing Concepts of the 'Domestic' Life of the Heroine." Massachusetts Review 14 (Spring 1973): 235-255.

SPENCE, CATHERINE HELEN

Wightman, Jennifer. "A Practical Dreamer: Catherine Helen Spence." Meanjin Quarterly 33 (March 1974): 89-92.

SPENSER, EDMUND

Entzminger, Robert L. "Courtesy: The Cultural Imperative." Philological Quarterly 53 (Summer 1974): 389-400.

Gilde, H. C. "The 'Sweet Lodge of Love and Deare Delight': The Problem of Amoret." Philological Quarterly 50 (January 1971): 63-74.

Goldberg, Jonathan. "The Mothers in Book III of The Faerie Queene." Texas Studies in Literature and Language 17 (Spring 1975): 5-26.

Moody, JoAnn. "Britomart, Imogen, Perdita, The Duchess of Malfi: A Study of Women in English Renaissance Literature." Ph.D. Dissertation, University of Minnesota, 1971.

Paolucci, Anne. "Women in the Political Love-Ethic of the Divine Comedy and the Faerie Queene." Dante Studies with the Annual Report of the Dante Society 90 (1972): 139-153.

Ruedy, Shirley Wallace. "Spenser's Britomart." Ph.D. Dissertation, Duke University, 1975.

STAËL, MADAME DE

Daemmrich, Ingrid G. "The Function of the Ruins Motif in Madame de Staël's Corinne." Romance Notes 15 (Winter 1973): 255-258.

Gutwirth, Madelyn. "Madame de Staël, Rousseau, and the Woman Question." PMLA 86 (1971): 100-109.

Lipton, Virginia Anne. "Women in Today's World: A

Study of Five French Women Novelists. " Ph. D.
Dissertation, The University of Wisconsin, 1972.

Moers, Ellen. "Mme. de Staël and the Woman of
Genius. " American Scholar 44 (Spring 1975): 225-
241.

West, Anthony. "Madame de Staël. " Mortal Wounds.
New York: McGraw-Hill, 1973, pp. 3-180.

STAFFORD, JEAN

White, Barbara Anne. "Growing Up Female: Adolescent
Girlhood in American Literature. " Ph. D. Dissertation, The University of Wisconsin-Madison, 1974.

STEAD, CHRISTINA

Burns, Graham. "The Moral Design of The Man Who
Loved Children. " Critical Review no. 14 (1971):
38-61.

"Christina Stead: An Interview. " Australian Literary
Studies 6 (May 1974): 230-248.

Geering, R. G. "Christina Stead. " In Contemporary
Novelists. Edited by James Vinson. London: St.
James Press, 1972; New York: St. Martin's Press,
1972.

Green, Dorothy. "The Man Who Loved Children: Storm
in a Tea-Cup. " In The Australian Experience, pp.
174-208. Edited by W. S. Ramson. Canberra:
Australian National University, 1974.

_____. Meanjin Quarterly 30 (Winter 1971): 251,
253. (Review of R. G. Geering's Christina Stead.)

STEIN, GERTRUDE

Bridgman, Richard. Gertrude Stein in Pieces. New
York: Oxford University Press, 1970.

Burnett, Avis. Gertrude Stein. New York: Atheneum,
1972.

Manley, Seon and Susan Belcher. O, Those Extraordinary

Women! Philadelphia: Chilton, 1972, pp. 247-251.

Mellow, James R. Charmed Circle: Gertrude Stein and Company. New York: Praeger, 1974.

Riding, Laura. Contemporaries and Snobs. St. Clair Shores, Michigan: Scholarly Press, 1971.

Secor, Cynthia. "Alice and Gertrude." In Female Studies VI: Closer to the Ground, pp. 150-151. Edited by Nancy Hoffman, Cynthia Secor, Adrian Tinsley. Old Westbury, N.Y.: Feminist Press, 1972.

Spacks, Patricia M. The Female Imagination. New York: Knopf, 1975.

Sutherland, Donald. "Alice and Gertrude and Others." Prairie Schooner 45 (1971): 284-299.

Thurman, Judith. "Gertrude Stein: A Rose Is a Rose Is a Rose." Ms. 2 (February 1974): 54-57.

Toklas, Alice B. Staying on Alone: Letters of Alice B. Toklas. New York: Liveright, 1973.

Weinstein, Norman. Gertrude Stein and the Literature of the Modern Consciousness. New York: Frederick Ungar, 1970.

STEINBECK, JOHN

Morita, Shoji. "Steinbeck's View of Womanhood: The Meaning of 'the time of waiting' in The Long Valley." Studies in American Literature 8 (1972): 39-52.

STERNE, LAURENCE

Faurot, R. M. "Mrs. Shandy Observed." Studies in English Literature 10 (Summer 1970): 579-589.

Spacks, Patricia Meyer. "Early Fiction and the Frightened Male." Novel 8 (Fall 1974): 5-15.

Stephenson, Richard John. "Sterne's Fiction." Ph. D. Dissertation, State University of New York at Buffalo, 1970.

STOWE, HARRIET BEECHER

Moore, Katharine. <u>Victorian Wives</u>. New York: St. Martin's Press, 1974.

Ruoff, John C. "Frivolity to Consumption: Or, Southern Womanhood in Antebellum Literature." <u>Civil War History</u> 18 (September 1972): 213-229.

Wood, Ann D. "The 'Scribbling Women' and Fanny Fern: Why Women Wrote." <u>American Quarterly</u> 23 (Spring 1971): 3-24.

STRINDBERG, AUGUST

Figes, Eva. <u>Patriarchal Attitudes</u>. New York: Stein & Day, 1970.

Hayes, Stephen G. and Jules Zentner. "Strindberg's Miss Julie: Lilacs and Beer." <u>Scandinavian Studies</u> 45 (Winter 1973): 59-64.

Lamm, Martin. <u>August Strindberg</u>. New York: Benjamin Blom, 1971.

Pampel, Brigitte C. G. "The Relationship of the Sexes in the Works of Strindberg, Wedekind, and O'Neill." Ph. D. Dissertation, Northwestern University, 1972.

SUCKOW, RUTH

White, Barbara Anne. "Growing Up Female: Adolescent Girlhood in American Literature." Ph. D. Dissertation, University of Wisconsin-Madison, 1974.

SVEVO, ITALO

Fifer, Elizabeth. "The Confessions of Italo Svevo." <u>Contemporary Literature</u> 14 (Summer 1973): 320-331.

SWENSON, MAY

<u>Poetry Is Alive and Well and Living in America</u>. Pleassantville, N. Y.: Educational Audio Visual Inc., n. d. (LP recordings and filmstrips.)

SWIFT, JONATHAN

Ehrenpreis, Irvin. "Letters of Advice to Young Spin-
sters." In Stuart and Georgian Moments, pp. 245-
269. Edited by Earl Miner. Berkeley: University
of California Press, 1972.

Landa, Louis A. "Of Silkworms and Farthingales and
the Will of God." In Studies in the Eighteenth Century, vol. 2, pp. 260-264. Edited by R. F. Brissenden. Toronto: University of Toronto Press,
1973.

Metcalfe, Joan Elizabeth. "Jonathan Swift and the Stage
of the World: A Study of Swift's Poetry, with Particular Reference to the Poems about Women."
Ph. D. Dissertation, The University of Florida, 1974.

Rees, C. "Gay, Swift and the Nymphs of Drury-lane."
Essays in Criticism 23 (January 1973): 1-21.

Schoppe, Linnea Pearson. "The Hound and the Hare,
the Rebel and the Fair: Four Critical Approaches
to the Love and Anti-Love Poetry of Jonathan
Swift." Ph. D. Dissertation, Northern Illinois University, 1973.

SWINBURNE, ALGERNON CHARLES

Jordan, John O. "The Sweet Face of Mothers: Psychological Patterns in Atalanta in Calydon." Victorian
Poetry 11 (Summer 1973): 101-114.

-T-

TEASDALE, SARA

Gabelnick, Faith. "Making Connections: American Wom-
en Poets on Love." Ph. D. Dissertation, American
University, 1974.

Walker, Cheryl Lawson. "The Women's Tradition in
American Poetry." Ph. D. Dissertation, Brandeis
University, 1973.

TEFFI, NADEZHDA

Haber, Edythe. "Nadezhda Teffi." Russian Literature Triquarterly no. 9 (Spring 1974): 454-472.

TENNYSON, ALFRED

Bergonzi, Bernard. "Feminism and Femininity in The Princess." The Turn of a Century. New York: Barnes & Noble, 1973. (Reprinted from The Major Victorian Poets: Reconsiderations. Edited by Isobel Armstrong. London: Routledge & Kegan Paul, 1969.)

Collins, Winston. "The Princess: The Education of the Prince." Victorian Poetry 11 (Winter 1973): 285-294.

Goslee, D. F. "Character and Structure in Tennyson's The Princess." Studies in English Literature 1500-1900 14 (Autumn 1974): 563-573.

Schlager, Herbert C. "The Marriage Theme in the Poetry and Plays of Alfred Tennyson." Ph. D. Dissertation, New York University, 1973.

THACKERAY, WILLIAM MAKEPEACE

Basch, Françoise. Relative Creatures: Victorian Women in Society and the Novel. New York: Schocken, 1974.

Berndt, David Edward. "'This Hard, Real Life': Self and Society in Five Mid-Victorian Bildungsromane." Ph. D. Dissertation, Cornell University, 1972.

Cabot, Frederick C. "The Two Voices in Thackeray's Catherine." Nineteenth-Century Fiction 28 (March 1974): 404-416.

Culross, Jack Lewis. "The Prostitute and the Image of the Prostitute in Victorian Fiction." Ph. D. Dissertation, The Louisiana State University and Agricultural and Mechanical College, 1970.

Detter, Howard Montgomery. "The Female Sexual Outlaw in the Victorian Novel: A Study in the Conventions of Fiction." Ph. D. Dissertation, Indiana University, 1971.

Halperin, John. Egoism and Self-Discovery in the Victorian Novel. New York: Burt Franklin, 1974, pp. 33-45.

Hardy, Barbara. The Exposure of Luxury: Radical Themes in Thackeray. Pittsburgh: University of Pittsburgh Press, 1972.

Heilbrun, Carolyn G. Toward a Recognition of Androgyny. New York: Knopf, 1973, pp. 57, 62, 63, 67-69.

Lubin, Sister Alice Mary. "I. Southwell's Religious Complaint Lyric. II. Becky Sharp's Role Playing in Vanity Fair. III. Grotesques in the Fictions of Flannery O'Connor." Ph. D. Dissertation, Rutgers University, The State University of New Jersey, 1973.

McMaster, Juliet. Thackeray: The Major Novels. Toronto: University of Toronto Press, 1971.

Moler, Kenneth L. "Evelina in Vanity Fair: Becky Sharp and Her Patrician Heroes." Nineteenth-Century Fiction 27 (September 1972): 171-181.

Moore, Katharine. Victorian Wives. New York: St. Martin's Press, 1974.

Peterson, M. Jeanne. "The Victorian Governess: Status, Incongruence in Family and Society." Victorian Studies 14 (September 1970): 7-23.

Rawlins, Jack P. Thackeray's Novels: A Fiction that Is True. Berkeley, Los Angeles, London: University of California, 1974.

Rogers, Katherine M. "A Defense of Thackeray's Amelia." Texas Studies in Literature and Language 11 (Winter 1970): 1367-1374.

_____. "The Pressure of Convention on Thackeray's Women." Modern Language Review 67 (April 1972): 257-263.

Swanson, Roger M. "Vanity Fair: The Double Standard." The English Novel in the Nineteenth Century, pp. 126-144. Edited by George Goodin. Urbana: University of Illinois Press, 1972.

THRALE, MRS. (Hester Lynch)

Miner, Earl, Jr., ed. Stuart and Georgian Moments.
Berkeley: University of California Press, 1972,
pp. 184, 288.

Spacks, Patricia Meyer. "'Ev'ry Woman is at Heart a
Rake.'" Eighteenth-Century Studies 8 (Fall 1974):
27-46.

_____. The Female Imagination. New York: Knopf,
1975.

_____. "Reflecting Women." Yale Review 63 (Octo-
ber 1973): 26-42.

TOLSTOY, COUNT LEO

Benson, Ruth Crego. Women in Tolstoy: The Ideal and
the Erotic. Urbana: University of Illinois Press,
1973.

Figes, Eva. Patriarchal Attitudes. New York: Stein &
Day, 1970.

Hardwick, Elizabeth. Seduction and Betrayal. New
York: Random House, 1974, pp. 193-196.

Heilbrun, Carolyn G. Toward a Recognition of Androgyny.
New York: Knopf, 1973, pp. 88-89.

Lieberman, Marcia R. "Sexism and the Double Standard
in Literature." In Images of Women in Fiction,
pp. 326-338. Edited by Susan Koppelman Cornillon.
Bowling Green, Ohio: Bowling Green University
Press, 1972.

Wagner, Geoffrey. Five for Freedom. Rutherford,
Madison, Teaneck, N.J.: Fairleigh Dickinson University Press, 1972, pp. 37, 45, 55, 88-90, 95, 96,
101, 143, 149, 174.

TOOMER, JEAN

Blake, Susan L. "The Spectatorial Artist and the

Structure of Cane." CLA Journal 17 (June 1974): 516-534.

Chase, Patricia. "The Women in Cane." CLA Journal 14 (March 1971): 259-273.

Duncan, Bowie. "Jean Toomer's Cane: A Modern Black Oracle." CLA Journal 15 (March 1972): 323-333.

Innes, Catherine L. "The Unity of Jean Toomer's Cane." CLA Journal 15 (March 1972): 306-322.

Kopf, George. "The Tensions in Jean Toomer's 'Theater.'" CLA Journal 17 (June 1974): 498-503.

Matthews, George C. "Toomer's Cane: The Artist and His World." CLA Journal 17 (June 1974): 543-559.

Reilly, John M. "The Search for Black Redemption: Jean Toomer's Cane." Studies in the Novel 2 (Fall 1970): 312-324.

Rosenblatt, Roger. Black Fiction. Cambridge: Harvard University Press, 1974.

Stein, Marion L. "The Poet-Observer and 'Fern' in Jean Toomer's Cane." Markham Review 2 (October 1970): 64-65.

Turner, Darwin T. In a Minor Chord: Three Afro-American Writers and Their Search for Identity. Carbondale and Edwardsville: Southern Illinois University Press, 1971.

Waldron, Edward E. "The Search for Identity in Jean Toomer's 'Esther.'" CLA Journal 14 (March 1971): 277-280.

Watkins, Patricia. "Is There a Unifying Theme in Cane?" CLA Journal 15 (March 1972): 303-305.

Westerfield, Hargis. "Jean Toomer's 'Fern': A Mythical Dimension." CLA Journal 14 (March 1971): 274-276.

TRITT, VICTORIA MAY

Urbas, Jeannette. "The Perquisites of Love." Canadian
Literature no. 59 (Winter 1974): 6-15.

TROLLOPE, ANTHONY

Aitken, D. "Anthony Trollope on 'The Genus Girl.'"
Nineteenth-Century Fiction 28 (March 1974): 417-
434.

Basch, Françoise. Relative Creatures: Victorian Women
in Society and the Novel. New York: Schocken,
1974.

Blinderman, Charles. "The Servility of Dependence:
The Dark Lady in Trollope." In Images of Women
in Fiction, pp. 55-67. Edited by Susan Koppelman
Cornillon. Bowling Green, Ohio: Bowling Green
University Press, 1972.

Culross, Jack Lewis. "The Prostitute and the Image
of the Prostitute in Victorian Fiction." Ph. D. Dissertation, The Louisiana State University and Agricultural and Mechanical College, 1970.

Decavalcante, Frank. "Sexual Politics in Four Victorian
Novels." Ph. D. Dissertation, Kent State University,
1974.

Glavin, J. J. "Trollope's Most Natural English Girl."
Nineteenth-Century Fiction 28 (March 1974): 477-485.

Levine, George. "Can You Forgive Him? Trollope's
Can You Forgive Her? and The Myth of Realism."
Victorian Studies 18 (September 1974): 5-30.

Lucas, Nancy Beissner. "Women and Love Relationships
in the Changing Fictional World of Anthony Trollope."
Ph. D. Dissertation, University of Illinois at Urbana-
Champaign, 1973.

McMaster, Juliet. "'The Meaning of Words and the
Nature of Things': Trollope's Can You Forgive
Her?" Studies in English Literature 14 (Autumn
1974): 603-618.

Moore, Katharine. Victorian Wives. New York: St.
Martin's Press, 1974.

Roberts, Ruth. The Moral Trollope. Athens: Ohio
University Press, 1971.

Skilton, David. Anthony Trollope and His Contemporaries.
London: Longman, 1972.

West, W. A. "Anonymous Trollope." Ariel 5 (January
1974): 46-64.

TSVETAEVA, MARINA

Taubman, Jane Andelman. "Tsvetaeva and Akhmatova:
Two Female Voices in a Poetic Quartet." Russian
Literature Triquarterly no. 9 (Spring 1974): 355-
369.

-U-

UPDIKE, JOHN

Allen, Mary Inez. "The Necessary Blankness: Women
in Major American Fiction of the Sixties." Ph. D.
Dissertation, University of Maryland, 1973.

Carlson, Constance Hedin. "Heroines in Certain American Novels." Ph. D. Dissertation, Brown University,
1971.

Hamilton, Alice and Kenneth. The Elements of John
Updike. Grand Rapids, Michigan: William B.
Eerdmans, 1970.

Markle, Joyce B. Fighters and Lovers: Theme in the
Novels of John Updike. New York: New York University Press, 1973.

Sharrock, Roger. "Singles and Couples: Hemingway's
A Farewell to Arms and Updike's Couples." Ariel
4, no. 4 (1973): 21-43.

Vargo, Edward P. Rainstorms and Fire: Ritual in the
Novels of John Updike. Port Washington, N. Y.:
Kennikat Press, 1973.

-V-

VALERA, JUAN

Tyrmand, Mary Ellen. "Women in Society in the Nineteenth-Century Spanish Novel." Ph. D. Dissertation,
Yale University, 1974.

VAN DUYN, MONA

Beis, Patricia Sharon. "Cold Fire: Some Contemporary
American Women Poets." Ph. D. Dissertation, Saint
Louis University, 1972.

Gabelnick, Faith. "Making Connections: American
Women Poets on Love." Ph. D. Dissertation, American University, 1974.

Zinnes, Harriet. "Seven Women Poets." Carleton Miscellany 14 (Spring-Summer 1974): 122-126.

VEDRES, NICOLE

Smith, Annette J. "Beyond Feminism: The Works of
Nicole Vedrès." Women's Studies 2 (1974): 79-90.

VEGA CARPIO, LOPE

McKendrick, Melveena. "The 'mujer esquiva': A Measure of the Feminist Sympathies of Seventeenth-Century
Spanish Dramatists." Hispanic Review 40 (1972):
162-197.

VILLON, FRANÇOIS

Pickens, Rupert T. "The Concept of the Feminine Ideal
in Villon's Testament: Huitain LXXXIX." Studies
in Philology 70 (January 1973): 42-50.

-W-

WALKER, ALICE

Callahan, John. "Reconsideration: The Higher Ground of Alice Walker." New Republic, 14 September 1974, pp. 21-22.

O'Brien, John. Interviews with Black Writers. New York: Liveright, 1973, pp. 185-211.

Smith, Barbara. "The Souls of Black Women." Ms. 2 (February 1974): 42-43, 78.

Washington, Mary Helen. "Black Women Image Makers." Black World 23 (August 1974): 10-18.

"Women on Women." American Scholar 41 (Fall 1972): 599-622. See also Patricia McLaughlin, "Comment," 41 (Fall 1972): 622-627.

WALKER, MARGARET

Emanuel, James A. "Margaret Walker." In Contemporary Novelists. Edited by James Vinson. London: St. James Press, 1972; New York: St. Martin's Press, 1972.

Giovanni, Nikki and Margaret Walker. A Poetic Equation: Conversations between Nikki Giovanni and Margaret Walker. Washington, D.C.: Howard University Press, 1974.

WARD, MRS. HUMPHRY

Colaco, Jill. "Mrs. Humphry Ward." Essays in Criticism 24 (April 1974): 207-212. (Review Essay.)

Colby, Vineta. "Light on a Darkling Plain: Mrs. Humphry Ward." The Singular Anomaly. New York: New York University Press, 1970, pp. 111-173.

Gorsky, Susan. "The Gentle Doubters: Images of Women in Englishwomen's Novels, 1840-1920." In Images of Women in Fiction, pp. 33, 35, 37, 42, 45. Edited by Susan Koppelman Cornillon. Bowling Green, Ohio: Bowling Green University Press, 1972.

————. "Old Maids and New Women: Alternatives to Marriage in Englishwomen's Novels, 1847-1915."

Journal of Popular Culture 7 (Summer 1973): 68-85.

Jones, Enid Huws. Mrs. Humphry Ward. New York: St. Martin's Press, 1973.

Musil, Caryn McTighe. "Art and Ideology: The Novels and Times of Mrs. Humphry Ward." Ph. D. Dissertation, Northwestern University, 1974.

Stone, Donald D. "Victorian Feminism and the Nineteenth-Century Novel." Women's Studies 1 (1972): 65-92.

Trevor, Meriol. The Arnolds: Thomas Arnold and His Family. New York: Scribner, 1973.

WARNER, SUSAN

Smith, Henry Nash. "The Scribbling Women and the Cosmic Success Story." Critical Inquiry 1 (September 1974): 47-70.

WEBB, MARY

Hannah, Barbara. Striving Toward Wholeness. New York: Putnam's for the C. G. Jung Foundation for Analytical Psychology, 1971.

WELTY, EUDORA

Brooks, Cleanth. "The Past Reexamined: The Optimist's Daughter." Mississippi Quarterly 26 (Fall 1973): 577-587.

Ginsberg, Elaine. "The Female Initiation Theme in American Fiction." Studies in Fiction 3 (Spring 1975): 27-37.

Hinton, Jane Lee. "'Out of All Times of Trouble': The Family in the Fiction of Eudora Welty." Ph. D. Dissertation, Vanderbilt University, 1974.

Howard, Zelma Turner. The Rhetoric of Eudora Welty's Short Stories. Jackson: University and College Press of Mississippi, 1973.

King, William Porter. "A Thematic Study of the Fiction of Eudora Welty." Ph.D. Dissertation, George Peabody College for Teachers, 1972.

McMillen, William E. "Conflict and Resolution in Welty's Losing Battles." Critique 15, no. 1: 110-124.

Manz-Kunz, Marie-Antoinette. Eudora Welty: Aspects of Her Short Fiction. Bern: Francke, 1971.

Marx, Paul. "Eudora Welty." In Contemporary Novelists. Edited by James Vinson. London: St. James Press, 1972; New York: St. Martin's Press, 1972.

Nelson, Doris Lowene. "The Contemporary American Family Novel: A Study of Metaphor." Ph.D. Dissertation, University of Southern California, 1970.

Spacks, Patricia M. The Female Imagination. New York: Knopf, 1975.

Tapley, Philip Allen. "The Portrayal of Women in Selected Short Stories by Eudora Welty." Ph.D. Dissertation, The Louisiana State University and Agricultural and Mechanical College, 1974.

Walker, Alice. "Eudora Welty: An Interview." Harvard Advocate 106 (Winter 1973): 68-72.

WHARTON, EDITH

Ammons, Elizabeth. "The Business of Marriage in Edith Wharton's The Custom of the Country." Criticism 16 (Fall 1974): 326-338.

_____. "Edith Wharton's Heroines: Studies in Aspiration and Compliance." Ph.D. Dissertation, University of Illinois at Urbana-Champaign, 1974.

Carlson, Constance Hedin. "Heroines in Certain American Novels." Ph.D. Dissertation, Brown University, 1971.

Cohn, Jan. "The Houses of Fiction: Domestic Architecture in Howells and Edith Wharton." Texas Studies in Literature and Language 15 (Fall 1973): 537-549.

Earnest, Ernest. The American Eve in Fact and Fiction, 1775-1914. Urbana, Chicago, London: University of Illinois Press, 1974, pp. 230-232.

Gargano, James W. "The House of Mirth: Social Futility and Faith." American Literature 44 (March 1972): 137-143.

Grumbach, D. "Reconsideration; Edith Wharton's Lily Bart in House of Mirth." New Republic, 21 April 1973, pp. 29-30.

Jacoby, Victoria A. D. "A Study of Class Values and the Family in the Fiction of Edith Wharton." Ph.D. Dissertation, Stanford University, 1972.

Kraft, Stephanie Barlett. "Women and Society in the Novels of George Eliot and Edith Wharton." Ph.D. Dissertation, The University of Rochester, 1973.

Lawson, Richard H. Edith Wharton and German Literature. Bonn: Bouvier Verlag Herbert Grundmann, 1974.

Lindberg, Gary. Edith Wharton and the Novel of Manners. Charlottesville: University Press of Virginia, forthcoming.

McDowell, Margaret B. "Viewing the Custom of Her Country: Edith Wharton's Feminism." Contemporary Literature 15 (Autumn 1974): 521-538.

McIlvaine, Robert. "Edith Wharton's American Beauty Rose." Journal of American Studies 7 (August 1973): 183-185.

Manley, Seon and Susan Belcher. O, Those Extraordinary Women! Philadelphia: Chilton, 1972, pp. 251-256.

Maynard, Moira. "The Medusa's Face: A Study of Character and Behavior in the Fiction of Edith Wharton." Ph.D. Dissertation, New York University, 1971.

Molley, Chester N. "The Artemis-Athene and Venus Polarity in the Works of Edith Wharton: A

Mythological Dimension with Psychological Implications." Ph. D. Dissertation, The Pennsylvania State University, 1971.

Montgomery, Judith H. "The American Galatea." College English 32 (May 1971): 890-899.

_____. "Pygmalion's Image: The Metamorphosis of the American Heroine." Ph. D. Dissertation, Syracuse University, 1971.

Parker, Jeraldine. "'Uneasy Survivors': Five Women Writers 1896-1923." Ph. D. Dissertation, University of Utah, 1973.

Phelps, Donald. "Edith Wharton and the Invisible." Prose no. 7 (Fall 1973): 227-245.

Sasaki, Miyoko. "The Sense of Horror in Edith Wharton." Ph. D. Dissertation, Yale University, 1973.

Semel, Sister Ann. "A Study of the Thematic Design in the Four Major Novels of Edith Wharton." Ph. D. Dissertation, University of Notre Dame, 1971.

Spacks, Patricia M. The Female Imagination. New York: Knopf, 1975.

Tuttleton, J. W. "The Age of Innocence (Edith Wharton)." (The Twentieth Century American Novel Series.) Deland, Fla.: Everett/Edwards, n. d. (Cassette.)

_____. "Edith Wharton: The Archeological Motive." Yale Review 61 (June 1972): 562-574.

Walton, Geoffrey. Edith Wharton: A Critical Interpretation. Rutherford, Madison, Teaneck, N. J.: Fairleigh Dickinson University Press, 1970.

Wolff, Cynthia Griffin. "Lily Bart and the Beautiful Death." American Literature 46 (March 1974): 16-40.

Wright, Dorothea Curtis. "Visions and Revisions of the 'New Woman' in American Realistic Fiction from 1880 to 1920: A Study in Authorial Attitudes."

Ph. D. Dissertation, University of North Carolina at Chapel Hill, 1971.

WHEATLEY, PHILLIS

Collins, Terence. "Phillis Wheatley; the Dark Side of the Poetry." Phylon 36 (March 1975): 78-88.

Jamison, Angelene. "Analysis of Selected Poetry of Phillis Wheatley." Journal of Negro Education 43 (Summer 1974): 408-416.

Matson, R. Lynn. "Phillis Wheatley--Soul Sister?" Phylon 33 (Fall 1972): 222-230.

Silverman, Kenneth. "Four New Letters by Phillis Wheatley." Early American Literature 8 (Winter 1974): 257-271.

Smith, Eleanor. "Phillis Wheatley: A Black Perspective." Journal of Negro Education 43 (Summer 1974): 401-407.

Walker, Alice. "In Search of Our Mothers' Gardens." Ms. 2 (May 1974): 64-70, 105.

WHITE, PATRICK

Beston, John B. "Love and Sex in a Staid Spinster: The Aunt's Story." Quadrant 73 (1971): 22-27.

_____. "Voss's Proposal and Laura's Acceptance Letter: The Struggle for Dominance in Voss." Quadrant 78 (1972): 24-30.

Core, George. "A Terrible Majesty: The Novels of Patrick White." Hollins Critic 11 (February 1974): 1-16.

Green, Dorothy. "Queen Lear or Cleopatra Rediviva? Patrick White's The Eye of the Storm." Meanjin Quarterly 32 (December 1973): 395-405.

McLeod, A. L. "Patrick White: Nobel Prize for Literature 1973." Books Abroad 48 (Summer 1974): 439-445.

Morley, Patricia. The Mystery of Unity: Theme and Technique in the Novels of Patrick White. Montreal and London: McGill-Queen's University Press, 1972.

WHITMAN, RUTH

McDonnell, Jane Taylor. "Beyond the Confessional." Carleton Miscellany 14 (Fall-Winter 1973-74): 107-111. (Review of The Passion of Lizzie Borden: New and Selected Poems.)

WILLIAMS, CHARLES

Myers, Doris T. "Brave New World: The Status of Women According to Tolkien, Lewis and Williams." Cimarron Review 17 (1971): 13-19.

Trowbridge, C. W. "Beatricean Character in the Novels of Charles Williams." Sewanee Review 79 (Summer 1971): 335-343.

WILLIAMS, TENNESSEE

Cate, Hollis L. and Delma E. Presley. "Beyond Stereotype: Ambiguity in Amanda Wingfield." Notes on Mississippi Writers 3 (1971): 91-100.

Lyons, Anne Ward. "Myth and Agony: The Southern Woman as Belle." Ph. D. Dissertation, Bowling Green State University, 1974.

Watson, Roy Alvin. "The Archetype of the Family in the Drama of Tennessee Williams." Ph. D. Dissertation, The University of Tulsa, 1973.

WILLIAMS, WILLIAM CARLOS

DeWitt, John Francis. "The Beautiful Thing: William Carlos Williams and Women." Ph. D. Dissertation, The University of Connecticut, 1973.

Weiss, Jeri Lynn. "The Feminine Assertion: Women in the World of William Carlos Williams." Ph. D. Dissertation, University of California, Los Angeles, 1973.

Westler, Max Jay. "The Sexual Orchard: A Study of

Masculine and Feminine Relationships in the Early
Poetry of William Carlos Williams." Ph. D. Dissertation, Columbia University, 1974.

WILMOT, JOHN

Brooks, Elmer L. "An Unpublished Restoration Satire
on the Court Ladies." English Language Notes 10
(March 1973): 201-208.

WILSON, ANGUS

Fletcher, John. "Women in Crisis: Louise and Mrs.
Eliot." Critical Quarterly 15 (Summer 1973): 157-
170.

Shaw, Valerie A. "The Middle Age of Mrs. Eliot and
Late Call: Angus Wilson's Traditionalism." Critical Quarterly 12 (Spring 1970): 9-27.

WILSON, ETHEL D.

Birbalsingh, Frank. "Ethel Wilson." Canadian Literature no. 49 (Summer 1971): 35-46.

Floody, Brian Edward. "Concepts of Love in the Work
of Ethel Wilson." M. A. Thesis, University of New
Brunswick, n. d.

MacDonald, R. D. "Serious Whimsy." Canadian Literature no. 63 (Winter 1975): 40-51.

McLay, C. M. "The Initiation of Mrs. Golightly."
Journal of Canadian Fiction 1 (Summer 1972): 52-55.

Trainor, William J. "Fate as an Outgrowth of Character
in the Novels of Ethel Wilson." M. A. Thesis, University of New Brunswick, n. d.

Urbas, Jeanette. "Equations and Flutes." Journal of
Canadian Fiction 1 (Spring 1972): 69-73.

_____. "Perquisites of Love." Canadian Literature
no. 59 (Winter 1974): 6-15.

WITTIG, MONIQUE

Beauman, Sally. New York Times Book Review, 10

October 1971, p. 5. (Review of Les Guérillères.)

Durand, Laura G. "Heroic Feminism as Art." Novel (Fall 1974): 71-77. (Review Essay.)

Sale, Roger. New York Review of Books, 16 December 1971, p. 23. (Review of Les Guérillères.)

Spraggins, Mary Pringle. "Myth and Ms.: Entrapment and Liberation in Monique Wittig's Les Guérillères." Paper presented at the Midwest Modern Language Association, St. Louis, 1 November 1974.

WOERNER, ULRIKA CAROLINA

Scholtz, Sigrid Gerda. "Images of Womanhood in the Works of German Female Dramatists 1892-1918." Ph.D. Dissertation, Johns Hopkins University, 1971.

WOOLF, VIRGINIA

Alexander, Jean. Venture of Form in the Novels of Virginia Woolf. Port Washington, N.Y.: Kennikat Press, 1974.

Ames, Kenneth J. "Elements of Mock-Heroic in Virginia Woolf's Mrs. Dalloway." Modern Fiction Studies 18 (Autumn 1972): 363-374.

Barnett, Alan W. Who Is Jacob? The Quest for Identity in the Writing of Virginia Woolf. Atlantic Highlands, N.J.: Humanities, forthcoming.

Bazin, Nancy Topping. Virginia Woolf and the Androgynous Vision. New Brunswick, N.J.: Rutgers University Press, 1973.

_____. "Virginia Woolf's Quest for Equilibrium." Modern Language Quarterly 32 (September 1971): 305-319.

Beja, Morris, ed. Virginia Woolf, 'To the Lighthouse': A Casebook. London: Macmillan, 1970.

Beker, Miroslav. "London as a Principle of Structure in Mrs. Dalloway." Modern Fiction Studies 18 (Autumn 1972): 375-385.

Bell, Millicent. "Virginia Woolf Now." Massachusetts Review 14 (Autumn 1973): 655-687.

Bell, Quentin. Virginia Woolf: A Biography. New York: Harcourt, Brace, Jovanovich, 1972.

Blanchard, Margaret. "Socialization in Mrs. Dalloway." College English 34 (November 1972): 287-304.

Chapman, R. T. "'The Lady in the Looking Glass': Modes of Perception in a Short Story by Virginia Woolf." Modern Fiction Studies 18 (Autumn 1972): 331-337.

Conklin, Anna Marie. "Historical and Sociocultural Elements in the Novels of Virginia Woolf." Ph. D. Dissertation, The University of North Carolina at Chapel Hill, 1974.

Corsa, Helen Storm. "To the Lighthouse: Death, Mourning and Transfiguration." Literature and Psychology 21 (1971): 115-131.

Cumings, Melinda Feldt. "Night and Day: Virginia Woolf's Visionary Synthesis of Reality." Modern Fiction Studies 18 (Autumn 1972): 339-349.

DiBattista, Maria Alba. "The Romance of Self: The Early Novels of Virginia Woolf." Ph. D. Dissertation, Yale University, 1973.

DiBona, Helene R. "The Fiction of Virginia Woolf: A Quest for Reality." Ph. D. Dissertation, University of California, Berkeley, 1970.

Donovan, Josephine. "Feminist Style Criticism." In Female Studies VI: Closer to the Ground, pp. 139-149. Edited by Nancy Hoffman, Cynthia Secor, Adrian Tinsley. Old Westbury, N. Y.: Feminist Press, 1972.

Drabble, Margaret. "How Not to be Afraid of Virginia Woolf." Ms. 1 (November 1972): 68-70, 72, 121.

Evans, Nancy Burr. "The Political Consciousness of Virginia Woolf: A Room of One's Own and Three Guineas." New Scholar 4 (Spring 1974): 167-180.

Fleishman, Avrom. Virginia Woolf: A Critical Reading. Baltimore: Johns Hopkins University Press, 1975.

Fox, Stephen D. "The Fish Pond as Symbolic Center in Between the Acts." Modern Fiction Studies 18 (Autumn 1972): 467-473.

Groves, Nora C. "The Case of Mrs. Dalloway." Virginia Woolf Quarterly 1 (Spring 1973): 51-59.

Hardwick, Elizabeth. Seduction and Betrayal. New York: Random House, 1974, pp. 125-139.

Harper, Howard M., Jr. "Mrs. Woolf and Mrs. Dalloway." In The Classic British Novel, pp. 220-239. Edited by Howard M. Harper, Jr. and Charles Edge. Athens: University of Georgia Press, 1972.

Haule, James Mark. "The Theme of Isolation in the Fiction of Dorothy M. Richardson, Virginia Woolf, and James Joyce." Ph. D. Dissertation, Wayne State University, 1974.

Heilbrun, Carolyn G. Toward a Recognition of Androgyny. New York: Knopf, 1973, pp. 76, 116-117, 126-127, 129, 130, 131-133, 149, 151-167, 169, 178.

Heine, Elizabeth. "The Evolution of the Interludes in The Waves." Virginia Woolf Quarterly 1 (Fall 1972): 60-80.

Hoffman, A. C. "Subject and Object and the Nature of Reality: The Dialectic of To the Lighthouse." Texas Studies in Literature and Language 13 (Winter 1972): 691-703.

Katz, Judith Nina. "Rooms of Their Own: Forms and Images of Liberation in Five Novels." Ph. D. Dissertation, The Pennsylvania State University, 1972.

Kelley, Alice Van Buren. The Novels of Virginia Woolf: Fact and Vision. Chicago: University of Chicago Press, 1973.

Latham, Jacqueline E. "Archetypal Figures in Mrs. Dalloway." Neuphilologische Mitteilungen 71 (1970): 480-488.

_____, ed. Critics on Virginia Woolf. Coral Gables, Fla.: University of Miami Press; London: Allen & Unwin, 1970.

Leaska, Mitchell A. "Virginia Woolf's The Voyage Out: Character Deduction and the Function of Ambiguity." Virginia Woolf Quarterly 1 (Winter 1973): 18-41.

_____. Virginia Woolf's "To the Lighthouse": A Study in Critical Method. New York: Columbia University Press, 1970.

Lewis, Thomas S. W., ed. Virginia Woolf: A Collection of Criticism. New York: McGraw-Hill, 1975.

Little, Judith. "Heroism in To the Lighthouse." In Images of Women in Fiction, pp. 237-242. Edited by Susan Koppelman Cornillon. Bowling Green, Ohio: Bowling Green University Press, 1972.

Love, Jean O. Worlds in Consciousness: Mythopoetic Thought in the Novels of Virginia Woolf. Berkeley: University of California Press, 1970.

Lubka, Nancy. "Virginia Woolf: A Feminist Appraisal." Women: A Journal of Liberation 2 (Fall 1970): 8-9.

McDowell, Margaret B. "Reflections on the New Feminism." Midwest Quarterly 12 (April 1971): 309-333.

McLaurin, Allen. Virginia Woolf: The Echoes Enslaved. London: Cambridge University Press, 1973.

Madison, Elizabeth Christen. "Reality and Imagery in the Novels of Virginia Woolf and Nathalie Sarraute." Ph.D. Dissertation, Indiana University, 1974.

Majumdar, Robin and Allen McLaurin, eds. Virginia Woolf: The Critical Heritage. Boston: Routledge & Kegan Paul, 1975.

Manley, Seon and Susan Belcher. O, Those Extraordinary Women! Philadelphia: Chilton, 1972, pp. 237-242, 301-306.

Morgan, Ellen. "Humanbecoming: Form and Focus in the Neo-Feminist Novel." In Images of Women in

Fiction, pp. 189- 190-192, 194. Edited by Susan Koppelman Cornillon. Bowling Green, Ohio: Bowling Green University Press, 1972.

Morganstern, Barry. "The Self-Conscious Narrator in Jacob's Room." Modern Fiction Studies 18 (Autumn 1972): 351-361.

Naremore, James. "A World Without a Self: The Novels of Virginia Woolf." Novel 5 (Winter 1972): 122-134.

_____. The World Without a Self: Virginia Woolf and the Novel. New Haven: Yale University Press, 1973.

Noble, Joan Russell, ed. Recollections of Virginia Woolf by her Contemporaries. New York: Morrow, 1972.

Novak, Jane. The Razor Edge of Balance: A Study of Virginia Woolf. Coral Gables: University of Miami Press, forthcoming.

Oates, Joyce Carol. New Heaven, New Earth: The Visionary Experience in Literature. New York: Vanguard Press, 1974.

Ozick, Cynthia. "Mrs. Virginia Woolf." Commentary 56 (August 1973): 33-44.

Peck, Ellen Margaret McKee. "Exploring the Feminine: A Study of Janet Lewis, Ellen Glasgow, Anaïs Nin, and Virginia Woolf." Ph. D. Dissertation, Stanford University, 1974.

Philipson, Morris. "Mrs. Dalloway, 'What's the Sense of Your Parties!'" Critical Inquiry 1 (September 1974): 123-148.

Phillips, Ann H. "The Anonymous Self: A Study of Virginia Woolf's Novels." Ph. D. Dissertation, Stanford University, 1972.

Pratt, Annis. "Sexual Imagery in To the Lighthouse: A New Feminist Approach." Modern Fiction Studies 18 (Autumn 1972): 417-431.

_____. "Women and Nature in Modern Fiction." Contemporary Literature 13 (Autumn 1972): 476-490.

Proudfit, Sharon W. "Lily Briscoe's Painting: A Key to Personal Relationships in To the Lighthouse." Criticism 13 (Winter 1971): 26-38.

_____. "Virginia Woolf: Reluctant Feminist in 'The Years.'" Criticism 17 (Winter 1975): 59-73.

Rachman, Shalom. "Clarissa's Attic: Virginia Woolf's Mrs. Dalloway Reconsidered." Twentieth Century Literature 18 (January 1972): 3-18.

Richardson, Betty. "Beleaguered Bloomsbury: Virginia Woolf, Her Friends, and Their Critics." Papers on Language & Literature 10 (Spring 1974): 207-221. (Review Essay.)

Richardson, Robert O. "Point of View in Virginia Woolf's The Waves." Texas Studies in Literature and Language 14 (Winter 1973): 691-709.

Richter, Harvena. [Review.] Modern Fiction Studies 19 (Winter 1973-74): 616-620.

_____. Virginia Woolf: The Inward Voyage. Princeton, N.J.: Princeton University Press, 1970.

Robinson, Deborah Sue. "'Frigidity' and the Aesthetic Vision: A Study of Karen Horney and Virginia Woolf." Ph.D. Dissertation, University of Rochester, 1974.

Robinson, Lillian S. "Who's Afraid of a Room of One's Own?" In The Politics of Literature, pp. 359-407 passim. Edited by Louis Kampf and Paul Lauter. New York: Pantheon Books, 1972.

Rogat, Ellen Hawkes. "A Form of One's Own." Mosaic 8 (Fall 1974): 77-90.

Rose, Phyllis. "Mrs. Ramsay and Mrs. Woolf." Women's Studies 1 (1973): 199-216.

Rosenbaum, S. P. "The Philosophical Realism of Virginia Woolf." In English Literature and British

Philosophy, pp. 316-356. Edited by S. P. Rosenbaum. Chicago: University of Chicago Press, 1971.

Ruotolo, Lucio P. "Clarissa Dalloway." Six Existential
Heroes: The Politics of Faith. Cambridge: Harvard
University Press, 1973, pp. 13-35.

Samuels, Marilyn Schauer. "The Symbolic Function of
the Sun in Mrs. Dalloway." Modern Fiction Studies
18 (Autumn 1972): 387-399.

Schlack, Beverly Ann. "A Freudian Look at Mrs. Dalloway." Literature and Psychology 23 (1973): 49-58.

Shanahan, Mary Steussy. "The Artist and the Resolution
of The Waves." Modern Language Quarterly 36
(March 1975): 54-74.

_____. "Between the Acts: Virginia Woolf's Final
Endeavor in Art." Texas Studies in Literature and
Language 14 (Spring 1972): 123-138.

Sharma, O. P. "Feminism as Aesthetic Vision: A Study
of Virginia Woolf's Mrs. Dalloway." Punjab University Research Bulletin (Arts) 2 (1971): 1-10.

_____. "Virginia Woolf's Night and Day." Indian
Journal of English Studies 12 (1971): 55-66.

Spacks, Patricia M. The Female Imagination. New
York: Knopf, 1975.

_____. "Taking Care: Some Women Novelists."
Novel 6 (Fall 1972): 36-51.

Sprague, Claire, comp. Virginia Woolf: A Collection
of Critical Essays. Englewood Cliffs, N. J.:
Prentice Hall, 1971.

Stevens, Michael. V. Sackville-West. New York:
Charles Scribner's Sons, 1974.

Stewart, Jack F. "Existence and Symbol in The Waves."
Modern Fiction Studies 18 (Autumn 1972): 433-447.

Sukenick, Lynn. "Sense and Sensibility in Women's

Fiction: Studies in the Novels of George Eliot, Virginia Woolf, Anaïs Nin, and Doris Lessing." Ph. D. Dissertation, The City University of New York, 1974.

Trautman, Joanne. The Jessamy Brides: The Friendship of Virginia Woolf and V. Sackville-West. University Park: The Pennsylvania State University, 1973.

_____. "A Talk with Nigel Nicolson." Virginia Woolf Quarterly 1 (Fall 1972): 38-44.

Vogler, Thomas A., comp. Twentieth Century Interpretations of "To the Lighthouse": A Collection of Critical Essays. Englewood Cliffs, N. J.: Prentice-Hall, 1970.

Watson, Sara Ruth. V. Sackville-West. New York: Twayne, 1972.

Weiser, Barbara. "Criticism of Virginia Woolf from 1956 to the Present: A Selected Checklist with an Index to Studies of Separate Works." Modern Fiction Studies 18 (Autumn 1972): 477-486.

Whitehead, Lee M. "The Shawl and the Skull: Virginia Woolf's 'Magic Mountain.'" Modern Fiction Studies 18 (Autumn 1972): 401-415.

Wyatt, Jean M. "Mrs. Dalloway: Literary Allusion as Structural Metaphor." PMLA 88 (May 1973): 440-451.

Zak, Michele Wender. "Feminism and the New Novel." Ph. D. Dissertation, Ohio State University, 1973.

WYCHERLY, WILLIAM

Freedman, W. "Impotence and Self-Destruction in The Country Wife." English Studies 53 (October 1972): 421-431.

Hallett, Charles A. "The Hobbesian Substructure of The Country Wife." Papers on Language and Literature 9 (Fall 1973): 380-395.

Jackson, Wallace. "The Country Wife: The Premises of Love and Lust." South Atlantic Quarterly 72 (1973): [540]-546.

Martia, Dominic Francis. "The Restoration Love Ethos and the Representation of Love in the Plays of William Wycherley." Ph. D. Dissertation, Loyola University of Chicago, 1972.

Schermerhorn, Karen Russell. "Women in Wycherley: Their Role in His Social Criticism." Ph. D. Dissertation, University of Minnesota, 1974.

Suwannabha, Sumitra. "The Feminine Eye: Augustan Society as Seen by Selected Women Dramatists of the Restoration and Early Eighteenth Century." Ph. D. Dissertation, Indiana University, 1973.

WYLIE, ELINOR

Gabelnick, Faith. "Making Connections: American Women Poets on Love." Ph. D. Dissertation, American University, 1974.

Homsley, Bonnie Sue. "The Life of Elinor Wylie." Ph. D. Dissertation, The University of Wisconsin, 1970.

Walker, Cheryl Lawson. "The Women's Tradition in American Poetry." Ph. D. Dissertation, Brandeis University, 1973.

-Y-

YEATS, WILLIAM BUTLER

Revard, Stella. "Yeats, Mallarmé, and the Archetypal Feminine." Papers on Language and Literature 8 (Supplement, Fall 1972): 112-127.

Runnels, James Alan. "Mother, Wife, and Lover: Symbolic Women in the Works of W. B. Yeats." Ph. D. Dissertation, Rutgers University, The State University of New Jersey, 1973.

YONGE, CHARLOTTE

Colby, Vineta. Yesterday's Woman: Domestic Realism in the English Novel. Princeton, N.J.: Princeton University Press, 1974.

Dennis, Barbara. "The Two Voices of Charlotte Yonge." Durham University Journal 34 (March 1973): 181-188.

Gorsky, Susan. "The Gentle Doubters: Images of Women in Englishwomen's Novels, 1840-1920." In Images of Women in Fiction, p. 35. Edited by Susan Koppelman Cornillon. Bowling Green, Ohio: Bowling Green University Press, 1972.

_____. "Old Maids and New Women: Alternatives to Marriage in Englishwomen's Novels, 1847-1915." Journal of Popular Culture 7 (Summer 1973): 68-85.

Moore, Katharine. Victorian Wives. New York: St. Martin's Press, 1974.

Showalter, Elaine Cottler. "The Double Standard: Criticism of Women Writers in England, 1845-1880." Ph.D. Dissertation, University of California, Davis, 1970.

-Z-

ZOLA, EMILE

Block, Haskell M. Naturalistic Triptych: The Fictive and the Real in Zola, Mann, and Dreiser. New York: Random, 1970.

Jennings, Chantal. "Zola feministe?" Cahiers Naturaliste 44 (1972): 172-187; 45:1-22.

Nelson, B. "Zola and the Ambiguities of Passion: 'Une Page d'amour.'" Essays in French Literature 10 (November 1973): 1-22.

Petrey, Sandy. "Stylistics and Society in La Curée." Modern Language Notes 89 (May 1974): 626-640.

Rosenberg, Rachelle A. "The Slaying of the Dragon:
An Archetypal Study of Zola's Germinal." Symposium: A Quarterly Journal in Modern Foreign Liter-
atures 26 (Winter 1972): 349-362.

GENERAL BIBLIOGRAPHY

Adburgham, Alison. Women in Print: Writing Women and Women's Magazines from the Restoration to the Accession of Victoria. London: Allen & Unwin, 1972.

Allen, Christine. "Plato on Women." Feminist Studies 2, nos. 2/3 (1975): 131-138.

Allen, Mary Inez. "The Necessary Blankness: Women in Major American Fiction of the Sixties." Ph.D. Dissertation, University of Maryland, 1973.

Alphonso-Karkala, John B. "Woman As Man's Resurrection in Kalevala and Mahabharata." Indian Literature 16 (1973): 70-83.

Arthur, Marylin B. "Early Greece: The Origins of the Western Attitude Toward Women." Arethusa 6 (Spring 1973): 7-58.

Atwood, Margaret. "Ice Women vs Earth Mothers." Survival: A Thematic Guide to Canadian Literature. Toronto: Anansi, 1972, pp. 195-212.

Backer, Dorothy Anne Liot. Precious Women. New York: Basic Books, 1974.

Barranger, Milly S. "The Cankered Rose: A Consideration of the Jacobean Tragic Heroine." CLA Journal 14 (December 1970): 178-186.

Basch, Françoise. Relative Creatures: Victorian Women in Society and the Novel. New York: Schocken, 1974.

Berg, Karin Westman. "Looking at Women in Literature." Scandinavian Review 63 (June 1975): 48-55.

Birky, Wilbur Joseph. "Marriage as Pattern and Metaphor in the Victorian Novel. " Ph. D. Dissertation, The University of Iowa, 1970.

Bitton, Livia E. "The Jewess as a Fictional Sex Symbol. " Bucknell Review 21 (Spring 1973): 63-86.

Blackwell, Frederick Warn. "Characterization of Women in Three Contemporary Hindi Playwrights: Jai Shankar Prasad, Lakshmi Narain Lal, and Mohan Rakesh. " Ph. D. Dissertation, The University of Wisconsin, 1973.

Boatner, Janet Williams. "Criseyde's Character in the Major Writers from Benoît through Dryden: The Changes and Their Significance. " Ph. D. Dissertation, The University of Wisconsin, 1970.

Bonin, Jane F. Major Themes in Prize-Winning American Drama. Metuchen, N. J. : Scarecrow Press, 1975.

Borenstein, Audrey F. "Reflections on Woman's Identity. " Georgia Review 26 (Summer 1972): 156-168.

Bradley, Sister Ritamary. "A Schema for the Study of the Characterization of Women in Medieval Literature. " Paper presented at the Midwest MLA meeting, St. Louis, November 1972. (Mimeographed.)

Brée, Germaine. Women Writers in France: Variations on a Theme. New Brunswick, N. J. : Rutgers University Press, 1973.

Brown, Russell M. "The Canadian Eve. " Journal of Canadian Fiction 3, no. 3 (1974): 89-93. (Review Essay.)

Broyard, A. "Woman as Stud: An Inquiry into Feminist Literature. " Mademoiselle 79 (July 1974): 98-99.

Buck, Janet T. "Pre-feudal Women. " Journal of the Rutgers University Library 34 (1971): 46-51.

Caldwell, Richard S. "The Misogyny of Eteocles. " Arethusa 6 (Fall 1973): 197-231.

Cassell, Anthony K. "Il Corbaccio and the Secundus Tradition. " Comparative Literature 25 (Fall 1973): 352-360.

Cazamian, Louis. The Social Novel in England 1830-1850. London and Boston: Kegan Paul, 1973.

Ch'en, Toyoko Yoshida. "Women in Confucian Society--A Study of Three T'an-Tz'u Narratives." Ph. D. Dissertation, Columbia University, 1974.

Chung, Ling. "Chinese Women and Literature--A Brief Survey." In The Orchid Boat: Women Poets of China, pp. 139-146. Edited by Kenneth Rexroth and Ling Chung. New York: McGraw-Hill, 1972.

Cicardo, Barbara Joan. "The Mystery of the American Eve: Alienation of the Feminine as a Tragic Theme in American Letters." Ph. D. Dissertation, St. Louis University, 1971.

Class, Bradley Mellon. "Fictional Treatment of Politics by Argentine Female Novelists." Ph. D. Dissertation, The University of New Mexico, 1974.

Clinton, Katherine B. "Femme et Philosophe: Enlightenment Origins of Feminism." Eighteenth-Century Studies 8 (Spring 1975): 283-299.

Codere, Annette. "The Evolving Role of Woman in Canadian Fiction in English and French." M. A. Thesis, University of Sherbrooke, 1973.

Cohn, Jan. "Women as Superfluous Characters in American Realism and Naturalism." Studies in American Fiction 1 (Autumn 1973): 154-162.

Colby, Vineta. The Singular Anomaly: Women Novelists of the Nineteenth Century. New York: New York University Press, 1970.

_____. Yesterday's Woman: Domestic Realism in the English Novel. Princeton, N. J.: Princeton University Press, 1974.

Cornillon, Susan Koppelman, ed. Images of Women in Fiction: Feminist Perspectives. Bowling Green, Ohio: Bowling Green University Press, 1972.

Cotter, James Finn. "Women Poets: Malign Neglect?" America, 17 February 1973, pp. 140-142.

Cottino-Jones, Marga. "Fabula vs Figura: Another Interpretation of the Griselda Story." Italica 50 (1973): 38-52.

Crain, Jane Larkin. "Feminist Fiction." Commentary 58 (December 1974): 58-62; Discussion, 59 (May 1975): 22-24.

Cranston, Edwin A. "A Bridge of Dreams." Monumenta Nipponica 27 (1972): 435-454. (Review of As I Crossed a Bridge of Dreams: Recollections of a Woman in Eleventh-Century Japan.)

Cumming, Alan. "Pauline Christianity and Greek Philosophy: A Study of the Status of Women." Journal of the History of Ideas 34 (October-December 1973): 517-528.

Cunningham, A. M. "We Have Seen the Future and It Is Feminine." Mademoiselle 76 (February 1973): 140-141.

Dean, Sharon Welch. "Lost Ladies: The Isolated Heroine in the Fiction of Hawthorne, James, Fitzgerald, Hemingway and Faulkner." Ph.D. Dissertation, University of New Hampshire, 1973.

Dickison, Sheila K. "Abortion in Antiquity." Arethusa 6 (Spring 1973): 159-166.

Dijkstra, Bram. "The Androgyne in Nineteenth-Century Art and Literature." Comparative Literature 26 (Winter 1974): 62-73.

Dinnick, Sarah Jane. "The Varied Roles of Women in Contemporary Canadian Fiction 1967-1972." M.A. Thesis, Université de Sherbrooke, n.d.

Dobbs, Jeanine. "Not Another Poetess: A Study of Female Experience in Modern American Poetry." Ph.D. Dissertation, University of New Hampshire, 1973.

Donovan, Josephine. "Feminist Style Criticism." In Female Studies VI: Closer to the Ground, pp. 139-149. Edited by Nancy Hoffman, Cynthia Secor, Adrian Tinsley. Old Westbury, N.Y.: Feminist Press, 1972. Also in Images of Women in Fiction, edited by Susan Koppelman Cornillon.

_____, ed. Feminist Literary Criticism: Explorations in Theory. Lexington: University of Kentucky Press, forthcoming.

Dover, K. J. "Classical Greek Attitudes to Sexual Behavior." Arethusa 6 (Spring 1973): 59-73.

Duffy, M. "Irate Accent." Time, 20 March 1972, pp. 98-99.

Duncan, Carol. "Happy Mothers and Other New Ideas in French Art." Art Bulletin 55 (December 1973): 570-583.

Earnest, Ernest. The American Eve in Fact and Fiction, 1775-1914. Urbana, Chicago, London: University of Illinois Press, 1974.

Edwards, Lee R., Mary Heath and Lisa Baskin, eds. Woman: An Issue. Boston: Little, Brown, 1972.

Evans, Nancy Burr. "The Value and Peril for Women of Reading Women Writers." In Images of Women in Fiction, pp. 306-312. Edited by Susan Koppelman Cornillon. Bowling Green, Ohio: Bowling Green University Press, 1972.

Feil, Doris. "The Female Page in Renaissance Drama." Ph.D. Dissertation, Arizona State University, 1971.

"Feminine Passivity in Fiction." Society 9 (March 1972): 12.

"Feminine Sensibility: A Forum." Harvard Advocate 106 (Winter 1973): 7-19.

Ferguson, Mary Anne. "Sexist Images of Women in Literature." In Female Studies V, pp. 77-83. Edited by Rae Lee Siporin. Pittsburgh: KNOW, 1972.

Ferguson, Moira Campbell. "Declarations of Independence: The Rebel Heroine, 1684-1800." Ph.D. Dissertation, University of Washington, 1973.

Ferrante, Joan M. Woman as Image in Medieval Literature: From the Twelfth Century to Dante. New York: Columbia University Press, 1975.

Fishel, Elizabeth. "Women's Fiction: Who's Afraid of Virginia Woolf." Ramparts, June 1973, pp. 45-48.

Fitzgerald, R. D. "Australian Women Poets." Texas Quarterly 15 (Summer 1972): 75-97.

"Five Important Playwrights Talk about Theatre without Compromise and Sexism." Mademoiselle 75 (August 1972): 288-289.

Flora, C. B. "Passive Female: Her Comparative Image by Class and Culture in Women's Magazine Fiction." Marriage and Family 33 (August 1971): 435-444.

Forrey, Carolyn. "The New Woman Revisited." Women's Studies 2 (1974): 37-56.

Fowler, Lois Josephs. "Sirens and Seeresses: Women in Literature and the High School Curriculum." English Journal 62 (November 1973): 1123-1126, 1159-1161.

Franklin, Phyllis. "Traditional Literary Study--In the Subjunctive Mood." In Female Studies VI: Closer to the Ground, pp. 38-56. Edited by Nancy Hoffman, Cynthia Secor, Adrian Tinsley. Old Westbury, N.Y.: Feminist Press, 1972.

Franz, Marie Luise von. Problems of the Feminine in Fairytales. New York: Spring, 1972.

Frederick, John T. "Hawthorne's 'Scribbling Women.'" New England Quarterly 48 (June 1975): 231-240.

Friedman, Leonard M. "The Nature and Role of Women as Conceived by Representative Authors of Eighteenth-Century France." Ph.D. Dissertation, New York University, 1970.

Friend, Beverly. "Virgin Territory: Women and Sex in Science Fiction." Extrapolation 14 (December 1972): 49-59.

Gabelnick, Faith. "Making Connections: American Women Poets on Love." Ph.D. Dissertation, American University, 1974.

Gant, Lisbeth. "The Black Woman in African Literature."

The New York Amsterdam News, 1 January 1972.

_____. "The Black Woman in American Literature."
The New York Amsterdam News, 27 November 1971.

García, E. Rosalinda. "The Picaresque Tradition of the
Female Rogue: Differences from and Similarities to the
Pícaro." Ph. D. Dissertation, Columbia University, 1973.

Gasiorowska, Xenia. "Two Decades of Love and Marriage
in Soviet Fiction." Russian Review 34 (January 1975):
10-21.

Getsi, Lucia. "Inventing Us: The Open Word." Mundus
Artium 7 no. 2 (1974): 7-9.

Gibson, Wendy. "Women and the Notion of Propriety in the
French Theatre (1628-1643)." Forum for Modern Language Studies 11 (January 1975): 1-14.

Ginsburg, Jane. "And Then There Was Good Old Nancy
Drew." Ms. 2 (January 1974): 93-94.

Goodwater, Leanna. Women in Antiquity: An Annotated
Bibliography. Metuchen, N. J.: Scarecrow Press, 1975.

Gorsky, Susan. "The Gentle Doubters: Images of Women in
Englishwomen's Novels, 1840-1920." In Images of Wom-
en in Fiction, pp. 28-54. Edited by Susan Koppelman
Cornillon. Bowling Green, Ohio: Bowling Green University Press, 1972.

_____. "Old Maids and New Women: Alternatives to
Marriage in Englishwomen's Novels, 1847-1915." Journal of Popular Culture 7 (Summer 1973): 68-85.

Gould, Mary Anne. "Women's Roles in Anglo-Saxon and
Eddic Poetry." Ph. D. Dissertation, University of Oregon, 1974.

Goulianos, Joan. "Women and the Avant-Garde Theater."
In Woman: An Issue, pp. 257-267. Edited by Lee R.
Edwards, Mary Heath and Lisa Baskin. Boston: Little,
Brown, 1972.

Griffin, Susan, Norma Leistiko, Ntozake Shange, and Miriam
Schapiro. "Women and the Creative Process: A

Discussion." Mosaic 8 (Fall 1974): 91-118.

Hallett, Judith P. "The Role of Women in Roman Elegy: Counter-Cultural Feminism." Arethusa 6 (Spring 1973): 103-124. Reply, 7 (Fall 1974): 211-217.

Halperin, John. Egoism and Self-Discovery in the Victorian Novel: Studies in the Ordeal of Knowledge in the Nineteenth Century. New York: Burt Franklin, 1974.

Halsband, Robert. "'The Female Pen': Women and Literature in Eighteenth-Century England." History Today 24 (October 1974): 702-709.

_____. "Ladies of Letters in the Eighteenth Century." In Stuart and Georgian Moments, pp. 271-291. Edited by Earl Miner. Berkeley: University of California Press, 1972.

Hampsten, Elizabeth. "A Woman's Map of Lyric Poetry." College English 34 (May 1973): 1075-1081.

Hansen, Carol Louise. "Woman as Individual in English Renaissance Drama: A Defiance of the Masculine Code." Ph. D. Dissertation, Arizona State University, 1975.

Hardwick, Elizabeth. Seduction and Betrayal: Women and Literature. New York: Random House, 1974.

Harris, Joseph. "'Maiden in the Mor Lay' and the Medieval Magdalene Tradition." Journal of Medieval and Renaissance Studies 1 (1971): 59-87.

Hastings, Marshall David. "Androgynous Imagery in Nineteenth-Century French Poetry." Ph. D. Dissertation, Stanford University, 1974.

Heilbrun, Carolyn. "Further Notes Toward a Recognition of Androgyny." Women's Studies 2 (1974): 143-149.

_____. "The Masculine Wilderness of the American Novel." Saturday Review 29 (January 1972): 41-44.

_____. Toward a Recognition of Androgyny. New York: Knopf, 1973.

Herman, Sondra R. "Loving Courtship or the Marriage

Market? The Ideal and Its Critics 1871-1911." American Quarterly 25 (May 1973): 235-252.

Heyob, Sharon Kelly. "The Cult of Isis among Women in the Graeco-Roman World." Ph. D. Dissertation, The Catholic University of America, 1973.

Hillman, Judith Zoe Stevinson. "An Analysis of Male and Female Roles in Two Periods of Children's Literature." Ph. D. Dissertation, University of Nebraska-Lincoln, 1973.

Hoekstra, Ellen. "The Pedestal Myth Reinforced: Women's Magazine Fiction, 1900-1920." In New Dimensions in Popular Culture. Edited by Russel B. Nye. Bowling Green, Ohio: Bowling Green University Popular Press, 1972.

Hoerchner, Susan Jane. "'I Have to Keep the Two Things Separate'; Polarity in Women in the Contemporary American Novel." Ph. D. Dissertation, Emory University, 1973.

Hoffman, Nancy. "Life in the Feminist Classroom." Ms. 2 (September 1973): 49-50, 84-85.

_____. "Reading Women's Poetry: The Meaning and Our Lives." College English 34 (October 1972): 48-62.

_____. "Women All Our Lives: Reading and Writing Women's Autobiographies." In Female Studies VI: Closer to the Ground, pp. 178-191. Edited by Nancy Hoffman, Cynthia Secor, Adrian Tinsley. Old Westbury, N. Y.: Feminist Press, 1972.

_____, Cynthia Secor, and Adrian Tinsley, eds. Female Studies VI: Closer to the Ground. Old Westbury, N. Y.: Feminist Press, 1972.

Hogeland, Ronald W. "'The Female Appendage': Feminine Life-Styles in America, 1820-1860." Civil War History 17 (June 1971): 101-114.

Howe, Florence. "Feminism and Literature." In Images of Women in Fiction, pp. 253-277. Edited by Susan Koppelman Cornillon. [Originally published as "Feminism, Fiction, and the Classroom." Soundings: An Interdisciplinary Journal (Fall 1972).]

Ifkovic, Edward J. "God's Country and the Woman: The Development of an American Identity in the Popular Novel 1893-1913." Ph.D. Dissertation, University of Massachusetts, 1972.

James, Katherine Harriett. "The Widow in Jacobean Drama." Ph.D. Dissertation, The University of Tennessee, 1973.

Janeway, Elizabeth. Between Myth and Morning: Women Awakening. New York: William Morrow, 1974.

Jones, James P. "Nancy Drew, WASP Super Girl of the 1930's." Journal of Popular Culture 6 (Spring 1973): 707-717.

Jong, Erica. "The Artist as Housewife." Ms. 1 (December 1972): 64-66, 100, 104-105. Also in The First Ms. Reader. New York: Warner Paperback Library, 1973, pp. 111-122.

Kaplan, Ann. "Feminist Criticism: A Survey with Analysis of Methodological Problems." Papers on Women's Studies 1 (February 1974): 150-176.

Kaplan, Sydney J. Feminine Consciousness in the Modern British Novel. Urbana: University of Illinois Press, forthcoming.

_____. "The Feminine Consciousness in the Novels of Five Twentieth-Century British Women." Ph.D. Dissertation, University of California, Los Angeles, 1971.

Karlinsky, S. "Fiction and Policy: The Hard-Worked Heroines." Nation, 21 September 1970, pp. 245-248. (Soviet fiction.)

Katz, Judith Nina. "Rooms of Their Own: Forms and Images of Liberation in Five Novels." Ph.D. Dissertation, The Pennsylvania State University, 1972.

Katz-Stoker, Fraya. "The Other Criticism: Feminism vs. Formalism." In Images of Women in Fiction, pp. 313-325. Edited by Susan Koppelman Cornillon. Bowling Green, Ohio: Bowling Green University Press, 1972.

Kaye, Melanie. "Diving Into the Wreck: The Woman Writer in the Twentieth Century." In Female Studies VI:

Closer to the Ground, pp. 68-77. Edited by Nancy Hoffman, Cynthia Secor, Adrian Tinsley. Old Westbury, N.Y.: Feminist Press, 1972.

Kazin, Alfred. "Cassandras: Porter to Oates." Bright Book of Life: American Novelists and Storytellers from Hemingway to Mailer. Boston and Toronto: Little, Brown, 1973.

Keene, Donald. "Feminine Sensibility in the Heian Era." Landscapes and Portraits: Appreciations of Japanese Culture. Tokyo: Kodansha, 1971; Palo Alto, Calif.: International, 1971, pp. 26-39.

Kennedy, Thomas Corbin. "Anglo-Norman Poems about Love, Women, and Sex from British Museum Ms. Harley 2253." Ph.D. Dissertation, Columbia University, 1973.

Keyser, Lester Joseph. "Joan of Arc in Nineteenth Century English Literature." Ph.D. Dissertation, Tulane University, 1970.

Klein, Norma. "Portraits of Women." Mademoiselle 80 (November 1974): 22.

Klinger, George Charles. "English She-Tragedy, 1680-1715; Its Characteristics and Its Relationship to the Sentimental Tradition." Ph.D. Dissertation, Columbia University, 1970.

Klotman, Phyllis R. "The White Bitch Archetype in Contemporary Black Fiction." Bulletin of the Midwest Modern Language Association 6 (Spring 1973): 96-110.

Koros, Carole Marie. "The Image of the Woman in Nonfiction and the Comedia during the Golden Age of Spain." Ph.D. Dissertation, University of Pennsylvania, 1973.

Kraus, Willis Keith. "A Critical Survey of the Contemporary Adolescent-Girl Problem Novel." Ph.D. Dissertation, Southern Illinois University, 1974.

Kutrieh, Marcia Geib. "Popular British Romantic Women Poets." Ph.D. Dissertation, Bowling Green University, 1974.

Lacy, Kluenter Wesley. "An Essay on Feminine Fiction, 1757-1803." Ph.D. Dissertation, The University of Wisconsin, 1972.

Lancashire, Anne. "The Second Maiden's Tragedy: A Jacobean Saint's Life." The Review of English Studies 25 (August 1974): 267-279.

Landa, Louis A. "Of Silkworms and Farthingales and the Will of God." In Studies in the Eighteenth Century, vol. 2, pp. 259-277. Edited by R. F. Brissenden. Toronto: University of Toronto Press, 1973.

Larson, Charles R. "Pamela in Africa: Onitsha Market Literature." The Emergence of African Fiction. Bloomington and London: Indiana University Press, 1971, pp. 66-92.

Lee, Barbara Gail. "Victim or Adventuress: Changing Perspectives on the Courtesan of the Nineteenth-Century French Stage." Ph.D. Dissertation, The Florida State University, 1972.

Lieberman, Marcia R. "Sexism and the Double Standard in Literature." In Images of Women in Fiction, pp. 326-338. Edited by Susan Koppelman Cornillon. Bowling Green, Ohio: Bowling Green University Press, 1972.

_____. "'Some Day My Prince Will Come': Female Acculturation through the Fairy Tale." College English 34 (1972): 383-395.

Lippert, Anne. "The Changing Role of Women as Viewed in the Literature of English- and French-Speaking West Africa." Ph.D. Dissertation, Indiana University, 1972.

Lipton, Virginia Anne. "Women in Today's World: A Study of Five French Women Novelists." Ph.D. Dissertation, the University of Wisconsin, 1972.

Loustanau, Martha Oehmke. "Mexico's Contemporary Women Novelists." Ph.D. Dissertation, The University of New Mexico, 1973.

Lowell, Sondra. "New Feminist Theater." Ms. 1 (August 1972): 17-18, 22-23.

Lupton, Mary Jane and Emily Toth. "Out, Damned Spot!" Ms. 2 (January 1974): 97-99.

Lyons, Anne Ward. "Myth and Agony: The Southern Woman as Belle." Ph. D. Dissertation, Bowling Green State University, 1974.

McDowell, Margaret D. "Reflections on the New Feminism." Midwest Quarterly 12 (April 1971): 309-334.

Mackay, B. "Women on the Rocks." Saturday Review World, 6 April 1974, pp. 48-49.

McKendrick, M. "Mujer esquiva--A Measure of the Feminist Sympathies of Seventeenth-Century Spanish Dramatists." Hispanic Review 40 (Spring 1972): 162-197.

McKendrick, Melveena. Woman and Society in the Spanish Drama of the Golden Age. London: Cambridge University Press, 1974.

McKenna, Isobel. "Women in Canadian Literature." Canadian Literature no. 62 (Autumn 1974): 69-78.

McRobbie, Kenneth. "Women and Love: Some Aspects of Competition in Late Medieval Society." Mosaic 5 (Winter 1971-72): 139-168.

"Madonna or Whore?" Human Behavior, October 1974, pp. 47-48.

Magaw, Barbara Louise. "The Female Characters in Prose Chivalric Romance in England, 1475-1603: Their Patterns and Their Influence." Ph. D. Dissertation, University of Maryland, 1973.

Manley, Seon and Susan Belcher. O, Those Extraordinary Women! or the Joys of Literary Lib. Philadelphia: Chilton, 1972.

Martines, Lauro. "A Way of Looking at Women in Renaissance Florence." Journal of Medieval and Renaissance Studies 4 (Spring 1974): 15-28.

Mattus, Martha Elizabeth. "The 'Fallen Woman' in the Fin de Siècle English Drama: 1884-1914." Ph. D. Dissertation, Cornell University, 1974.

Mayor, Mara. "Fears and Fantasies of the Anti-Suffragists."
Connecticut Review 7 (April 1974): 64-74.

Melani, Lilia. "Hidden Motives: A Study of Power and Wom-
en in British Periodical Fiction, 1864." Ph. D. Dissertation, Indiana University, 1973.

Meldrum, Barbara. "Images of Women in Western American
Literature." (Western American Writers Series) Deland,
Fla.: Everett/Edwards, n. d. (Cassette.)

Miller, Nancy Kipnis. "Gender and Genre: An Analysis of
Literary Femininity in the Eighteenth-Century Novel."
Ph. D. Dissertation, Columbia University, 1974.

Miller, Robert P. "The Wounded Heart: Courtly Love and
the Medieval Antifeminist Tradition." Women's Studies
2, no. 3 (1974): 335-350.

Millett, Kate. "The Debate over Women: Ruskin versus
Mill." Victorian Studies 14 (September 1970): 63-81.

_____. Sexual Politics. New York: Avon, 1971.

Miner, Earl, ed. Stuart and Georgian Moments. Berkeley:
University of California Press, 1972.

Moers, Ellen. "Money, the Job, and Little Women." Commentary 35 (January 1973): 57-65. Reply with rejoinder:
E. Kaledin 55 (May 1973): 26.

Mollenkott, Virginia R. "The Bible and Women Today."
Texas Quarterly 16 (Autumn 1973): 58-65.

Moore, Katharine. Victorian Wives. New York: St. Martin's Press, 1974.

Morgan, Ellen. "Humanbecoming: Form and Focus in the
Neo-Feminist Novel." In Images of Women in Fiction,
pp. 183-205. Edited by Susan Koppelman Cornillon.
Bowling Green, Ohio: Bowling Green University Press,
1972.

_____. "Neo-Feminism and Modern Literature." Ph. D.
Dissertation, University of Pennsylvania, 1972.

Mullet, Olive Gale. "The War with Women and Words:

Lady Gregory's Destructive, Celtic Folklore Woman."
Ph. D. Dissertation, The University of Wisconsin, 1973.

Nagarkar, Jyotee Kamala Kant. "The Medea Theme in
French Dramatic Literature." Ph. D. Dissertation,
Wayne State University, 1971.

Nelson, Gayle. "The Double Standard in Adolescent Novels."
English Journal 64 (February 1975): 56-58.

Nin, Anaïs. "On Feminism and Creation." Michigan
Quarterly Review 13 (Winter 1974): 4-13.

Norton, David. "Toward an Epistemology of Romantic Love."
Centennial Review 14 (Fall 1970): 421-443.

Odd, Frank Lynn. "The Women of the Romancero." Ph. D.
Dissertation, University of Colorado, 1974.

Osmond, Rosalie E. "Body, Soul, and the Marriage Relationship: The History of an Analogy." Journal of the
History of Ideas 34 (April-June 1973): 283-290.

Oyler, Margaret Mary. "An Examination of the Heroine of
the Junior Novel in America as Reflected in Selected
Junior Novels, 1850-1960." Ed. D. Dissertation, Columbia University, 1970.

Parekh, Kishor. "Sensuous Women of Sigiriya." Orienta-
tions 1, no. 8 (August 1970): 30-39.

Parker, Jeraldine. "'Uneasy Survivors': Five Women
Writers 1896-1923." Ph. D. Dissertation, University of
Utah, 1973.

Parotti, Phillip Elliott. "The Female Warrior in the
Renaissance Epic." Ph. D. Dissertation, The University
of New Mexico, 1972.

Patai, D. "Utopia for Whom?" Aphra 5 (Summer 1974):
2-16.

Perry, Ruth. "Women, Letters, and the Origins of English
Fiction: A Study of the Early Epistolary Novel." Ph. D.
Dissertation, University of California, Santa Cruz, 1974.

Pomeroy, Sarah B. "Selected Bibliography on Women in

Antiquity." <u>Arethusa</u> 6 (Spring 1973): 125-157.

Potter, Vilma R. "New Politics, New Mothers." <u>CLA Journal</u> 16 (December 1972): 247-255. (Black women in Black drama.)

Pratt, Annis. "Archetypal Approaches to the New Feminist Criticism." <u>Bucknell Review</u> 21 (Spring 1973): 3-14.

_____. "The New Feminist Criticism." <u>College English</u> 32 (May 1971): 872-878.

_____. "Women and Nature in Modern Fiction." <u>Contemporary Literature</u> 13 (Autumn 1972): 476-490.

Pratt, Linda Ray. "The Abuse of Eve by the New World Adam." In <u>Images of Women in Fiction</u>, pp. 155-174. Edited by Susan Koppelman Cornillon. Bowling Green, Ohio: Bowling Green University Press, 1972.

Register, Cheryl. "Feminist Ideology and Literary Criticism." Ph.D. Dissertation, University of Chicago, 1973.

Reichert, William O. "Woman, Violence, and Social Order in America." <u>Centennial Review</u> 15 (Winter 1971): 1-22.

Reuben, Elaine. "Can a Young Girl from a Small Mining Town Find Happiness Writing Criticism for the New York Review of Books?" <u>College English</u> 34 (October 1972): 39-47.

Rich, Adrienne. "When We Dead Awaken: Writing as Re-Vision." <u>College English</u> 34 (October 1972): 18-30.

Roberts, W. D. "The Heroine Doesn't Have to Be an Idiot: Gothic Novels." <u>Writer</u> 88 (January 1975): 12-14.

Robinson, Lillian S. "Dwelling in Decencies: Radical Criticism and the Feminist Perspective." <u>College English</u> 32 (May 1971): 879-889.

_____. "Monstrous Regiment: The Lady Knight in Sixteenth-Century Epic." Ph.D. Dissertation, Columbia University, 1974.

_____. "Who's Afraid of a Room of One's Own?" In

The Politics of Literature, pp. 354-411. Edited by Louis Kampf and Paul Lauter. New York: Pantheon Books, 1972.

_____ and Lise Vogel. "Modernism and History." In Images of Women in Fiction, pp. 278-305. Edited by Susan Koppelman Cornillon. [Originally published in New Literary History 3 (Autumn 1971): 177-197.]

Roemer, Kenneth M. "Sex Roles, Utopia, and Change: The Family in Late Nineteenth-Century Utopian Literature." American Studies 13 (1972): 33-48.

Rosenstein, Harriet. "On Androgyny." Ms. 1 (May 1973): 38-43.

Rosenthal, Peggy. "Feminism and Life in Feminist Biography." College English 36 (October 1974): 180-184.

Rossi, Alice S. The Feminist Papers: From Adams to de Beauvoir. New York: Columbia University Press, 1973.

Rout, Savitri. Women Pioneers in Oriya Literature. Cuttack: Manorama Rout, 1971.

Rubin, Barbara L. "'Anti-Husbandry' and Self-Creation: A Comparison of Restoration Rake and Baudelaire's Dandy." Texas Studies in Literature and Language 14 (Winter 1973): 583-592.

Rudolf, Jo-Ellen Schwartz. "The Novels that Taught the Ladies: A Study of Popular Fiction Written by Women, 1702-1834." Ph.D. Dissertation, University of California, San Diego, 1972.

Russ, Joanna. "The Image of Women in Science Fiction." In Images of Women in Fiction, pp. 79-94. Edited by Susan Koppelman Cornillon. Bowling Green, Ohio: Bowling Green University Press, 1972. (Reprinted from Red Clay Reader.)

_____. "What Can a Heroine Do? Or Why Women Can't Write." In Images of Women in Fiction, pp. 3-20. Edited by Susan Koppelman Cornillon. Bowling Green, Ohio: Bowling Green University Press, 1972.

Salingar, Leo. "Medieval Stage Heroines." Shakespeare

and the Traditions of Comedy.   London: Cambridge
University Press, 1974.

Sargent, Lyman Tower.   "Women in Utopia."   Comparative
Literature Studies 10 (December 1973):   302-316.

Sargent, Pamela.   "Introduction: Women and Science Fiction."
Women of Wonder.   New York: Vintage, 1974.

Sass, Janet.   "A Literature Course of Our Own: Women's
Studies Without Walls."   In Female Studies VI: Closer
to the Ground, pp. 79-87.   Edited by Nancy Hoffman,
Cynthia Secor, Adrian Tinsley.   Old Westbury, N. Y. :
Feminist Press, 1972.

Scanlon, Leone.   "Essays on the Effect of Feminism and
Socialism Upon the Literature of 1880-1914."   Ph. D.
Dissertation, Brandeis University, 1973.

Schechter, Harold.   "Kali on Main Street: The Rise of the
Terrible Mother in America."   Journal of Popular Culture 7 (Fall 1973):   251-263.

Schmidt, Dolores Barracano.   "The Great American Bitch."
College English 32 (May 1971):   900-905.

Scholtz, Sigrid Gerda.   "Images of Womanhood in the Works
of German Female Dramatists: 1892-1918."   Ph. D.
Dissertation, Johns Hopkins University, 1971.

Schulman, Grace.   "Women the Inventors."   Nation, 11
December 1972, pp. 594-596.

Schupf, Harriet Warm.   "Single Women and Social Reform in
Mid-Nineteenth Century England: The Case of Mary Car-
penter."   Victorian Studies 17 (March 1974):   301-317.

Sebenthall, R. E.   "Too Much of a Good Thing?"   Arts in
Society 11 (Spring-Summer 1974):   165-166.   (Review
Essay.)

Shafer, Y. B.   "Liberated Women in American Plays of the
Past."   Players Magazine 49 (Spring 1974):   95-100.

Shaw, Sharon K.   "Medea on Pegasus: Some Speculations on
the Parallel Rise of Women and Melodrama on the Jacobean
Stage."   Ball State University Forum 14, no. 4 (1973):
13-21.

Shinn, Thelma J. Wardrop. "A Study of Women Characters in Contemporary American Fiction 1940-1970." Ph. D. Dissertation, Purdue University, 1972.

Showalter, Elaine. "Killing the Angel in the House: The Autonomy of Women Writers." Antioch Review 32 (June 1973): 339-353.

_____. "Women Writers and the Female Experience." Notes from the Third Year: Women's Liberation. P. O. Box AA, Old Chelsea Station, N. Y., 1971.

Simmons, Sarah Tawil. "Attitudes de Hamilton, Marivaux, Crebillon fils et Laclos envers la femme d'apres leurs oeuvres romanesques." Ph. D. Dissertation, University of Colorado, 1970.

Skeeter, Sharyn J. "Black Women Writers: Levels of Identity." Essence 4 (May 1973): 58-59, 76, 89.

Sloman, Judith. "The Female Quixote as an Eighteenth-Century Character Type." In Transactions of the Samuel Johnson Society of the Northwest, pp. 86-101. Edited by Robert H. Carnie. Calgary, Alberta: Samuel Johnson Society of the Northwest, 1972.

Slotkin, Richard. Regeneration through Violence: The Mythology of the American Frontier. Middletown, Conn.: Wesleyan University Press, 1973, pp. 491-506.

Smith, Henry Nash. "The Scribbling Women and the Cosmic Success Story." Critical Inquiry 1 (September 1974): 47-70.

Smith, Leslie. "Through Rose-Colored Glasses: Some American Victorian Sentimental Novels. In New Dimensions in Popular Culture, pp. 90-106. Edited by Russel B. Nye. Bowling Green, Ohio: Bowling Green University Popular Press, 1972.

Snow, Kimberly. "Images of Woman in the American Novel." Aphra 2 (Winter 1970): 56-68.

Spacks, Patricia M. The Female Imagination. New York: Knopf, 1975.

_____. "Fiction Chronicle." Hudson Review 27 (Summer

1974): 283-295. (Review Essay.)

_____. "Free Women." Hudson Review 24 (Winter 1971-72): 559-573.

_____. "Reflecting Women." Yale Review 63 (October 1973): 26-42.

Stanford, Ann. "Introduction." The Women Poets in English. New York: McGraw-Hill, 1972.

Steeves, Edna L. "Pre-Feminism in Some Eighteenth-Century Novels." Texas Quarterly 16 (Autumn 1973): 48-57.

Stein, Karen F. "Reflections in a Jagged Mirror: Some Metaphors of Madness." Aphra 6 (Spring 1975): 2-11.

Stern, Paula. "The Womanly Image: Character Assassination through the Ages." Atlantic Monthly 225 (March 1970): 87-90.

Stone, Donald D. "Victorian Feminism and the Nineteenth-Century Novel." Women's Studies 1 (1972): 65-92.

Sudrann, Jean. "Hearth and Horizon: Changing Concepts of the 'Domestic' Life of the Heroine." Massachusetts Review 14 (Spring 1973): 235-255.

Suwannabha, Sumitra. "The Feminine Eye: Augustan Society as Seen by Selected Women Dramatists of the Restoration and Early Eighteenth Century." Ph. D. Dissertation, Indiana University, 1973.

Swidler, Leonard. Women in Judaism. Metuchen, N. J.: Scarecrow Press, forthcoming.

Symes, Dal Streenan. "The Heroine's Search for Salvation in Later Nineteenth-Century British Popular Fiction." Ph. D. Dissertation, University of New Mexico, 1973.

Tayler, Irene. "The Woman Scaly." Bulletin of the Midwest Modern Language Association 6 (Spring 1973): 74-87.

Theodore, Terry. "A Critical Study of Domestic Themes in American Comedy from 1900-1918." Ph. D. Dissertation, The University of Michigan, 1971.

Thomas, C. G. "Matriarchy in Early Greece: The Bronze and Dark Ages." Arethusa 6 (Fall 1973): 173-195.

Thomas, Clara. "Journeys to Freedom." Canadian Literature 51 (1972): 11-19. (Nineteenth-Century female writers.)

Thompson, Roger. Women in Stuart England and America: A Comparative Study. London and Boston: Routledge & Kegan Paul, 1974.

Tobias, Richard C. "Popular Studies of Victorian Life." Victorian Studies 17 (December 1973): 209-215.

Toth, Susan Allen. "Sarah Orne Jewett and Friends: A Community of Interest." Studies in Short Fiction 9 (Summer 1972): 233-242.

Tufte, Virginia. The Poetry of Marriage: The Epithalamium in Europe and Its Development in England. Berkeley: California University Press, 1970.

Turco, Lewis. "The Matriarchy of American Poetry." College English 34 (May 1973): 1067-1074.

Twitchell, James. "Lolita as Bildungsroman." Genre 7 (September 1974): 272-278.

Vicinus, Martha, ed. Suffer and Be Still: Women in the Victorian Age. Bloomington: Indiana University Press, 1972.

Vos, F. "The Rôle of Women in Tokugawa Classicism." Acta Orientalia Neerlandica. Leiden: Brill, 1971, pp. 206-213.

Voth, Ruth Anne. "The Lyric Strain: A Study of the Heroine of the Old South." Ph. D. Dissertation, The George Washington University, 1970.

Wagner, Geoffrey. Five for Freedom: A Study of Feminism in Fiction. Rutherford, Madison, Teaneck, N. J. : Fairleigh Dickinson University Press, 1972.

Waidner, Maralee Layman. "From Reason to Romance: A Progression from an Emphasis on Neoclassic Rationality to Romantic Intuition in Three English Woman Novelists."

Ph. D. Dissertation, The University of Tulsa, 1973.

Walker, Alice. "In Search of Our Mothers' Gardens." Ms. 2 (May 1974): 64-70, 105.

Walker, Cheryl Lawson. "The Women's Tradition in American Poetry." Ph. D. Dissertation, Brandeis University, 1973.

Waller, Jennifer R. "'My Hand a Needle Better Fits': Anne Bradstreet and Women Poets in the Renaissance." Dalhousie Review 54 (Autumn 1974): 436-450.

Warren, Larissa Bonfante. "The Women of Etruria." Arethusa 6 (Spring 1973): 91-101.

Watson, Colin. "Girls Who Kept Cool." Snobbery with Violence: Crime Stories and Their Audience. New York: St. Martin's Press, 1971.

Wells, Nancy. "Women in American Literature." English Journal 62 (November 1973): 1159-1162.

Wender, Dorothea. "Plato: Misogynist, Paedophile and Feminist." Arethusa 6 (Spring 1973): 75-90.

Wheeler, Helen Ripplier. Womanhood Media Supplement. Metuchen, N. J.: Scarecrow Press, 1975.

Wilding, Faith and Chris Rush. "In the Beginning." Los Angeles: Pacifica Tape Library, 1972. (Discussion of the new feminist poetry.)

Williams, Ora. American Black Women in the Arts and Social Sciences: A Bibliographic Survey. Metuchen, N. J.: Scarecrow Press, 1973.

Winthrop, Henry. "Sexuality in Literature." Colorado Quarterly 21 (Winter 1973): 337-358.

Wolff, Cynthia Griffin. "A Mirror for Men: Stereotypes of Women in Literature." Massachusetts Review 13 (Winter Spring 1972): 205-218. Reprinted in Edwards, Heath and Baskin, Woman: An Issue, pp. 205-218.

Women and Literature: An Annotated Bibliography of Women Writers. Cambridge, Mass.: Sense & Sensibility Collective, 57 Ellery St., 1971.

Women in Literature. Pleasantville, N.Y.: Educational
    Audio Visual, n.d. (Recordings and filmstrips.)

Wood, Ann Douglas. "The Literature of Impoverishment:
    The Women Local Colorists in America 1865-1914."
    Women's Studies 1 (1972): 3-46.

_____. "The 'Scribbling Women' and Fanny Fern: Why
    Women Wrote." American Quarterly 23 (Spring 1971):
    3-24.

Yeazell, Ruth. "Fictional Heroines and Feminist Critics."
    Novel 8 (Fall 1974): 29-38.

Yee, Carole Zonis. "Why Aren't We Writing About Our-
    selves?" Off Our Backs (February-March 1972). Also
    in Images of Women in Fiction. Edited by Susan Koppel-
    man Cornillon. Bowling Green, Ohio: Bowling Green
    University Press, 1972.

Yeh, Shang-Lan Sophia. "The Portrayal of Women in the
    Icelandic Family Sagas." Ph.D. Dissertation, The
    University of Iowa, 1974.

Zahler, William Paul. "The Husband Wife Relationship in
    American Drama from 1919 to 1939." Ph.D. Disserta-
    tion, Kent State University, 1973.

Zerbe, Evelyn Accad. "Veil of Shame: Role of Women in
    the Modern Fiction of North Africa and the Arab World."
    Ph.D. Dissertation, Indiana University, 1974.

INDEX OF CRITICS AND EDITORS